THE POLITICS OF AID, TRADE AND INVESTMENT

COMPARATIVE POLITICAL ECONOMY AND
PUBLIC POLICY SERIES
Volume II: The Politics of Aid, Trade and Investment

Series Editors:

CRAIG LISKE, *University of Denver*
WILLIAM LOEHR, *University of Denver*
JOHN F. McCAMANT, *University of Denver*

Editorial Board:

Luis Quiros-Varela, *Instituto de Ciencia Politica,
    Universidad Catolica de Chile, Santiago, Chile*
Miguel S. Wionczek, *Secretaria Technica del Plan Nacional
    de Ciencia y Technologia, Mexico*
Richard I. Hofferbert, *Inter-University Consortium for
    Political Research, University of Michigan*
Todd M. Sandler, *Department of Economics,
    Arizona State University*
Steven Sinding, *Agency for International Development,
    Washington, D.C.*
Martin O. Heisler, *Department of Political Science,
    University of Maryland*
Vincent B. Khapoya, *Department of Political Science,
    Oakland University*
William Mitchell, *Department of Political Science,
    University of Oregon*

THE POLITICS OF AID, TRADE AND INVESTMENT

Edited by

SATISH RAICHUR
CRAIG LISKE

University of Denver

SAGE PUBLICATIONS

Halsted Press Division
JOHN WILEY & SONS
New York – London – Sydney – Toronto

Distributed by Halsted Press, a Division of
John Wiley & Sons, Inc., New York

Printed in the United States of America

Library of Congress Cataloging in Publication Data
Main entry under title:

The politics of aid, trade and investment.

(Comparative political economy and public policy series; v. 2)

    1. International economic relations—Addresses, essays, lectures.
2. Economic assistance—Addresses, essays, lectures.   3. Commercial policy—Addresses, essays, lectures.   4. Investments—Addresses, essays, lectures.   I. Raichur, Satish.   II. Liske, Craig.
HF1411.P5913   338.91   75-31886
ISBN 0-470-54117-2

FIRST PRINTING

CONTENTS

INTRODUCTION

The first volume in the Comparative Political Economy and Public Policy Series dealt with domestic policy formulation. The eight chapters in this volume examine factors affecting bilateral economic and military aid, multilateral aid, private capital flows, trade policy, and military intervention. While all the chapters are carefully documented, the kind of information used and the analyses performed on the data range from a careful accounting of nonquantitative information to the statistical estimation of a social field theory model. Their pedagogical value lies both in their substantive content as well as the methodological approaches employed. They indicate the usefulness of formulating hypotheses in a testable form and confronting them with data in order to understand more fully and systematically foreign policy processes.

The first chapter, by Van Atta and Robertson, focuses on Soviet foreign policy behavior. It attempts to explain Soviet trade and aid activity on the basis of the political, social, and economic characteristics of the Soviet Union relative to other international system member states. Aid and trade behavior are examined in conjunction with conflictual and political-diplomatic relationships. They find that by the 1960s Soviet behavior had changed from a power-based relation to one emphasizing development and cultural variables. The piece is a good pedagogical example of imaginative and careful empirical research in the area of international relations.

The next three chapters, by Pearson, Petersen, and Bennett and Guzman, examine U.S. policy with respect to military intervention, economic aid, military aid, and multilateral aid. The three chapters either explicitly or implicitly test alternative models of foreign policy behavior, including what may be generally referred to as a neo-Marxist or imperialist explanation. Pearson tests three major explanations of American military intervention abroad during the period 1950-1967. The explanations are economic imperialism, anticommunism, and major power strategic interest. While none of the explanations fully accounts for American intervention, factors associated with economic and military dependence on the United States and those associated with American competition with major and/or communist powers seem to be the most salient. The chapters by Petersen, and Bennett and Guzman examine aspects of U.S. foreign policy with respect to Latin America. Petersen examines U.S. foreign policy behavior (operationalized in terms of economic aid, military aid, and diplomatic personnel) within three contexts: neo-Marxist (i.e., imperialist), security-defensive, and paternalistic-benevolent. His findings lead to the rejection of the last explanation of American foreign policy. There appears to be no overriding concern for supporting democratic institutions, opposing military regimes, or for the economic need of Latin American nations. Petersen finds, as does Pearson, that the neo-Marxist and strategic-defensive explanations work well in explaining U.S. foreign policy behavior. The Bennett and Guzman chapter isolates and tests the saliency of political allegiance in explaining the distribution of multilateral aid to Latin American countries in 1971. An examination of IBRD and IDB aid reveals that political allegiance to the United States as reflected in the voting record of the General Assembly of the OAS does not explain aid distribution. The finding is, of course, interesting when placed in conjunction with the results obtained by Pearson and Petersen, who indicated that an imperialist explanation does offer at least partial insight into related aspects of American foreign policy. The results are not contradictory. The neo-Marxist explanations are phrased primarily in terms of the predominance of the economic motive in explaining American interaction with other nation-states. Bennett and Guzman find a positive and significant correlation between multilateral aid and per capita incomes and annual growth rates in the GNP of recipient countries. This corroborates Petersen's rejection of the paternalistic-benevolent explanation of U.S. foreign economic behavior in addition to emphasizing the importance of the economic motive in American foreign policy. Finally, to the extent that American control of both IBRD and IDB allocations is not absolute, a weighting of aid allocations by percentage of votes controlled by the United States may well provide a closer fit for the Bennett/Guzman regression model.

The pieces by Rock and by Franco examine two key aspects of American foreign economic behavior: private and public capital flows. The Rock chapter examines the determinants of U.S. foreign private investment in manufacturing to sixty-five Third World countries and analyzes the impact of American aid policies on foreign investment activity. It is a comprehensive test of foreign investment activity, examining the relative importance of economic and non-economic variables in the size-distribution of private capital flows to the Third World. It goes on to trace the implications of foreign investment, trade, and the multilateralization of aid on American foreign economic policy. Franco is concerned with the implications of the untying or multilateralization of American economic aid activity. The whole question of bilateral versus multilateral aid is complex. Its overtones are both political and economic in nature. Bilateral aid is strongly identified with the possible (and/or) actual compromising of recipient sovereignty. Economically, bilateral aid, also more likely to be tied, calls into question the real transfer of resources in any given aid package. Divergence between world market prices and donor prices leads to resource transfers below the face value of the aid package itself. The United States generally followed an aid policy which tied procurement of commodities to U.S. sources. The Nixon procurement policy formulated in 1970 led to a partial multilateralization of American aid. Partial, since procurement from key DAC countries was forbidden because of their refusal to untie their own aid programs. Untying of aid has obvious implications for the export performance of the donor's industry. Franco carefully reviews the bilateral-multilateral debate and puts forward a simple model to estimate the relative shifts in aid-generated exports if aid were untied. The results indicate that aid-related exports from the United States could be expected to fall substantially if aid were unconditionally untied. The beneficiaries of the redirection of aid-related exports to Third World countries would be the DAC countries. Franco is concerned exclusively with the "first-round" effects of aid-giving. In fact, in addition to generating first-round exports, aid programs also generate secondary exports. The latter are additional exports generated from an increase in the recipient's foreign exchange reserves. In his chapter, Rock also points to the implications of untying of aid on the flow of private capital from the United

States to Third World countries. If Rock's suggestion that untying may well reduce private capital flows to the Third World is correct, then the entire question of multilateralization of aid must be looked at afresh in terms of its redistributive effects among Third World countries, the United States, and the DAC countries. This is an area which needs a much closer examination before the euphoria with multilateralization leads to major swings in policy.

The last two chapters are different both substantively and methodologically. In part, they reflect our appreciation of nonquantitative approaches to the study of foreign policy processes as well as the importance of purely domestic factors in their formulation of policy which governs inter-nation interaction. The chapter by Hultman examines the question of export controls. Export controls are used to (1) raise prices of commodities and hence enhance foreign exchange earnings, (2) achieve political objectives, (3) alleviate domestic shortages and thereby curtail domestic inflationary pressures, and (4) implement international commodity agreements. Historically, Third World countries have used export controls for the first and fourth reasons, although the oil embargo by OPEC was directed at achieving political objectives along with increasing revenues. The United States has used export control primarily for the second and third reasons. The Trade Reform Act of 1974 contains an "access to supplies" provision that calls for institutional arrangements to be set up to guarantee American access to commodities not readily produceable domestically. Hultman examines this provision, discusses the implementation problems, and traces the implications for the countries involved.

Arnold's chapter is an interesting comparison of governmental efforts to promote manufacturing exports during the democratic regime in Brazil (1956-1964) and the authoritarian regime of 1964-1974. The two regimes are compared in terms of three issue areas: program organization, export incentives, and private sector mobilization. It includes a careful examination of the claim made by the authoritarian regime that it revolutionized policy-making by insulating key decision makers from partisan politics and permitting decisions to be made on purely technical grounds. Arnold's chapter is a good example of an examination of domestic factors as they impinge on policy formulation which affects external relations as well as a nonstatistical study executed with sufficient care that it yields results qualitatively equally acceptable as those reached by studies using more sophisticated "statistical numerology."

The first volume in this series dealt with domestic public policy. This volume, the second in the series, deals with foreign policy. Like the first, it is essentially representative of the kind of research which we believe is necessary if the fringes of public policy research are to be extended further. Finally, it contributes to a better understanding of some of the key components of American and Soviet foreign policy behavior.

Satish Raichur

Chapter 1

AN ANALYSIS OF SOVIET FOREIGN ECONOMIC BEHAVIOR
FROM THE PERSPECTIVE OF SOCIAL FIELD THEORY

RICHARD VAN ATTA

CACI, Inc.-Federal

and

DALE B. ROBERTSON

American University

INTRODUCTION

The movement of the East-West struggle toward "coexistence" has been described as a process of maturation or modernization in Soviet and American policies (Gehlen, 1967). The progressive shifting of Soviet foreign economic policy away from the autarkic perspective of the Stalin era to a broader policy based jointly on political and economic considerations is an important aspect of this reorientation of Soviet foreign policy (Pisar, 1970: 29-43). The objective of this study is to explicate the quantitative and qualitative change in Soviet foreign economic aid and trade from a political perspective. We analyze first the aid and trade variables within the context of the broader spectrum of foreign policy behavior focusing specifically on the relationship of the economic variables to such international activities as conflict, diplomatic relations, and tourism. Second, the trade and aid of the Soviet Union is analyzed from the perspective of R. J. Rummel's "social-field" theory, which states that the behavior between two states is a function of relative differences of these states on their political, social, and economic characteristics. The question addressed here is to what extent Soviet trade and aid can be accounted for by the position of the USSR relative to other nations in the international system.

HISTORICAL CONTEXT OF SOVIET FOREIGN ECONOMIC BEHAVIOR

The Stalin era could be characterized as a period of establishing "fortress Russia." The major economic emphasis was upon the development of a solid industrial base within the Soviet Union, while internationally Stalin sought (after 1945) to keep a tight grip on the Eastern European countries and China. It was thought that isolationism was the way to counter the military and economic pressure exerted from the NATO alliance and the Marshall Plan and to hasten the inevitable collapse of the capitalist system. The influence of the Western countries in the Third World was not directly challenged, since Stalin perceived that ties with the West would erode naturally as Marxist economic determinism took its course.

Gehlen suggests that change in Soviet foreign economic policy from this autarkic stance resulted from both an attempt to shift the Cold War struggle to the less dangerous arena of economic competition and an attempt to return to the original economic orientation of Marx (Gehlen, 1967: 157-158). The leadership that emerged during the post-Stalin period was much more capable of adapting to the international environment. They recognized the viability of the capitalist states. Moreover, they were willing to utilize trading opportunities with the West to hasten the industrialization of the Soviet Union. Thus, Pisar comments, the new Soviet leaders looked upon the United States and its allies in more pragmatic terms. They saw that the economic cycles predicted by the deterministic ideology of their predecessors were not occurring. Furthermore, the diversity and intensity of growth in the West demanded enormous quantities of raw materials—products that Russia could supply in exchange for much-needed machines and technology. At the same time, a look at the Third World revealed that, as colonial ties were breaking apart, opportunities for economic intrusion were appearing (Pisar, 1970: 29-43).

Goldman cites three reasons for increased aid and trade to the underdeveloped countries. First, Russia desired and needed new trade opportunities. The desired symbiotic relationship among the members of Comecon had not materialized. Second, humanitarian reasons cannot be discounted. The Third World countries were perceived as having been plundered by their colonial masters, and the Soviets felt a desire to help. However, Goldman cites political self-interest as the paramount factor in foreign aid. To illustrate this point, he recounts cases where the Soviet Union had bought unneeded goods, such as coffee, in hopes of countering the economic losses with political gains (Goldman, 1967: 185-187). Tansky (1966) gives similar reasons for Soviet foreign assistance, contending that economic penetration was the major motivation. In addition to gaining entry into developing countries, the Soviets were attempting to eliminate Western influence. In discussing the new Soviet foreign economic policy, both Pisar (1970: 41) and Tansky (1966: 955) comment upon the technique, which Pisar calls "distinctive," of emphasizing heavy industrial development. Pisar perceives this as a natural tendency to export one's own method of developing, while Tansky attributes to the Soviet Union the more tactical motivation of attempting to preempt the industrial sector.

In order for the Soviet Union to assume the leadership position that it sought in the industrialization of the less-developed countries, real sacrifices had to be made in terms of restructuring foreign economic policy so that significant levels of industrial commodities could be exported. In fact, it was not until the sixties that the trade balance of the Soviet Union allowed it to make such sales in significant amounts (Pisar, 1970: 40). Until then, trade with the underdeveloped countries was fostered through the acceptance of commodities in payment for loans and the purchasing of primary commodities (Gehlen, 1967: 189).

Statistics on aid and trade in the post-Stalin decade reveal a great deal about the extent of the changes that were occurring. From 1946 to 1953, trade with the other Comecon countries increased from $777 million to $4.773 billion. The new leaders apparently decided that emphasis on intrabloc trade was too high. By 1957, the percentage of Soviet trade with its allies had decreased from a high of 83 percent to 73 percent. The rift with China and Albania precipitated a further decrease (Pisar, 1970: 15). From 1958 to 1964, trade with Western countries had increased by 126 percent. The peak year in Soviet economic initiatives to the West was 1961, with 206 accords being signed with 32 countries (Gehlen, 1967: 130). Changes in aid patterns were equally dramatic. In 1954, $6 million worth of assistance was extended, while in 1965 the figure rose to $5 billion (Tansky, 1966: 949).

This review demonstrates that some fundamental changes have occurred in the foreign political and economic policies of the Soviet Union in the years following the death of Stalin. In the next section, we shall put forth an analysis of Soviet foreign relations, focusing on economic behavior, that seeks to elaborate and clarify this shift in policy.

THE ANALYSIS OF SOVIET FOREIGN ECONOMIC BEHAVIOR

While changes in foreign policy can often be attributed to individual policy makers and explained in terms of political exigencies, the question of the systematic relationship of foreign economic policy to broader international political concerns can also be raised. The Soviet Union's leaders themselves apparently concluded that the earlier policies centered around autonomy and self-sufficiency were not appropriate for the complex international environment with which they had to contend. What we explore in this study is, first, the extent to which there existed during this period (1955 to 1963) systematic patterning between the aid and trade relations of the Soviet Union and its other foreign behavior; and, second, the relationship between aid and trade activity and a set of variables which specify the relative position of the Soviet Union to other nations in the international system.

The context in which this research is developed is "social-field theory" as elaborated by R. J. Rummel (1965). This theoretical perspective asserts that the foreign behavior of one nation-state to another (dyadic behavior) is a function of the relative position of these actors in the system regarding their attribute properties. The relative similarities and differences between actors on their political, social, and economic characteristics engender the interaction between the actors. This perspective (which we shall subsequently discuss more extensively) has been utilized to assess the individual foreign behavior patterns of the United States (Rummel, 1972b), the People's Republic of China (Rhee, 1971), and the Union of Soviet Socialist Republics (Choi, 1973; Robertson, 1974), and also a large number of nations in a more comparative manner (Van Atta, 1973). These studies are all broadly focused on foreign behavior in general. In the research presented here, our interest is to maintain this breadth of focus, but to channel it specifically to the analysis of the foreign economic behavior of the Soviet Union.

This focus for assessing Soviet foreign economic behavior can be related to other efforts to analyze political and societal impacts on Soviet interaction. There are three categories of research that we can use to classify the empirical research that has been conducted on Soviet aid and trade: attribute theory, behavior theory, and relative attribute or "field" theory. Those studies in which the descriptive characteristics or attributes of a country are hypothesized to be the major determinants of the foreign behavior of that country have been classified as attribute theories (Rummel, 1972b). Some researchers see international behavior as both the dependent and the independent variables, focusing often on the interactive relationships in foreign policy. These studies we call behavior theories. Finally, there are studies that use the concept of relative attributes, positing that behavior is influenced by the relative differences and similarities between nations.

Traditional examinations of Soviet foreign relations have generally relied upon what we have called "attribute theory." Attribute theories focus on the internal characteristics of a single nation. Those studies which depend upon historical, ideological, or geographical variables are examples of this approach (see Brody and Vesecky, 1969, for an extensive list of attribute studies of the Soviet Union). Integration theory provides us with several examples of the use of national attributes in quantitative research. Much of the literature dealing with international integration assumes that domestic characteristics are key variables. Simon (1969) uses attribute concepts as dependent variables in an attempt to avoid the trap of defining integration in terms of interaction and then using interaction variables as independent variables. He defines integration as a political condition in which certain states have a disposition to be cohesive. This condition would be recognized by a similarity of value systems, internal value structures, and elite attitudes, all of which are domestic attributes. Simon then focuses his study on political and economic interaction scales. High scores on these variables are considered as necessary, but not sufficient, for integration to occur. Specifically, Simon is looking for patterns of interaction between the Soviet Union and the developing states. The major conclusion of the study is that the Soviet Union has concentrated its attention upon the smallest and least developed countries.

Some scholars have selected the actions of competitors as the major predictor of foreign behavior. These studies we have classified as "behavior theories." The Triska and Finley (1965) multiple symmetry model is an example of a study which concentrates on interstate behavior rather than domestic attributes. Policy direction is posited to be a function of either a creative attempt to move ahead of an opponent or a reflexive movement to correct a perceived imbalance. The central proposition of the model is that, if a nation is to remain in balance with an opponent, it must respond to a unilateral initiative (e.g., in weaponry, technology, espionage, or alliances) on exactly that dimension. For example, if all other things were equal and the United States were to develop a new missile system, the Soviets would have to respond with a similar development in order to stay in balance. Triska and Finley specifically mention Comecon as a response to EEC. The model could also be used to explain Soviet expansion into the aid field.

Beim's research (1964) is another example of a behavior theory. He uses the conceptual tools of game theory to elaborate the Communist bloc's motivations for giving aid to less developed countries. In the framework of game theory, a nation's strategy is dependent upon such things as perception of payoff and feedback, which are both behavior concepts. Beim divides the world into three player groups—Western bloc, Communist bloc, and Third World. He sees the first two as active, aggressive players trying to increase their influence with the third group, which is basically passive, using the international game for pursuing the goal of domestic growth. Influence over the developing nations can be gained by such methods as:

(1) promoting goodwill and solidifying friendly relations,
(2) making recipient countries dependent upon the donor,

(3) cultivating a natural ideological ally over the long run, and
(4) obtaining military advantage (Beim, 1964: 785-788).

Beim concludes from his analysis of interaction that the Communist strategy is mixed but basically oriented toward establishing a dependency relation.

Galtung (1966) moves beyond simple attribute theory, assuming that behavior is influenced by the relative differences and similarities between states on attribute dimensions. First, he ranks states according to the characteristics of size, wealth, power, and development. The initial hypothesis that he tests is that a nation's position on one scale determines its position on other scales: nations that are high on one dimension will tend to be high on all others. The second hypothesis, what Galtung calls the ordering principle, holds that interaction between nations is rank dependent "in the sense that there is much interaction between nations high in the ranking system, less between one nation that is high and another that is low, and much less between two nations low in the system" (p. 146). Galtung has gone beyond the theory of attributes influencing behavior and has proposed that a nation's behavior is influenced by its position vis-à-vis other nations. To predict the interaction between nations "A" and "B," we need to know the status of both on the relevant dimensions.

For two basic reasons, we have chosen attribute distance or field theory as our research mode. In the first place, it provides a framework capable of incorporating many of the prevailing theoretical efforts in international relations.[1] The second reason for selecting the attribute distance approach is that the competition between the two "dominant" powers in the post-World War II era, in which being "number one" is of paramount importance, can best be understood using a theory focusing on the differences and similarities between countries (Van Atta, 1974).

FIELD THEORY

In this section, we shall briefly discuss the field-theoretic perspective that is utilized in this study. The field concept was adopted from physics and initially applied to the social sciences by scholars such as Lewin and Wright. Lewin conceptualized social units in a spatial framework in which groups or individuals existed concurrently with relevant ecological units. He hypothesized that the distance between the elements influenced the behavior of the actors.

In the study of international relations, Rummel presents a formalized field theory within a linear algebraic system. Rummel calls his theory "social field theory" and builds it upon three basic assumptions:

(1) International relations is a field consisting of all nation attributes and interactions and their complex relationships through time.

(2) The international field comprises a Euclidean attribute space defining all nation attributes and a Euclidean behavior space defining all nation dyadic interactions.

(3) The attribute distances between nations in attribute space at a particular time are social forces determining the location of dyads in behavior space at that time [Hilton, 1973].

To understand field theory, one must appreciate the difference between attributes and attribute distances. An attribute is a descriptor that characterizes a nation, differentiating it from all others. It is an informational unit restricted in time and space. Examples of nation-state attributes are the gross national product of the Soviet Union in 1955 and the size of the Brazilian air force in 1963. Meehan calls such isolated properties facts and contends that they have little meaning unless they are systematically related, in which case they become concepts (Meehan, 1967: 11). Field theory provides a perspective for interrelating observations of the nation-state system into a set of concepts which together define the international field. The distances between nations within this field are seen as a basic element determining the interaction from one nation to another.

Figure 1 gives a geometric depiction of "attribute space," where points P_1 and P_2 are determined from the values of each nation on a particular attribute property (e.g., population, energy production). Lines are then drawn from the origin to the points, forming a vector space. The relationship between the vectors is given by the angle θ (the cosine of which is the correlation of the variables). From the intercorrelated variables, a set of independent *dimensions* can be determined which defines the space of variables. It is these dimensions which are the independent variables in the field theory model. It is on these dimensions that the differences between nations are assessed which are utilized to ascertain the nations' behavioral relations.

Figure 2 illustrates three possible dimensions of attribute space and shows the relative plotting of the Soviet Union and the United States within the space. A distance vector d is derived by subtracting the American and Soviet scores on the various dimensions.

The distance or difference measure provides information about nation-states that their individual attribute scores do not. What we obtain are measures by which we can specify the relative properties of actors. For instance, instead of knowing that Panama has an army of a certain size, we know that relative to the other nations in the system, the size of this army is very small. This type of concept points to a thrust that has been evoked frequently in social theory, where power, status, and homogeneity are all *relational* concepts based upon the inherent characteristics of the actors. Rousseau, for instance, asserted that a nation "feels weak so long as there are others stronger than itself. Its safety and preservation demand that it makes itself stronger than its neighbors" (quoted in Forsyth et al.,

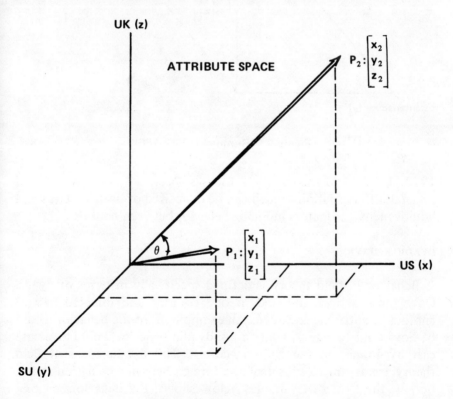

Figure 1. (Rummel, 1965: 186)

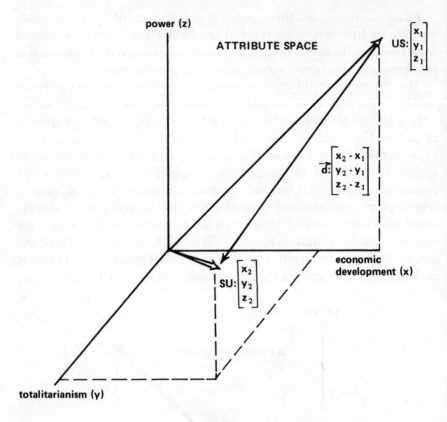

Figure 2. (Rummel, 1965: 186)

1970: 170). Field theory, then, focuses specifically on political and societal differentiation—which can be conceived of both as status and homogeneity—as factors inducing behavior between nations.

DYADIC BEHAVIOR

Behavior in field theory is defined specifically in terms of dyads. Only those actions initiated in one country and directed toward another country are included. An example of dyadic behavior would be Soviet aid to Egypt, while a nondyadic behavior would be a vote cast by France in the United Nations. This dyadic focus of field theory treats only a subset of the foreign behavior of nation-states, but, as the listing of variables below shows, the behaviors encompassed are substantial.

In approaching this study from the perspective of field theory, the aid and trade variables are included in a set of foreign policy variables. This allows the assessment of the economic policy variables within the context of the overall behavioral relations of actors in the system, raising the question of what variables in the array of foreign behavior variables are related to aid and trade within "behavior space." Table 1 lists the foreign behavior variables used in this study and the sources from which they were derived. The set of variables was selected on the basis of prior analyses of dyadic foreign inter-action, particularly Rummel's study of U.S. behavior (Rummel, 1972b) and Rhee's analysis of Communist Chinese interaction (Rhee, 1971).

The behavior variables listed were selected to range across several generic domains. Aid and trade are both ostensibly "economic" variables. The international conflict index is a gross measure of the hostile behavior of the Soviet Union directed toward other nations.[2]

TABLE 1

Data for Soviet International Behavior 1955 and 1963

	Variable	Source
1	Aid	Goldman, Marshall I. *Soviet Foreign Aid* New York: Praeger, 1967.
2	Trade	*UN Statistical Yearbook*
3	Tourists	*UN Statistical Yearbook*
4	Diplomatic Representation	*The Statesman's Yearbook* 1 = Embassy 2 = Legation 3 = Relations but no representatives
5	Treaty	DON data
6	Treaty Propensity	Treaties (1950-1957 or 1958-1965)
7	Comparative Treaties	USSR Treaty Propensity/U.S. Treaty Propensity
8	Conflict	DON data—aggregation of all conflict indicators (all data is in the form USSR → j)
9-12	Visits to (T) and from (F) the USSR (two levels each)	*U.S. Foreign Information Broadcasting Service Daily Report,* and *New Times*

The political-diplomatic sector is represented by the treaty variables, diplomatic representation, and the various levels and types of foreign visits. Given the nature of Soviet society, very little information is available on what might be termed the "salience" variables such as the flow of mail, student exchanges, immigration, or book translations. One variable included in this study, tourism, does seem to represent this domain. In the Appendix, a more complete description of the individual variables analyzed is given. Initially the visits were categorized into four levels for both "to" and "from": (1) Head of State, (2) Minister, (3) other government official, and (4) nongovernment visitor. A factor analysis of the 1955 visits revealed that the three "to" visit levels below the Head of State level were highly correlated. The three categories were, therefore, aggregated. The "from" visits were sufficiently intercorrelated to warrant the formation of a single measure. The final indicators were named T_1, T_{234}, and F_{tot}. The 1963 aggregation is similar except the "from" visits are divided into F_1 and F_{234}.

TRADE AND AID AS ASPECTS OF BEHAVIOR SPACE

The initial research question raised from the field-theoretic perspective is what the relationship of the economic behavior variables, trade and aid, is to the other indices of foreign behavior. Does Soviet behavior show a similar patterning across all of the variables, or do separate patternings result for specific subsets of variables? The technique of factor analysis is appropriate to this question as it provides a set of independent dimensions so positioned as to represent clusterings of interrelated variables. Table 2 shows the results of the factor analysis of the eleven Soviet foreign behavior variables for 1955, and Table 3 gives the factor analysis results for the twelve indices of 1963 Soviet behavior. (The different number of variables for the two years is due to the combining of F_1 with F_{234} for 1955 into F_{tot}, as noted above.)

The factor analysis for 1955 behavior shows that four dimensions are required to depict the set of variables. The first dimension, accounting for thirty-three percent of the total variation in the behavior variables, shows both trade and aid clustering together with the variables Tourists, Treaty Propensity, and Comparative Treaties. The nations which show high factor scores on this dimension, not surprisingly, are Poland, China, Czechoslovakia, Rumania, East Germany, Hungary, and Bulgaria (see Table 4). The Communist bloc

TABLE 2

Factor Analysis of 1955 Soviet Foreign Behavior Variables[a]

| Variable | Orthogonal Rotation[b] | | | | h_i^{2}[c] |
	F_1	F_2	F_3	F_4	(R^2)
Aid	.87	− .07	− .05	− .00	.770
Tourists	.85	− .07	.08	− .01	.727
Trade	.85	.10	.23	.01	.786
Treaty Propensity	.69	.47	.37	− .02	.843
Comparative Treaties	.74	.15	.11	.04	.596
T_{234}	.47	.69	.36	− .01	.827
F_{tot}	.43	.51	.53	− .01	.732
Treaty	− .05	.79	.12	− .08	.645
Conflict	− .03	.80	− .23	.06	.703
T_1	.09	− .03	.88	.01	.779
Diplomatic Representation	.01	− .02	.01	.99	.994

a. Values $\geq |.50|$ are in bold type.

b. Varimax solution.

c. h_i^2 is the communality of each variable. It is equal to the sum of the common loadings
$(h_i^2 = a_i^2 + a_2^2 + \ldots + a_n^2)$.

TABLE 3

Factor Analysis of 1963 Soviet Foreign Behavior Variables[a]

| Variable | Orthogonal Rotation[b] | | | | | h_i^2 |
	F_1	F_2	F_3	F_4	F_5	(R^2)
Tourists	.76	.04	.27	.25	.03	.731
Trade	.83	.08	.37	.20	.01	.874
F_1	.88	− .01	− .12	.08	.01	.802
F_{234}	.76	.56	.05	.04	.06	.897
T_{234}	.36	.79	.32	.09	.04	.861
Treaty Propensity	.23	.50	.18	.67	.02	.791
Conflict	− .10	.88	− .15	.22	− .04	.852
Aid	.14	.23	.81	− .04	.05	.734
T_1	.07	− .12	.78	.14	− .05	.663
Comparative Treaties	.13	.01	.50	.68	.01	.736
Treaty	.17	.14	− .12	.88	− .01	.841
Diplomatic Representation	.02	− .00	− .01	− .00	.99	.996

a. Values $\geq |.50|$ are in bold type.

b. Varimax solution.

orientation of Soviet economic behavior, both aid and trade, is accompanied by supportive treaty relations and a similar concentration of tourism in Eastern Europe.

The second dimension, accounting for approximately twenty percent of the variation, represents the conflict domain. Nations which receive relatively large amounts of conflict interaction from the USSR, such as the United States, Yugoslavia, and the United Kingdom, are singled out on this factor. It is interesting that the diplomatic variables Treaty, T_{234}, and F_{tot} appear in this dimension. The inference that might be drawn from this is that the treaties concluded in 1955, as well as the visits from the USSR to other

TABLE 4

Factor Scores on Soviet "Trade and Aid" and "Conflict" Dimensions for 1955
(for highest fifteen countries plus additional Communist bloc countries)

Trade and Aid			Conflict		
Nation	Rank	Score	Nation	Rank	Score
Poland	1	5.445	United States	1	6.604
PRC	2	5.410	Yugoslavia	2	3.764
Czechoslovakia	3	3.205	United Kingdom	3	2.534
Rumania	4	1.499	Austria	4	1.135
GDR	5	1.084	Afghanistan	5	1.062
Hungary	6	.743	GDR	6	.946
Bulgaria	7	.505	Rumania	7	.881
North Korea	8	.243	France	8	.841
Sweden	9	.198	Hungary	9	.729
United Kingdom	10	.140	Japan	10	.634
France	11	.054	Czechoslovakia	11	.631
Japan	12	.008	Bulgaria	12	.574
Norway	13	-.006	Sweden	13	.415
Mongolia	14	-.006	Greece	14	.378
Denmark	15	-.007	Iran	15	.239
Yugoslavia	27	-.222	Albania	26	-.147
Albania	75	-.356	PRC	28	-.168
			Poland	81	-1.238

nations (F_{tot}) and visits to the USSR below the level of Head of State (T_{234}) were to some degree connected with the negotiation of conflict issues. This diplomatic-conflict aspect of Soviet foreign behavior in 1955 is essentially unrelated to the bloc-oriented focus of USSR foreign economic behavior. Indeed, as Table 4 shows, five bloc members rank in the top fifteen recipients of Soviet conflict among the eighty-one nations analyzed, while Albania and China are intermediate in rank, and Poland ranks eighty-first.

The interrelation of Soviet foreign behavior variables for 1963 gives a rather different picture. Trade and aid are not found jointly clustering on a dimension. Rather, the trade variable, along with tourists, and visits from the USSR (F_1 and F_{234}), form one cluster of variables. The aid variable loads on another dimension together with Head of State visits to the USSR (T_1). Conflict behavior still clusters with some diplomatic variables in a dimension separate from the economic variables, while a relatively distinct "treaty" dimension emerges as well. As with 1955, the diplomatic representation variable is unrelated to the rest of the set.

Scrutinizing the array of nations on the 1963 behavior dimensions (Table 5), we see that the first factor (trade) portrays essentially an Eastern European involvement. Noticeable in 1963 is the descent of the People's Republic of China from the list of nations with high scores on this dimension. The third factor, with aid as a primary loading variable, shows the thrust of the USSR into new political-diplomatic arenas. High-scoring nations on this factor include bloc members Bulgaria, Mongolia, Hungary, Rumania, and Czechoslovakia. Other nations with high values on the aid dimension are Cuba, India, Egypt, Finland, and some smaller Third World nations. There remains some residual involvement with China.

While the aid variable does emerge on a dimension separate from trade, the presence of several Soviet bloc members shows that aid was not only an instrument of penetrating into new areas, but also integral to a policy of resuscitating relations with allies. The period of unrest in the late 1950s was followed by very substantial increases in Soviet aid outlays to most of the Eastern European bloc members (Goldman, 1967: 32). Concurrent with the effort to enhance relations with these allies, the Soviet Union engaged in an outward thrust toward selected Third World nations. The relationship between these two efforts is that they are two parts of a general policy of the USSR during this period to establish a presence in the international arena as

TABLE 5

Factor Scores on Soviet "Trade," "Aid," and "Conflict" Dimensions for 1963
(for highest fifteen nations plus additional Communist bloc countries)

Trade			Aid			Conflict		
Nation	Rank	Score	Nation	Rank	Score	Nation	Rank	Score
GDR	1	5.7.7	Bulgaria	1	4.731	United States	1	5.991
Poland	2	4.116	Cuba	2	4.389	PRC	2	2.222
Czechoslovakia	3	3.104	Mongolia	3	2.757	India	3	1.686
Yugoslavia	4	2.707	India	4	2.503	Indonesia	4	1.000
Rumania	5	1.177	Hungary	5	2.365	United Kingdom	5	.900
Iran	6	1.457	Finland	6	1.904	Iraq	6	.854
Finland	7	1.158	Egypt	7	1.278	Yugoslavia	7	.848
Norway	8	.357	Laos	8	1.229	Egypt	8	.690
Bulgaria	9	.213	Rumania	9	1.114	North Vietnam	9	.668
Italy	10	.207	Nepal	10	.861	Afghanistan	10	.510
FRG	11	.181	Ceylon	11	.824	Italy	11	.476
North Vietnam	12	.157	Czechoslovakia	12	.765	Rumania	12	.420
PRC	13	.153	Demark	13	.751	GDR	13	.272
Sweden	14	.073	Iraq	14	.560	Japan	14	.232
France	15	.061	Afghanistan	15	.511	France	15	.188
Hungary	19	-.082	PRC	18	.237	Poland	16	.177
Albania	75	-.436	GDR	31	-.305	Bulgaria	18	.097
			Poland	33	-.310	Albania	30	-.158
			Albania	39	-.339	Hungary	80	-.872
						Czechoslovakia	81	-.984

a coequal with the United States. To assert its position as a competitor, the Soviet Union had to solidify its existing alignment structure as well as attempt to attract new actors to support its policies.

The conflict dimension provides some intriguing results compared to the aid and trade findings. The overall pattern of scores remains similar to those for 1955 with the United States the major recipient of Soviet conflict and a mix of Western, nonaligned, and bloc members filling out the remaining top ranks. However, there is a marked increase of Asian conflict patterns, China being the most pronounced, with India, Indonesia, and North Vietnam also ranking in the first ten conflict recipients. Two other Third World nations, Iraq and Egypt, also become major targets of Soviet conflict activity in 1963.

It is interesting that some of the major recipients of aid behavior, notably India, Egypt, Iraq, Rumania, and Afghanistan, also appear in the upper echelon of conflict behavior targets. These results are consistent with the situation for 1955, where the major Eastern European recipients of Soviet economic behavior also were major conflict parties. What is most intriguing regarding the 1963 situation is that the "nonaligned" aid recipients—Egypt, India, and Iraq—join with the Soviet bloc actors as major conflict recipients, while in the previous time frame none of these three was a major target of either Soviet conflict or Soviet economic behavior. While the coupling here might be merely coincidental, it may be indicative of a more general orientation of the USSR toward nations it considers within its "camp." The involvement of the Soviet Union with these nations produces stresses resulting in both conflictual interaction and diplomatic activity.

ASSESSMENT OF SOVIET AID AND TRADE FROM THE PERSPECTIVE OF FIELD THEORY

Field theory posits a linear linkage between the independent variable, attribute distance, and the dependent variable, dyadic behavior. The model can be expressed by the equation:

$$W_{i \to j,k} = \sum_{\ell = 1}^{p} a_{\ell i} d_{\ell, i - j}$$

The dependent variable, $W_{i \to j,k}$, is the behavior of nation i (in this case the USSR) toward nation j on the kth dimension. The independent variables, denoted by $d_{\varrho,i-j}$, are the distances between the actors i and j on the dimensions of the attribute space weighted by the parameters $\alpha_{\varrho i}$.[3]

In this study, the specific hypothesis to be tested is that the dyadic aid and trade behavior of the USSR is predicted by the differences between the USSR and the recipient nation on attribute dimensions. Our examination of Soviet behavior shows in 1955 homogeneity in aid and trade patterns. It is hypothesized that this single foreign economic dimension formed by aid and trade will probably vary directly with similarities on the development and political orientation dimensions. There are several reasons why we anticipate this relationship. In 1955, the Soviet Union was in great need of trading partners. However, due to external imposition as well as internal choice, it was isolated from the major industrial powers. The USSR, therefore, had only the Communist bloc nations to look to for economic alliances. Most of these countries were as much in need of aid to shoreup their war-ravaged economies as they were in need of trade. The result was a combined pattern of aid and trade which not only served to provide the USSR with trade outlets but also to satisfy the ideological goal of strengthening world Communism. We therefore hypothesize a unitary pattern in which trade and aid are associated with developed, Communist-oriented countries. In the 1963 analysis of Soviet aid and trade, patterns differed. This differentiation raises the possibility that divergent political objectives were served by these interactions. Trade is hypothesized to increase as power and development similarities increase, while aid should decrease as power and development similarities increase.

Figure 3 outlines the strategy by which the attributes and behavior spaces were determined and the field theory hypothesis was tested. In stage one, the raw data sets were collected and prepared for the analysis. The basic attribute variables were from the Dimensionality of Nations (DON) project. From the DON attribute set, those variables containing behavior aspects were eliminated. Among those discarded were indicators characterizing nations as to their UN voting pattern, bloc membership, receipt of U.S. aid, and trade patterns. The final set is listed in Table 6.[4]

The second step in the research design was the factor analysis of the attribute and behavior data sets, reducing the large number of

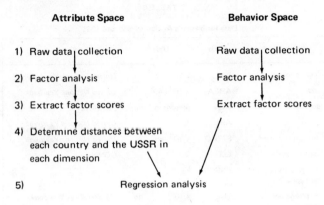

Figure 3.

variables in each to a set of dimensions. The scores for each nation were calculated on the attribute dimensions, and the differences between the Soviet scores and those of other nations were obtained. The final step in the research was the regression of the attribute difference scores onto the scores of Soviet aid and trade behavior with these nations. The results of this analysis are presented below.

The results of the attribute space analysis for 1955 and 1963 are given in Tables 7 and 8, respectively. The dimensions have been provided with labels depicting the substantive thrust of the variables which load most highly on them. For 1955, eight dimensions were obtained:[5] "Power," "Development," "Culture," "Oriental," "Agriculture," "Political Orientation," "Defense," and "Domestic Violence." These results conform to Rummel's analysis of the attributes of nations for 1955 (Rummel, 1969). The results that were obtained for the 1963 data on nation-state attributes give a less distinct structure. The first factor shown, F_1, appears to combine several variables which in the 1955 study appeared on different dimensions. The factor represents both defense preparation (DEFEX, COMPL) and social welfare or development (PHY, GNPPC), with linguistic diversity also loading on the dimension (LANG). We left this factor unlabeled, yet were intrigued at the interrelation shown between defense outlay and social welfare variables. The remaining factors correspond fairly closely to the 1955 findings, except that the political orientation variables (GOPPO and COMST) get absorbed by other factors, rather than forming a distinct dimension on their own.

TABLE 6

Data for Nation's Attribute 1955 and 1963

Variable Name	Code	Unit	Source
population	POP	x 10^4 persons	*United Nations Yearbook*
area	AREA	x 10^3 km^2	*United Nations Yearbook*
density	DEN	persons in 1 km^2	POP/AREA
arable land	ARLND	%	*United Nations Yearbook*
steel production[a]	STPRO	x 10^3 ton	*United Nations Yearbook*
literacy rate[a]	LIT	%	DON data
energy consumption per capita[a]	ENCON	kg	same as ENPRO
telephone per capita[b]	TEL	x 10^{-5}	*UN Statistical Yearbook*
population per physician	PHY	x 10	*UN Statistical Yearbook*
GNP per capita[a]	GNPPC	US$	GNP/POP
nonagricultural population[b]	NAGPO	%	*UN Statistical Yearbook*
geographical distance from USSR	GEODS	cm	distance between capitals on 30 cm. globe
size of armed forces[b]	FORCE	x 10^3 persons	Coward, H. R. *Military Technology in Developing Countries.* Cambridge, Mass., 1967. Sellers, R. C. *The Reference Handbook of the Armed Forces of the World*, II, 1967.
number of combat airplanes[a]	COMPL	number	main source: Sellers (1967).
Communist Party membership	COMST	ratio to POP x 10^{-5}	DON data
killed in domestic violence	KILLD	number	DON data
colonialism	COLON	0: colonized 1: no 2: possessed	*Worldmark Encyclopedia*
Roman Catholic	CATH	%	DON data
Protestant	PROTS	%	DON data
Moslem	MOSLM	%	DON data
Buddhist	BUDDH	%	DON data
language	LANG	number	DON data
Chinese population	CHINS	code (see def. in main text)	*UN Demographic Yearbook*
freedom of group opposition	GOPPO	index	DON data
defense expenditure	DEFEX	million US$	main sources: Coward (1967) for '55, and DON data for '63

a. Used in 1963 study only.

b. Used in 1955 study only.

TABLE 7

Factor Analysis of 1955 Raw Attribute Variables[a]

Variable	F1 (Power)	F2 (Development)	F3 (Culture)	F4 (Oriental)	F5 (Agriculture)	F6 (Political Orientation)	F7 (Defense)	F8 (Domestic Violence)	h^2_i $(\bar{R}^2)$
POP	**.83**	-.11	-.04	.10	.18	.04	-.02	.13	.759
AREA	**.82**	.21	.04	.00	-.28	-.08	-.03	-.03	.809
DEN	-.04	.09	.04	.14	**.87**	.08	-.01	-.03	.794
ARLND	-.01	.07	.01	-.19	**.79**	-.31	.02	.17	.784
TEL	.07	**.83**	-.01	-.04	.01	.19	.37	-.01	.870
PHY	-.11	-.07	-**.53**	.08	-.30	.11	-.19	.05	.448
NAGPO	-.01	**.76**	.37	-.09	.25	.08	.19	.08	.825
GEODS	-.15	.07	**.67**	-.43	.45	.15	.04	.03	.898
FORCE	**.89**	.11	-.01	.08	.04	-.17	.23	-.03	.901
COMST	.01	.05	.04	.07	.25	**.80**	.00	.22	.760
KILLD	.05	-.01	.03	-.03	.08	.19	.01	**.93**	.920
COLON	.08	**.50**	.36	-.29	.18	-.05	.24	-.23	.613
CATH	-.13	-.14	**.87**	-.22	-.08	.04	.00	.08	.862
PROTS	.08	**.91**	.20	-.05	-.05	-.02	-.17	-.01	.915
MOSLM	-.04	-.41	-**.66**	-.47	-.10	.09	.15	.03	.864
BUDDH	-.09	-.20	-.22	**.85**	-.01	-.08	.02	.11	.840
LANG	**.50**	-.08	-.31	.11	-.05	.10	-**.62**	.00	.761
CHINS	.43	-.02	-.09	**.72**	-.01	.16	.08	.12	.760
GOPPO	-.12	.21	.18	.06	.10	**.85**	.02	-.00	.824
DEFEX	.42	.21	-.04	.00	.03	.06	**.73**	.01	.770

Orthogonal Rotation

a. Values $\geq$ |.50| are in bold type.

TABLE 8

Factor Analysis of 1963 Raw Attribute Variables[a]

| Variable[b] | | Orthogonal Rotation | | | | | | h^2 |
	F_1 (Unnamed)	F_2 (Power)	F_3 (Agriculture)	F_4 (Culture)	F_5 (Development)	F_6 (Oriental)	F_7 (Colonial)	$(\bar{R}^2)$
POP	-.01	**.80**	.12	-.03	-.09	.12	-.06	.688
AREA	.02	**.84**	.21	-.09	.16	-.11	-.01	.805
DEN	-.11	-.13	**.64**	.01	.19	.29	.11	.578
ARLND	-.00	-.06	**.85**	-.05	.03	-.12	.01	.757
STPRO	.32	**.75**	.11	.01	.19	.00	.28	.797
LIT	-.25	.05	.25	.20	**.75**	.00	.00	.738
ENCON	.10	.25	.21	-.09	**.78**	-.25	.13	.835
PHY	**.82**	-.13	-.03	-.11	-.12	-.00	-.41	.893
GNPPC	**.89**	-.01	.07	-.03	.37	-.06	.10	.957
GEODS	-.06	-.07	-.40	**-.68**	.02	-.37	.29	.863
COMPL	**.79**	.11	-.08	.00	-.17	.10	**.50**	.931
COMST	-.05	.17	**.66**	.16	.05	-.21	-.06	.541
KILLD	.05	-.05	-.04	-.00	-.06	.48	.01	.244
COLON	.14	.06	.08	.12	.20	.09	**.87**	.848
CATH	-.10	-.09	-.02	**.92**	.05	.20	.01	.907
PROTS	.09	.04	-.16	-.42	**.61**	-.14	.41	.772
MOSLM	-.11	-.04	-.16	-.49	**-.51**	-.38	-.04	.679
BUDDH	-.05	.02	-.02	-.24	-.13	**.79**	-.18	.732
LANG	**.81**	-.01	-.09	-.03	-.25	.11	.42	.916
CHINS	-.01	.49	-.03	-.12	.03	**.69**	.10	.740
GOPPO	.15	-.13	-.38	.35	**.50**	-.09	-.02	.567
DEFEX	**-.81**	.33	.00	.03	.10	-.02	-.01	.793

a. Values $\geq |.50|$ are in bold type.

b. Tables 7 and 8 were originally composed of identical variable sets. However, in order to obtain determinate solutions it was necessary to reduce the colinearity in the variable set by eliminating highly correlated variables leaving surrogates to represent clusters. The remaining sets for the two years are, therefore, conceptually compatible.

REGRESSION RESULTS

The technique of stepwise multiple regression was used to assess the predictability of Soviet aid and trade behavior from the attribute difference scores. The stepwise procedure enters each independent variable into the equation in order of its ability to explain the remaining variance in the dependent variable. The dependent variables in the regression equations are the Soviet economic behavior dimensions as determined by factor analysis. Therefore, aid and trade are represented by a single factor in 1955, but are separated in 1963. As shown in Table 9, for 1955, almost forty percent of the variance in the "Aid and Trade" dimension is accounted for by the attribute difference variables. Power and Political Orientation together account for thirty-one percent of the variance, while the remaining five variables add only seven percent to the explained variance.

The correlation of Power and Political Orientation with Soviet foreign economic behavior in 1955, while moderate, is substantial enough to warrant further interpretation. The relative magnitude and direction of the effect of these variables is demonstrated by the standardized regression equation shown below:

$$\text{Soviet Economic Behavior} = -.41 \text{ Power difference}$$
$$-.13 \text{ Domestic Violence}$$
$$-.08 \text{ Culture}$$
$$-.08 \text{ Culture}$$
$$-.03 \text{ Defense}$$
$$+.03 \text{ Development } (R^2 = .38)$$

From this equation, we see that Power and Political Orientation are inversely related to economic behavior; that is, the less powerful and the less politically oriented toward the USSR a nation is, the less economic behavior the Soviet Union will direct toward it.

In the 1963 analysis, thirty-one percent of the variance in the Trade factor is explained by the independent variable set, but only twelve percent of the Aid factor is accounted for by attribute differences. However, these equations reveal some interesting patterns.

TABLE 9

Summary of Stepwise Multiple Regression Analysis

Dependent Variable	Independent Variables					
	1955			1963		
	Variable	Multiple R	R²	Variable	Multiple R	R²
Aid and Trade	Power	.374	.14			
	Political Orientation	.556	.31			
	Agriculture	.594	.35			
	Domestic Violence	.608	.37			
	Culture	.614	.38			
	Defense	.615	.38			
	Development	.616	.38			
Trade				Agriculture	.489	.24
				Oriental	.531	.28
				Development	.549	.30
				Culture	.558	.31
				Unnamed	.559	.31
				Power	.559	.31
Aid				Agriculture	.272	.07
				Unnamed	.304	.09
				Culture	.331	.10
				Development	.340	.12
				Oriental	.345	.12
				Colonial	.349	.12
				Power	.350	.12

Trade Behavior = $-.14$ Agriculture
$+.21$ Oriental
$-.14$ Development
$+.10$ Culture
$+.03$ Unnamed
$-.02$ Power $(R^2 = .31)$

Aid Behavior   = $-.27$ Agriculture
$+.14$ Unnamed
$+.13$ Culture
$+.07$ Development
$-.06$ Oriental
$+.05$ Colonial
$-.04$ Power $(R^2 = .12)$

For both economic dimensions, the Agriculture factor explains the major portion of the variance. Referring to Table 8, we note that this dimension includes Communist Party membership as well as the agriculture indicators. The regression equations for the 1963 data, therefore, show that agricultural and ideological dissimilarity between a country and the USSR is related to the amount of behavior directed toward it on the two types of behavior. This trend can be contrasted to the 1955 analysis in which homogeneity was the major basis of predicting economic behavior. Qualitatively, Soviet behavior changed from a power-based relation to one emphasizing development and cultural variables. Power, in fact, becomes one of the least useful predictors of Soviet economic actions in 1963.

In sum, the results of the regression analyses show that the relatively homogeneous international transaction variable in 1955, encompassing trade, aid, and also tourism and treaties, is relatively well predicted by attribute differences, especially those on the Political Orientation and Development factors. In 1963, the behavior space itself is much less homogeneous and the results of the regression analyses correspondingly diminish. The first behavior dimension, with trade, tourists, and visits *from* the USSR as major loaders, is still moderately predicted by attribute differences. The lack of a distinct "Political Orientation" dimension in 1963, though reflective of the more complex political environment at this time, makes comparison with the 1955 results less direct. Aid as a separate variable appears to be unpredicted from the field-theoretic perspective. The aid outlays of the USSR are not systematically related to the attribute difference between the Soviet Union and other nations.

This result, while discouraging perhaps for advocates of a field-theoretic approach, is not overly shocking. If aid is essentially given out on the basis of political-strategic considerations and is therefore based on the political and diplomatic maneuvering of nations vis-à-vis one another in the international system, it would be somewhat surprising that the relatively static properties of attribute difference would be much related to it. What would most likely be required for predicting aid activity of this type is a model of the competitive interrelationship of the USSR and the United States. Difference in attribute characteristics could still be brought to bear in such a model, but within a general perspective of competitive interaction (Van Atta, 1974). Field theory is not itself adequate to assess behavior which is contingent upon the behavior of another actor in the system.

CONCLUSION

This study has explored the possibility of analyzing Soviet foreign economic behavior from the perspective of social field theory. Our results indicate the field-theoretic perspective has some inherent limitations for analyzing the changing interrelationships of Soviet foreign behavior. During the earlier period (1955), when Soviet policy was less complex, the results of the field theory approach are reasonably good. Attribute differences account for about forty per-cent of the variance in the economic behavior dimension. For 1963, the ability to account for either the "Trade" dimension or the "Aid" dimension with attribute differences is reduced. First, the behavior pattern itself is more complex, there being two dimensions of "eco-nomic" behavior, rather than just a single dimension. Second, neither dimension for 1963 is accounted for as well as the single dimension in the 1955 study. On the positive side, the analyses do indicate that a relatively general model of international interaction can be of some use as the starting place for assessing Soviet economic behavior. However, the model would have to be elaborated to deal with the interactive developments of Soviet behavior as they relate to the United States and other actors as well.

We see the analyses conducted here as establishing a *starting place* for assessing Soviet foreign economic behavior from a political perspective. The underlying notion of field theory, that relative attribute differences are predictive of foreign behavior, provides a base point for assessing behavior. Attribute differences should be considered as the most basic factors which impinge upon nations—much like gravity is seen as a basic physical force. Yet, as the movements of physical objects are due to many other forces which counter gravitational pull, the behavior of nations must encompass the interactive forces of strategy and decision, as well as the more static impacts of attribute properties. What is notable, given this perspective, is the degree of predictability that we obtain, particularly for the 1955 period. The international environment for the Soviet Union would seem to have been defined at this time in terms of the most basic elements. The positions of other nations relative to Soviet interests were for the most part clear. But the 1963 results are indicative of a more complex, differentiated, and ambiguous perspective. Thus, the notion that over this period of time a basic shift in the Soviet perspective toward the international environment had occurred would seem to be credible. Our analysis using the field-theoretic perspective has been of some value in depicting this shift. The analysis does not provide an explanation of this shift, nor does the perspective employed provide a means of elaborating the implications of such a shift. For these, other theoretical perspectives must be brought to bear.

NOTES

1. See Rummel's (1972b) study of U.S. foreign relations, where he tests (1) the linkage "pre-theory" of James Rosenau, (2) the social-status theory of Johan Galtung, (3) the distance theory of Quincy Wright, (4) the power transition theory of A. F. K. Organski, (5) the integration-regional findings of Bruce Russett, and (6) several propositions about geographic distance.

2. The conflict index is an accumulation of all of the conflict events directed toward a particular nation-state by the USSR for a given year. The events used were those coded by the DON project from the New York *Times* according to its "Foreign Conflict Behavior Code Sheet" (Rummel, 1966). Due to the low number of events in the category breakdowns, only the total number of events was used in this analysis.

3. This model, with the actor-specific weightings $a_{\ell i}$, is the second of two models developed by Rummel. Model I treated differences and similarities as forces acting equally

on all countries. Studies of 1955 data (Rummel, 1969) and a retest using 1963 data (Van Atta, 1973) show that Model I has virtually no predictive capacity. In both studies, only thirteen percent of the variation in B-space was explained by A-space. Therefore, this study confines itself to the less deterministic Model II.

4. Table 6 shows the set of attribute data that was used in the field theory analysis. A larger set of variables was initially selected, but the multicolinearity among the original variables necessitated reducing the set. A non-linear dependent matrix was obtained by eliminating highly correlated variables from the data set leaving one to represent the group.

5. In the factor analyses, the number of factors selected were determined by the eigenvalue associated with the factors. The criterion utilized was that all factors with an eigenvalue equal to or exceeding 1.00 were rotated to varimax orthogonal position. Additional factors beyond those meeting the eigenvalue criterion were examined, but for the attribute dimensions, none was included. Oblique rotations also were assessed, but, as they differed only slightly from the orthogonal, the orthogonal were used in this study.

REFERENCES

BEIM, D. (1964) "The Communist bloc and the foreign aid game." Western Political Quarterly 17 (December): 784-799.

BRODY, R. A. and J. F. VESECKY (1969) "Soviet openness to changing situations: a critical evaluation of certain hypotheses about Soviet foreign policy behavior," pp. 353-386 in J. Triska (ed.) *Communist Party States: Comparative and International Studies.* New York: Bobbs-Merrill.

CHOI, C. (1973) "The contemporary foreign behavior of the U.S. and the USSR: an application of Rummel's status-field theory." University of Hawaii, Dimensionality of Nations Project Research Report 68.

FORSYTH, M. G., H.M.A. KEENS-SOPER, and P. SAVAGER (1970) *Trietschke.* London: Allen and Unwin.

GALTUNG, J. (1966) "East-West interaction patterns." Journal of Peace Research 3: 146-177.

GEHLEN, M. P. (1967) *The Politics of Coexistence: Soviet Methods and Motives.* Bloomington: University of Indiana Press.

GOLDMAN, M. I. (1967) *Soviet Foreign Aid.* New York: Frederick A. Praeger.

HERMAN, L. M. (1966) "Soviet foreign trade and the United States market," pp. 935-947 in *New Direction in Soviet Economy,* Studies prepared for the Subcommittee on Foreign Economic Policy of the Joint Economic Committee, Congress of the United States.

HILTON, G. (1973) "A review of the Dimensionality of Nations Project." Sage Professional Papers in International Studies 02-015. Beverly Hills: Sage Publications.

MEEHAN, E. F. (1967) *Contemporary Political Thought: A Critical Study.* Homewood, Ill.: Dorsey.

PISAR, S. (1970) *Coexistence and Commerce: Guidelines for Transactions Between East and West.* New York: McGraw-Hill.

RHEE, S. (1971) "Communist China's foreign behavior: an application of field theory model II." University of Hawaii, Dimensionality of Nations Project Research Report 57.

ROBERTSON, D. B. (1974) "A field theory analysis of Soviet foreign behavior with special emphasis on alternative research strategies." M.A. thesis. American University.

RUMMEL, R. J. (1965) "A field theory of social action with application to conflict within nations." General Systems Yearbook 10: 183-211.

––– (1966) "A foreign conflict behavior code sheet." World Politics 18: 283-296.

––– (1969) "Field theory and indicators of international behavior." University of Hawaii, Dimensionality of Nations Project Research Report 29.

——— (1970) "A status-field theory of international relations." University of Hawaii, Dimensionality of Nations Project Research Report 50.

——— (1972a) *The Dimensions of Nations.* Beverly Hills: Sage Publications.

——— (1972b) "U.S. foreign relations: conflict, cooperations, and attribute distances," pp. 71-114 in B. M. Russett (ed.) *Peace, War, and Numbers.* Beverly Hills: Sage Publications.

RUSSETT, B. M. (1968) "Delineating international regions," in J. D. Singer (ed.) *Quantitative International Politics: Insights and Evidence.* New York: Free Press.

SIMON, M. D. (1969) "Communist system interaction with developing Afro-Asian states," in J. Triska (ed.) *Communist Party States: Comparative and International Studies.* New York: Bobbs-Merrill.

TANSKY, L. (1966) "Soviet foreign aid to the less developed countries," pp. 947-974 in *New Directions in the Soviet Economy,* Studies prepared for the Sub-committee on Foreign Economic Policy of the Joint Economic Committee, Congress of the United States.

TRISKA, J. [ed.] (1969) *Communist Party States: Comparative and International Studies.* New York: Bobbs-Merrill.

——— and D. D. FINLEY (1965) "Soviet-American relations: a multiple symmetry model." Journal of Conflict Resolution 9 (March): 37-53.

VAN ATTA, R. H. (1974) "Competitive interdependence in a bipolar international system." Ph.D. dissertation. Indiana University.

——— (1973) "Field theory and national-international linkages," in J. Wilkenfeld (ed.) *Conflict Behavior and Linkage Politics.* New York: David McKay.

APPENDIX

Attribute Space Variables

VARIABLE	SOURCE	
Aid	Goldman, Marshall I. *Soviet Foreign Aid.* New York: Praeger, 1967	Data for economic aid include amounts expended on grants or long-term loans in cash on time, including within the latter category the provision of service as well as its commodities.
Trade	*U.N. Statistical Yearbook*	Exports (USSR → j)
Tourists	*U.N. Statistical Yearbook*	USSR → j
Diplomatic Representation	*The Statesman's Yearbook*	1 = Embassy, 2 = Legation, 3 = Relations but no representative
Treaty	Dimensionality of Nations Project (DON)	All bilateral and multilateral treaties and agreements filed with the Secretary General of the United Nations. Accessions, supplementary agreements, and exchanges of notes were counted also.

APPENDIX

Attribute Space Variables

VARIABLE	SOURCE	
Treaty Propensity	Transformation	Total treaties (1950-1957 or 1958-1965)/8
Comparative Treaties	Transformation	USSR treaty propensity/ U.S. treaty propensity
Conflict	DON	Aggregation of all DON conflict data (USSR →j)
Visits to and from the USSR	U.S. Foreign Broadcast Information Service, Daily Report and New York Times	All reported visits to and from the Soviet Union classified into four categories: Head of State, Minister, other government official, and non-government.

Chapter 2

AMERICAN MILITARY INTERVENTION ABROAD: A TEST OF ECONOMIC AND NONECONOMIC EXPLANATIONS

FREDERIC S. PEARSON

University of Missouri—St. Louis

INTRODUCTION

While some have maintained that U.S. military intervention—i.e., movement of troops to foreign states—is relatively unlikely in the post-Vietnam setting, such judgments seem premature since we know little about the factors that have generally led to U.S. interventions. The fact that in 1973 U.S. troops were put on worldwide military alert in response to supposed Soviet intentions in the Middle East seems to indicate that U.S. military intervention is not precluded. Therefore, it is necessary to see which ones might fit future conflict environments. In particular, with growing major power needs for resources and trade, it is necessary to determine the effects of economic interests on military intervention decisions.

AUTHOR'S NOTE: Note that sources for data collection do not appear in References but rather only in Notes. The author is grateful to Joel Blassman Richard Hayes, E. T. Jones, and Robert Sorensen for methodological and substantive suggestions, as well as to Robert Baumann and Gordon Folkman for their assistance in data preparation. This research is generously supported by the Center for International Studies, University of Missouri—St. Louis. Of course, all inclusions are the responsibility of the author.

Three major explanations of U.S. interventions will be tested: (1) the economic-imperialism explanation; (2) the anti-Communist explanation; and (3) the major power strategic interest explanation. Each of these should be familiar to students of U.S. foreign policy, and some have been treated recently in explaining U.S. diplomatic ties to Latin America (see Chapter 3 of this volume, by Petersen). No one has yet empirically applied these alternative approaches to the study of U.S. troop movements. Together, the three constitute a rough model of U.S. intervention decision-making, since presumably a country ranking high in all three types of U.S. interest would be of more concern to U.S. decision makers and more subject to military intervention than one ranking high on two, one, or none. This model will be tested, along with the validity of each separate explanation.

Those positing the economic imperialism explanation extend Leninist argument to the post-World War II era: U.S. corporate capitalists constantly seek overseas markets, profits, and workers, and through their influence on the U.S. government, see to it that the army and flag follow the investor (see, for instance, Kolko, 1969; Magdoff, 1969). Testing these assumptions for U.S. policies in general, rather than intervention in particular, Petersen has found that in Latin America, U.S. policies, such as economic and military assistance and diplomatic representation, correlate rather strongly with measures of U.S. private economic interest (described in Chapter 3, below). While many have speculated about the relations of imperialism or economic domination on the one hand, and war or intervention on the other, few have provided clear empirical tests. (For a theoretical approach, see Kramer and Bauer, 1972; for an initial test of a structural theory, see Galtung, 1971.) Indeed, imperialism itself has often been posited as the dependent variable.

Empirical evidence belies some Leninist assumptions, since few major powers have fought each other in competition over weak countries. Instead, major powers have most frequently been at war with those smaller countries themselves, and, even more frequently, small countries have fought each other (see Pearson, 1974c). While major powers individually have been the most warlike countries, proponents of the economic-imperialist explanation have been hard-pressed to account for the relative scarcity of major power economic interests in war zones such as Vietnam. However, rejoinders often stress the growth of major power economic penetration of such areas once fighting begins, as well as the strategic value of such places for maintaining economic access to entire regions; Vietnam itself may not be economically important, but Japan, Taiwan, the Philippines, etc., are. Thus, the respective arguments rage on, and careful weighing of evidence remains imperative.

Some intervention theorists have described U.S. interventionary behavior mainly in terms of anti-Communist power competition while others have described behavior that could be typical of any major power (or even many minor powers) in a position of world leadership—Britain in the nineteenth century, Rome in the first century, etc.—i.e., a desire to maintain maximum possible influence in any area, and to forestall undesired policy changes in foreign countries. Tillema (1973) sets out decision rules about the U.S. intervention based on two factors: the degree of Communist threat in a country, and the degree to which a country is of "special interest" to the United States. Both of these factors are ambiguous. We know now, although North Korea possibly did not know in 1949, that South Korea is of special interest to the United States, though we may not know why. The concept "special interest" remains rather vague and could include such factors as economic investment, geographic proximity, cultural similarity, strategic location, prior involvements, etc. As for U.S. anti-Communism, some theorists (see Barnet, 1968) have maintained that the United States has intervened in some targets where the threat of Communism was mainly imaginary or contrived. It is possible that even if there had been no Russian revolution, the United States would still be a highly interventionary major power, since the acquisition of power often brings increased perceived need and ability to manipulate events in foreign countries—to avert undesired policies which could negatively affect the major power's far-flung interests. This is, of course, a circular process in which greater power, affording greater ability to affect conditions abroad, leads to greater interest in what goes on abroad, which leads to greater perceived need for "security," which leads to greater quest for power. While Tillema indicates that the reasons for U.S. interventions changed drastically after World War II,[1] Barnet and others place U.S. postwar interventions in the tradition of nineteenth- and twentieth-century U.S. and great power interventions—designed to prevent uncontrolled or revolutionary change, oppose world domination by other major powers, and assure manipulation of events in certain regions (see Morris, 1973: 37).

The three predominant explanations of U.S. foreign policy decisions are hardly mutually exclusive. The events that a major power might like to influence in a given region could include those that would threaten economic interests or increase the power of "Communists." The United States may oppose other major powers in its world "police officer" role, but anti-Communism cannot be fully separated from great power competition since the major power rivals of the United States happen to be "Communist" states. The major power competition explanation is larger than and, in a way, subsumes the other two.

It should be possible to determine whether U.S. interventions can be explained by either the more limited and specific economic and/or anti-Communist schools, or whether it is necessary to include other variables generally descriptive of major power strategically oriented foreign policies. We must first determine the circumstances of U.S. interventions and the amount of various types of U.S. interests in target states. Suppose a U.S. naval base comes under siege in a local dispute in a small country with which the United States has few economic relations and in which there are no communists. A U.S. military intervention might be aimed at continued U.S. preparedness to resist moves by Communist states in the area, but the immediate interest is in military access to the base. Therefore, the great power strategic explanation would come closest to fitting the circumstances. The key variables which led to and which could be controlled to prevent the need for U.S. intervention relate to the tendency of major powers to seek overseas military bases. In this study, we will search for the variables and interests which most directly and immediately led to interventions. If there are no concrete U.S. economic, or strategic, or anti-Communist interests in a country, the particular explanation of U.S. intervention corresponding to the missing interests will be discounted, though certainly not disproven. Explanations associated with interests which are present could be valid. It is necessary to determine joint probabilities of intervention given combinations of such interests if validation is to be achieved.

In this study, it is assumed that economic interests are reflected in levels of U.S. trade and investment in foreign countries as well as in those countries' economic dependence on the United States.[2] It is also assumed that there are three basic types of U.S. major power strategic interests in smaller powers: (1) diplomatic interest—i.e., the use of foreign countries as important listening posts and points of diplomatic leverage in a region—indicated by the size of diplomatic mission concerned with the particular country;[3] (2) military interest—in the small power's regional role and in U.S. military access to the region, indicated by grants of military aid;[4] and (3) interest in spreading life styles to make foreign areas more amenable to U.S. influence by attempting to export U.S. values—this has been indicated by "nation-building" efforts, cultural exchanges, and the bilateral distribution of U.S. economic aid.[5] Anti-Communism may be related to all these interests, but they are broader as well— concerning the ease with which Americans may contact and influence events in foreign states (see Morris, 1973: 37). Anti-Communist interests themselves are indicated in the strength of Communist parties in foreign states and in the amount of Soviet or Chinese economic and political penetration of those states.[6] U.S. decision makers may worry about the "potential" for Communism in a state, but if no concrete Communist strength (aid, party strength, training programs, informational exchanges, etc.) in a state can be shown, the anti-Communist explanation for intervention in that state will be discounted (see Barnet, 1968: chs. 4-5).

The mere existence of U.S. interests in a foreign state is not enough to trigger U.S. military intervention. There must also be a perceived threat to or an opportunity to expand those interests. In this study, such threat or opportunity are operationalized in terms of the amount of civil violence and disruption occurring in potential intervention targets.[7] Of course, such disruption also represents a potential cost to an intervener, since intervening troops may get bogged down in a long, bloody civil conflict and since political goals may be difficult to achieve in such an environment. However, severe civil disruption in a country in which the United States has great strategic, economic, or ideological interests may leave few evident alternatives to intervention—at least as perceived by U.S. decision makers. (On the effects of time and crisis on perceived alternatives, see Holsti, 1972: 14-15.)

The balance among interests, alternatives, and costs conditions nearly all human decisions, and the balance varies from situation to situation. It is difficult to specify a particular balance which may cause an intervention, since different decision makers are sensitive to different factors in the interest-cost-alternative equation. Nevertheless, it should be possible to describe situations in which the balance indicates that intervention is likely. (On alternatives and costs, see Pearson, 1974a; Young, 1968: 180-181; Sullivan, 1969.) By determining the frequency of U.S. military as opposed to non-military responses when threats to major interests were great, evidence is gathered on whether the threat factor increases or decreases perceived costs of and alternatives to military intervention.

FINDINGS

Foreign military intervention is defined as the movement of troops or military forces by one independent country, or a group of countries in concert, across the border of another independent country (or colony of an independent country), or actions by troops already stationed in the target country. It is relatively easy to identify such troop or force movements, and this definition avoids the ambiguities of others which dwell on actions "aimed at authority structures," "convention-breaking" actions which disrupt normalized relations, and actions designed to "force changes" in the target country (see Rosenau, 1968, 1969; Sullivan, 1969; Beloff, 1968). For purposes of the present study, only intervention in which troops undertook some direct military action, as opposed to longer-term relatively inactive encampment on bases (such as by U.S. troops in West Germany), were analyzed for the period 1950-1967.

Analyses of data on interventions and U.S. interests have been performed separately for each region of the world so that patterns peculiar to each region can be discovered. The U.S. Department of State is organized in large part along regional lines, and it is possible that State Department specialists in certain regions have different conceptions of "intervenable" issues. This may affect U.S. decision-making at higher echelons. There has certainly been an asymmetry to U.S. military interventions since World War II, with the bulk occurring in Asia; it may be important to determine whether Asian crises or interests have systematically differed from those of other regions. Furthermore, researchers have previously been quick to downplay the effects of economic interests on U.S. military and political policy in "less-developed" regions because most U.S. trade and investment centers in Europe, Canada, Japan, and some Latin American countries. However, these dominant worldwide economic interests may obscure relatively important U.S. economic interests in each individual region.[8] Conceivably, there are key economic interests in each region for which the United States might intervene, but which might not seem so great when compared to overall U.S. trade and investment. Thus, analyses are presented according to region, and time lags are controlled so that measurements of U.S. interests are always taken *prior* to the interventions which they might predict.

In general, U.S. foreign military interventions from 1950-1967 (see Table 1) were mainly friendly to the target government, often aiding the government against rebel groups. The United States used troops mainly to shore up favored regimes rather than to tear down hostile regimes. There were exceptions to the pattern of friendly interventions, of course, as in U.S. bombardment of North Korea and North Vietnam. The goal in these actions may have been to bring down a Communist regime, but U.S. leaders probably would have settled for effectively punishing and weakening the regimes. In general, though, the U.S. military was kept out of a direct role in such subversive operations as the Bay of Pigs invasion; there were evidently more appealing covert and nonmilitary means of bringing down relatively uncooperative foreign governments, while means short of military intervention may frequently fail to strengthen weak unpopular pro-U.S. regimes (of course, military action may also fail). Those who speculate about possible U.S. intervention to wrest Saudi oil wells from an uncooperative Saudi government do not have much precedent on their side. The United States does not usually discipline old friends with military interventions, though conceivably Washington could attempt to engineer a coup in Saudi Arabia or elsewhere and intervene to "protect" the new regime and its right to sell oil. Indeed, if historical patterns hold true, the most likely spots for future U.S. military interventions would be in countries like Jordan, where interests built over long periods of time could be destroyed by a coup d'état.

U.S. military interventions have most frequently concerned regional power balances, ideological competition, and protection of military or diplomatic installations, personnel, or interests. American armed forces were also frequently used to evacuate foreign nationals thought to be endangered by civil disputes in "less- developed" countries; sometimes, as in the Congo and Dominican Republic, such

TABLE 1

List of U.S. Interventions, 1950-1967[a]

	DATE	TARGET
II, c, d	June, 1950	Taiwan
II, 2, b, d	June 27, 1950	South Korea
I, 2, c, d	July 2, 1950	North Korea
I, 2	August 27, 1950	China
II, 1	October 25, 1951	Philippines
II, 2, b	January 1955	Taiwan
II, 1, c, d	July 15, 1958	Lebanon
II, 1, d	July 17, 1958	Jordan
III, a	July 28, 1958	Cuba
II, 2, c, d	September 4, 1958	Taiwan
II, 1, c	March 1961	Laos
II, 1, c, d	December 11, 1961	South Vietnam
II, 2, c, d	May 17, 1962	Thailand
II, 2, c, d	November 1962	India
III, b	January 13, 1964	Zanzibar
2, c, d	March 19, 1964	Cambodia
III, b	April 1964	Gabon
II, 1, c, d	May 1964	Laos
I, 2, c, d	August 4, 1964	North Vietnam
II, 1	August 13, 1964	Congo (Kinshasa)
II, 1, b	November 23, 1964	Congo (Kinshasa)
II, 1, a, c, d	March 7, 1965	South Vietnam
II, 1, a, b, c, d	April 28, 1965	Dominican Republic
II, 1	July 10, 1967	Congo (Kinshasa)

Key: I = Hostile; II = Friendly; III = Neutral or Nonsupportive; 1 = In Domestic Dispute; 2 = To Affect Policies or Conditions if No Dispute; a = Military-Diplomatic Protective; b = Evacuation; c = Ideological; d = Regional Power Balance.

a. The United States also bombed Soviet territory during the Korean War, but while the action took place in Asia, the intervention is not included here because of the concern with "Third World" interventions and USSR classification as "European."

evacuations constituted opening wedges for more profound political and military interference. Economic motives were seldom expressed by U.S. intervention decision makers, and while some U.S. intervention targets (e.g., the Dominican Republic and Taiwan) had many U.S. enterprises, the United States did little business in other targets prior to intervention (e.g., Vietnam). Since it can be argued that U.S. officials view certain countries as strategic pivots for influence in a region, and loss of influence in a total region as bad for U.S. business, it is necessary to examine American economic relations with regions and intervention targets more carefully (see next paragraph). Territorial and social interests in foreign countries seemed almost totally unrelated to U.S. interventions, although these interests frequently characterized military interventions by small powers throughout the world—e.g., Greek and Turkish interventions in Cyprus (see Pearson, 1974c).

Looking more closely at particular types of U.S. intervention targets, investment data (Table 2) indicate that the regions in which the United States most frequently intervened were generally not those with the most investment. Latin America and Europe (along with Canada) traditionally have been the prime grounds for U.S. investments, with Asia coming next and gaining on Latin America throughout the years since World War II. If military forces were used primarily to pacify regions of great economic interest, the relative scarcity of military interventions in Latin America—and the Middle East, for that matter—does not fit the predicted pattern. Conceivably, investors do not like to do business in regions so subject to political instability that the use of U.S. troops must be contemplated. Africa, with five U.S. military interventions from 1950-1967 (Central and East Asia had fifteen reported and one alleged intervention; the Middle East, two; and Latin America, two reported and one alleged), seemed a more frequent intervention arena than might be predicted by U.S. economic interest alone. The major U.S. African investments in 1966 were in Liberia, Libya, and South Africa, where no U.S. interventions occurred.

Countries in which the U.S. intervened which ranked high in U.S. regional direct investments prior to intervention were Cuba (ranked first in Central America-Caribbean in 1957), Colombia (prior to 1948), the Dominican Republic (ranked fifth in Central America-Caribbean in 1960), India (ranked fourth in region in 1960), and the

TABLE 2

U.S. Direct Investments Abroad by Region[a]
(millions of dollars)

	1950	1957	1966
Latin America	4,445	7,434	9,826
	(45)	(1,163)	(276)
Central-Caribbean	1,488	2,234	2,723
South America	2,957	5,200	7,102
Europe	1,733	4,151	16,209
	(121)	(287)	(1,970)
EEC	637	1,680	7,584
Other	1,096	2,471	8,624
Africa	287	664	2,074
	(33)	(9)	(108)
North	56	106	―――
East	12	30	―――
West	42	147	―――
Central-South	177	381	―――
Asia	1,001	2,019	3,896
	(79)	(144)	(180)
Mid-East	692	1,138	1,669
	(63)	(71)	(68)
Far East	309	881	2,227
	(16)	(73)	(112)
India	38	113	243
Japan	19	185	756
Philippines	149	306	579
Other	104	277	649
Oceania	256	698	2,069
	(25)	(-4)	(189)
Canada	3,579	8,769	16,999
	(287)	(718)	(1,336)

a. Figures in parentheses indicate capital flows to the United States from these areas.

Philippines (first in the region in 1950). Thus, Asia and Latin America are two regions in which U.S. interventions could have been designed in part to protect investment interests. U.S. African interventions did not seem related to investment, although, as shown further, the Congo was a major U.S. regional trade partner, and British or Belgian economic concerns might have affected Washington's intervention decisions. Naturally, African interventions could have been designed to pave the way for future economic enterprise, but in the 1970s Africa still had the least overall U.S.

investment—though Africa had gained considerably on Asia in this regard.

In general, extensive economic interests, as measured by U.S. trade, were not as prevalent in U.S. intervention targets as U.S. strategic interests (see Table 3).[9] For the three years prior to each intervention, average U.S. trade was calculated in each region for the countries which were not intervention targets and compared to average trade for the intervention targets. U.S. intervention targets in Central Asia (India) and Central America (Cuba and the Dominican Republic) had above-average trade with the United States for their region over the three years prior to intervention. The Congo was also a primary U.S. trade partner in Africa in both 1964 and 1967, although Gabon and Zanzibar were not. Trade seemed a less important factor in U.S. East Asian interventions, although the Philippines (1951) and Taiwan (1955) were important trade markets.

While overall U.S. trade with intervention targets was not consistently above regional averages, the U.S. imperialism theory is not totally discredited. Except for the 1962 and 1964 interventions in Asia, U.S. intervention targets in the 1960s were more dependent on U.S. imports (as a percentage of their total imports) than the average of non-targets in their region. African targets seemed especially dependent in this regard. Obviously, this does not prove that President Johnson sent troops to the Congo or the Dominican Republic to preserve a U.S. economic toehold on those countries, but when considered in conjunction with the other variables, the effect of economic interests is not negligible.

Economic effects are complicated, however. For example, in 1958 the Congo had been the second largest supplier of African goods to the United States, but by 1964 had fallen to eighth amid massive internal dislocation and upheaval. Thus, concrete U.S. interest declined prior to intervention while remaining above the regional average; but U.S. intervention decision makers may have desired to restabilize the Congo in order to regain access to Congolese resources. Concrete economic interests were also relatively low in Jordan and Lebanon, scenes of U.S. interventions in 1958. But at that time, Iraq, ranking fifth among Middle Eastern countries in exports to the United States, had undergone a violent coup which threatened its Western-oriented strategic and economic policy. Intervention in Jordan and Lebanon thus could have related as well to desire for

TABLE 3

Amount of U.S. Economic and Noneconomic Interests in Intervention Targets Compared to Non-Targets by Region[a]

E. Asia	1950	1951	1955	1958	1961	1962	1964	1965
FS	+2	+	+	+	+	+	−	+2
	(−)	(+)	(±)	(+)	(+)	(+)	(±)	+2
TR	−	+2	+	−	−2	−2	−2	−2
	(−2)	(+2)	(−)	(−)	(−2)	(−2)	(−2)	(−2)
MA	+2	+2	+2	+2	−	−	−2	+2
	(+2)	(+2)	(+2)	(+2)	(−2)	(−2)	(−2)	(+2)
AA	+2	−	−2	−2	−	−2	+	+2
	(−2)	(±)	(−2)	(−2)	(−)	(−2)	(+)	(+2)
CP					−2	−	+2	−2
					(−2)	(−)	(−2)	(+2)
% USSR IMP					−	=	=	≡
					(−)	(=)	(±)	(≡)
% PRC IMP					−	≡	≡	−
					(−)	(−)	(=)	(−)
% USIMP					+	≡	−2	+2
					(±)	(−)	(−)	(+2)
USSRECAID					+2	−	−	−
					(+)	(−)	(=)	(−)
PRCECAID					=	=	=	=
					(=)	(=)	(=)	(=)
USECAID					+	+	+	+
					(+)	(+)	(+)	(+)
USSRNS					≡	−	+	−
					(=)	(−)	(+)	(−)
PRCNS					≡	−	+	−
					(=)	(−)	(=)	(=)
USSRSTU					−	−	+2	−
					(≡)	(=)	(−2)	(−)
PRCSTU					−	−2	+2	−
					(−)	(±)	(≡)	(≡)
USSTU					−2	+2	−2	−
					(−2)	(+2)	(−2)	(−)

	Central Asia	Africa		Middle East	Central Americas	
	1962	1964	1967	1958	1958	1965
FS	+2 (+2)	-2 [+]	+	+	+	- (-)
TR	+2 (+2)	- [+]	+	-2	+2	+ (±)
MA	- (-)	- [-]	+2	-2	+2	+2 (+)
AA	+2 (+2)	+2 [+2]	+2	-2	+2	+ (+2)
CP	+2	- [-]				-
% USSRIMP	-2	≡ [≡]				- (=)
% PRCIMP	=	≡ (≡)	≡			≡ (=)
% USIMP	+	+2 [+2]	+2			+ (+)
USSRECAID	=					
PRECAID	-					
USECAID	-	-2 [-]	+			-2 (-2)
USSRNS	=	- [+]	-			≡ (=)
PRCNS	=	+ [+]	-			≡ (≡)
USSRSTU	+2	-2 [-2]				- (-)
PRCSTU	+2	+2 [+2]				- (=)
USSTU	+2	-2 [-]				-2 (-)

a. "+" indicates that average scores for intervention targets were above the regional average for non-targets; "+2" indicates that target's average scores were more than twice the non-target average; "-" indicates that targets were below the non-target regional average; "-2" indicates at least two times below the non-target average; "=" indicates that target and non-target regional averages were equal; "≡" indicates that targets were only slightly below non-target averages; "±" indicates slightly above non-target averages. Parentheses indicate results after Communist bloc countries have been deleted from the regional calculations; brackets indicate results after evacuation interventions have been deleted from regional calculations.

(note continued on p. 50)

Data on USSR and PRC interactions, as well as U.S. economic aid were readily available only after 1959. Abbreviated variable titles: FS—size of U.S. foreign service mission; TR—total U.S. Trade (exports + imports); MA—U.S. military aid; AA—armed attacks (internal political violence); CP—size of local Communist Party; % USSR (PRC) (US)—percentage of state's imports coming from USSR (PRC) (US); USSR (PRC) (US) ECAID—economic aid from USSR (PRC) (US); USSR (PRC) NS—news services of USSR (PRC) in state; USSR (PRC) (US) STU—state's students studying in the USSR (PRC) (US).

continued or increased access to resources. Indeed, Lebanon itself has become a major banking and investment center. It is difficult to pinpoint economic motives for U.S. interventions because economic interests seldom occur wholly separately from strategic interests, although factor analysis shows that the two types of interests are not consistently correlated. Generally, there were probably somewhat fewer U.S. Middle Eastern interventions in the 1950s and 1960s than the economic importance of that region to the West would suggest, and slightly more interventions in Africa and Indochina than suggested by their economic importance. Thus, economic interests alone are not the best intervention predictors. However, in Latin America, parts of Asia, and Africa, economic interests are not irrelevant to an understanding of U.S. military moves. Furthermore, the United States has used or armed many regional proxies in efforts to stabilize the economically important Middle East without direct U.S. intervention: Turkey against Syria, Israel and Jordan against Palestinians, Saudi Arabia against the U.A.R., Iran against Iraq and other revolutionaries.

Judging from Table 3, the major power strategic explanation of U.S. interventions best describes intervention decisions, though qualifications according to region and time period are necessary and though anti-Communism is hardly irrelevant. Military and diplomatic strategy and concern over targets' ability to compete militarily in their region seemed the major reasons for U.S. East Asian interventions in the 1950s. Prior military assistance seemed the best predictor of such interventions, as the United States committed itself to a series of alliances in Asia. Taiwan, South Korea, and the Philippines were rather dwarfed by Japan in terms of economic importance to the United States. But they were strategically located in relation to China, were willing to cooperate militarily, to compete with Communist states in the region, and came to represent important diplomatic arenas for U.S. influence—as reflected by the size of U.S. diplomatic missions assigned. These interventions and interests were spurred by and came to represent the legacy of the Korean War.

U.S. interventions in South Korea and Taiwan were mainly aimed at protecting these states against external attack and thus preserving a military balance in the region favorable to the United States. Of course, South Korea's violent conflict with the North can be interpreted as a civil conflict. The Philippines also suffered from acute internal political violence at the time of intervention in 1951, though its record on violence had been only slightly above regional averages for non-Communist states for the prior three years.

In part, this Korean War pattern seemed to change in the East Asian interventions of the 1960s. Except for Vietnam in 1965, targets had not received unusually large (for the region) amounts of military aid prior to intervention, though in a per capita calculation, Laos received especially high levels of aid. Indeed, military assistance to Vietnam skyrocketed *after* the 1961 intervention there, as it had in many targets after U.S. interventions. Note, though, that Vietnam ranked fourth in U.S. military aid to Asia in 1960, even before the U.S. intervention. Gradually, in the 1960s, U.S. Asian policy obtained the added dimension of "nation-building," a strategy aimed at reorienting the political loyalties and values of foreign citizens so that they would support political systems compatible with the U.S. mode. The United States sought not only to preserve the strength of regional allies, but to counteract the appeal of revolution and compete ideologically for new adherents. Now intervention targets were strife-torn countries where Communism was considered a potential if not immediate threat. Change threatened to get out of U.S. control, and the remedy was thought to be the promotion of controlled and gradual reform. When reform failed, and in the midst of internal chaos, anti-insurgency intervention would be used. Diplomatic interest in these intervention targets was generally high and economic interest relatively low, but U.S. economic aid to such targets was consistently high relative to non-targets prior to intervention. While military aid was the best predictor of Asian interventions in the 1950s, economic aid—indicating the major power nation-building strategy—became one of the best predictors in the 1960s. The United States embarked on interventions not simply in the territory of firm allies, but in countries torn by civil conflict and in some cases formally pledged to neutralism. Indochinese interventions were directed at the regional balance of power, but indirectly, through attempts at changing internal conditions in the target state rather than equipping the target to "deter" Communist states in the region.

These distinctions are not ironclad, of course, since the Philippines in 1951 was preoccupied with domestic turmoil, and since Thailand was part of the American alliance and "deterrence" system of the 1960s. However, in the Philippines, American-oriented "nation-building" was carried out under the colonial administration of the early twentieth century. By 1951, the task was to keep the established regime in power. The regimes the United States sought to help in Laos and Vietnam were less-well-established, and the political tasks involved in military intervention were much greater than in the Philippines in 1951.

U.S. interventions in Central Asia, Africa, and Central America in the 1960s also reflected this concern with internal turmoil in the target, though nation-building, as reflected by economic aid, was not as seriously pursued in non-Asian targets. Armed attacks by domestic opposition groups were far above regional averages in U.S. intervention targets in these regions, and seemed to threaten more economic and diplomatic than military interests. Domestic turmoil threatened economic interests and regional military policy vis-à-vis Cuba in Central America and the Caribbean, threatened diplomatic and economic access to India—the largest counterpoint to Chinese political and economic influence in Central Asia—and threatened the economic ties of the United States and its allies to the Congo. In the Middle East, though the level of internal disruption was relatively low, the bloody conflict in Iraq seemed likely to spread and threaten friendly governments in geographically important diplomatic listening posts. U.S. military strategy in the Middle East had been stymied by Nasser in the mid-fifties, and the United States, without extensive formal alliances and bases, had to maneuver diplomatically through proxies. Hence, the importance of Jordan and Lebanon, as well as the willingness to move militarily to show Nassar that such moves could be made if deemed necessary.

The importance of targets' internal political disruption to U.S. intervention decisions is further underscored by the fact that all seventeen "friendly" (aid target government or oppose rebels) U.S. military interventions were in targets with at least some violent political conflict just prior to or at the time of intervention. Twelve of the seventeen interventions were preceded (in the same year or the prior year) by over fifty politically related deaths in the target—indicating rather high-intensity violence. U.S. exports to six of these twelve also ranked high in the given region, while exports to two of the five targets without much violent conflict ranked high in the region. Thus, there was a tendency for the United States to intervene militarily to prop up regimes threatened by rather severe domestic violence, and in roughly half of these interventions there was considerable U.S. economic interest in the target. Furthermore, violence was great prior to nine of the twelve interventions in states which were major (top five ranks) regional recipients of U.S. military aid at the time of intervention. Thus, the mixture of strategic military interest and violent internal disturbance characterized a majority of U.S. friendly interventions.

The United States intervened in eight targets which were neither major export markets nor major military aid recipients. However, these tended to be rather quick evacuation interventions to remove endangered personnel from places like Gabon or Zanzibar, or interventions in countries which suddenly took on new importance for U.S. decision makers when a crisis emerged in the region—South Korea, 1950, Indochina as the Laos accords broke down in 1961-1962, and Jordan in 1958 after the Iraqi monarchy fell. These cases seem to contrast with U.S. reaction when interests which had grown over a period of years were threatened in the Philippines, Congo, Taiwan, the Dominican Republic, and Vietnam (1965) by progressively developing crises which finally reached the acute stages.

If we turn the calculations around and look at the probability of being intervened in, given high rank in U.S. trade, military or economic aid, foreign service missions, etc., we find that the probabilities of military intervention by the United States seem greatest for those countries highly dependent on U.S. imports (an average across years of twenty percent), and high in U.S. military aid (seventeen percent) and internal disruption (armed attacks by organized political groups—eighteen percent). (See Table 4.) U.S. imports, military aid, and internal political violence are also the variables with the most significant differences in intervention probabilities for high-versus low-ranking states. States ranking low on PRC and USSR imports are also significantly more likely to be intervened in by the United States than are high-ranking states. This reflects the U.S. propensity for friendly interventions. Thus, although no single variable explains much of the variance in U.S. interventions, the mode of postwar U.S. military moves has been to protect governments which have already been defined as strategically important and/or which confront rather massive domestic conflicts.

TABLE 4

Average Percentage of High and Low Ranking States
Which Were U.S. Intervention Targets[a]

	High	Low	Significance	
For Srv	.09	.04	t = 1.0	p < .5
Trade	.08	.08	t = 0	
Military Aid	.17	.05	t = 2.4	p < .05
Armed Attacks	.18	.03	t = 5.0	p < .002
C.P. Membership	.09	.14	t = .862	p < .5
% Imp-USSR	.03	.14	t = 2.24	p < .05
% Imp-PRC	.03	.15	t = 4.01	p < .002
% Imp-USA	.20	.06	t = 2.99	p < .05
Ec Aid-USSR	.10	.11	t = .20	p > .80 N = 6
Ec Aid-PRC	.00	.09	t = 3.0	p < .05 N = 3
Ec Aid-USA	.11	.11	t = 0	

a. "High" is defined as the upper five ranks within each region; "low" as the lower five ranks. On variables such as PRC economic aid, with few non-zero scores, countries with non-zero scores are rated "high" and those with zero scores "low." Ties are all included in the same rank, so that many more than five countries could be classified "high" or "low." In these calculations Central and East Asia have been combined, and Central and South America have been combined.

Averages are calculated across thirteen U.S. intervention years from 1950-1967 for foreign service, trade, military aid, and armed attacks, and generally across seven years in the 1960s for the other variables. Significance tests have been run, although the thirteen intervention years are not a sample and we cannot necessarily assume that the distribution of interventions across years is normal. However, with N = 7 or thirteen years for both the high- and low-scoring countries, the t statistic should give valid indications of the probability of these differences in average percentages if we were dealing with samples (see Hays, 1963: 322). In essence, also, we are sampling from the total number of U.S. intervention years in history (past and future).

While civil disruption was a catalyst that often brought U.S. intervention to protect or expand economic or strategic military or diplomatic interests, the direct threat of Communist takeover was not frequently involved. Communist party strength was above regional averages (Table 3) only in India, 1962, and Vietnam (the North in 1964 and the South in 1965) among U.S. intervention targets. Looking at cases from the 1950s, where data were missing, there was direct threat of Communist success in Korea and, to an extent, in the Philippines. The People's Republic of China did not seem seriously to contemplate attack on Taiwan (see Sigal, 1970), and Communist threats to Lebanon and Jordan were negligible.

Soviet or Chinese economic penetration played little or no role in U.S. interventions, at least as measured by countries' dependence on Communist states for imports.

When the United States became concerned with "nation-building," competition with the Soviet Union in the distribution of economic aid ensued; this competition evidently related to Indochinese interventions (Laos especially) in 1961 (see Table 3). However, this was the only reflection of worry about Communist economic involvement in U.S. intervention targets. Competition with USSR and the PRC was also reflected in the U.S. intervention in India, as evidenced in the relatively high level of Indian cultural exchanges with both East and West. But competition had not been keen enough to make India a prime recipient of U.S. economic aid in the prior three years, and if there had been no acute border war with China, the United States might not have sent forces to bolster the Indians in a purely domestic dispute. In Africa, the Congo was relatively open to Soviet and Chinese cultural penetration, which interacted with the severe violence and economic interests to bring U.S. intervention. However, it is again clear that the narrower explanations of U.S. intervention decisions—the threat of Communism or threats to economic interests—are not sufficiently powerful, and that they must be combined with factors of the major power strategic explanation. U.S. decision makers sought to "contain" Soviet and Chinese influence in Asia, the Middle East, and Africa, and to contain Cuban influence in Latin America, but this generalized competition was not a reaction to immediate threats of Communist takeover (except in Vietnam, 1965). Rather, it was characteristic of a dominant major power's attempts to prevent uncontrolled political, economic, or military changes in any region of the world, and to maintain political, economic, and military access to all regions.

While the relative lack of variance in the dependent variable—U.S. military interventions (most countries were not intervened in) —makes the use of multivariate data analysis techniques relatively fruitless,[10] we should determine whether more interventions occurred in countries high on several indicators of U.S. interest than in those high on few indicators (see Table 5). Averaged across the years from 1950-1959 in which there was at least one U.S. intervention, thirty-three percent of countries ranking high on all four indicator variables were intervened in. However, this figure is a bit deceiving, since there were only three cases (in three separate years,

TABLE 5

Average Percentages of Countries High on One or More Variables Prior to Intervention[a]

Years 1950-1959

Number of Highs[b]	Yearly Average Percentage of Interventions
4	.33 (N = 3 Region-years)
3	.18 (N = 5 Region-years)
2	.12 (N = 5 Region-years)
1	.06 (N = 6 Region-years)
0	.06 (N = 6 Region-years)

Years 1960-1967

Number of Highs[c]	Yearly Average Percentage of Interventions
7	.00 (N = 1 Region-year)
6	.04 (N = 4 Region-years)
5	.00 (N = 4 Region-years)
4	.14 (N = 6 Region-years)
3	.07 (N = 7 Region-years)
2	.09 (N = 7 Region-years)
1	.06 (N = 7 Region-years)
0	.01 (N = 7 Region-years)

a. In these calculations, Central and East Asia have been combined, and Central and South America have been combined.

b. Variables included: Foreign Service, Trade, Military Assistance, Armed Attacks.

c. Variables included: Foreign Service, Trade, Military Assistance, Armed Attacks, Communist Party Membership, % Imports-USSR, % Imports-PRC, % Imports-USA, Econ. Aid-USSR, Econ. Aid-PRC, Econ. Aid-USA.

hence N = 3) in which countries ranked high on all four variables. In the 1950s, countries high on several variables seemed more intervention-prone than those high on few or none, but this pattern broke down in the 1960s, as countries high on from one to four variables seemed most intervention-prone. None of the percentages is high enough to conclude that, even taken in combination, these are the key variables to explain U.S. interventions. Military aid and armed attacks again seem the most important explanatory variables for 1950s interventions; of the intervention targets with few high scores, military aid and armed attacks were the most frequently high. In the one case in which armed attacks and military aid were concurrently high, there was a U.S. intervention; this compares to one of three cases for concurrent highs in U.S. trade and armed attacks. Furthermore, highs in military aid and armed attacks occurred concurrently in two other interventions, along with highs in foreign service mission size and trade. China had been high on foreign service mission size, U.S. trade, and armed attacks in the three years prior to U.S. Korean war attacks, and there were no reported data on U.S. military aid to China.

Turning to the 1960s, there is no evidence that countries simultaneously high on many U.S. interest indicators were especially subject to intervention. Countries with a moderate number of high scores seemed most intervention-prone, but even here only between seven and fourteen percent received interventions. Although all possible combinations of eleven variables are difficult to calculate, two main sets of U.S. interests characterized intervention targets. One set reflected targets' dependence on the United States as measured by percentage of imports from U.S. trade, U.S. economic aid, military aid, and foreign service mission size. Combinations of two, three, or four of these variables interacted with high levels of threat to incumbent governments—as reflected in armed attacks and/or high Communist Party strength—in South Vietnam in 1961 and 1965, Laos in 1964, and the Congo in 1964 and 1967. Furthermore, Thailand, without many armed attacks, ranked high in both military and economic aid prior to intervention in 1962. This set of variables characterizes U.S. intervention in states already dependent on the United States and contrasts somewhat with the set of variables characterizing U.S. interventions in neutralist states. USSR economic aid and high percentage of USSR or PRC imports interacted with high levels of armed attacks, Communist Party membership, or U.S. economic penetration in the Laos-1961, India-1962, and Cambodia-1964 interventions. These variables characterize the second main form of U.S. intervention: competitive intervention to preclude other major power penetration, and to gain the political allegiance, of uncommitted states.

CONCLUSION

Judging from the generally low percentages of variance in U.S. military intervention associated with the independent variables in this study, two conclusions may be drawn:

(1) The three major explanations of U.S. foreign policy common in the literature do not fully explain U.S. military interventions.

(2) Or the particular variables used to measure U.S. economic, strategic, or ideological interests are not valid.

Conceivably, factors peculiar to U.S. domestic politics or bureaucratic decision-making (for instance, the role of the U.S. ambassador or the State Department) helped condition intervention decisions; domestic political factors have not been measured here. More likely, though, no one factor or even one set of factors can be expected to explain all U.S. interventions. In this analysis, there is evidence that at least two sets of factors apply in various circumstances: (1) factors associated with dependence on the United States—especially economic and military dependence; (2) factors associated with U.S. competition with major and/or Communist powers. One group of interventions took place in U.S. "client" states, and another group took place in states still subject to U.S.-USSR-PRC contention.

Clearly, neither the economic nor the anti-Communist explanation of U.S. interventions is, in itself, sufficient, and factors of U.S. strategic interest must be added. Military aid to countries suffering from severe domestic disruption, or severe disruption in countries highly economically dependent on the United States (as compared to other states of the region) tended to precede U.S. interventions. Generally, with the exception of Vietnam, Communist Party strength was not great inside U.S. intervention targets, and Communist penetration was limited to economic aid or trade. There was also some regional variation, as major power competition took different forms in Asia—with "nation-building" in Indochina—and Africa—with competitive intervention in the resource-rich Congo. U.S. economic interests seemed better intervention predictors in Latin America than in other regions. Patterns of U.S. intervention also seemed to change over the years. Strategic military (aid) and diplomatic (foreign service) interests best predicted U.S. interventions in the 1950s, while economic dependence, internal violence, and U.S. economic aid became better predictors in the 1960s. Indeed, regionally high levels of U.S. economic penetration were present in some form (trade, aid, or percentage of imports) in nine of thirteen intervention targets in the 1960s, and seemed threatened by high domestic violence in five.

Since no single explanation of intervention seems to suffice across regions and years, and since the major power strategic explanation can comprise economic and anti-Communist factors, perhaps it is time to discard some traditional U.S. foreign policy interpretations. One is tempted to adopt the major-power strategic explanation as most comprehensive and promising, but it, too, has drawbacks in its vagueness and generality. It comes close to a tautology, since any U.S. action could be interpreted as designed to increase U.S. influence in and access to regions. The results of this analysis indicate that perhaps foreign policy researchers should spend less time seeking broad explanations and instead better distinguish U.S. policy toward allies, protectorates, and clients from U.S. policy toward neutrals or uncommitted states. Rather than describing the pursuit of economic, military, or ideological goals—goals which are all highly interrelated— perhaps we should determine the degree to which dependence on the United States in economic, military, and ideological relations makes a state more or less subject to U.S. military or nonmilitary intervention. If the United States is a major power out to maximize worldwide influence, does neutralism or a noncommitted foreign policy raise, lower, or have no effect on the degree of manipulation attempted by the U.S. government? Does alliance partnership affect such penetration and manipulation? These are the kinds of questions left so far unanswered for policy makers in other countries, and yet it appears that questions about the intended and unintended consequences of policies restricting or encouraging foreign ties are the key ones for the study of foreign policy.

NOTES

1. According to Tillema, prior to World War II, reasons for U.S. overt military intervention included suppression of piracy, suppression of slave trading, protection of American lives and property, initiatives by local commanders, and desire to put down revolutionaries in Latin America and Asia. One of the major shortcomings of Tillema's study is the failure to identify certain key U.S. interventions both before and after World War II: President Wilson's move into the newly formed USSR; President Eisenhower's airlift of British troops to Jordan; President Johnson's airlift of Belgian troops to the Congo; the use of U.S. combat personnel in Laos, etc.

2. Economic dependence is measured by the percentage of a country's imports coming from the United States. The source of data was: CADY, R., F. MOGDIS, and K. TIDWELL (1973) Major Power Interactions with Less Developed Countries. Ann Arbor, Mich.: Inter-University Consortium for Political Research.

The sources of U.S. import and export data are:

1947-1964 data: U.S. Department of Commerce, Bureau of the Census (1968) Foreign Commerce and Navigation of the United States 1964. Washington, D.C.: Government Printing Office, 60-75.

1965 data: U.S. Department of Commerce, Bureau of the Census (1970) Foreign Commerce and Navigation of the United States 1965, Vol. I, Standard International Trade Classification (SITC), Commodity by Country. Washington, D.C.: Government Printing Office, 8-13.

1966-1968 data: U.S. Department of Commerce, Bureau of the Census (1969) Statistical Abstract of the United States 1969. Washington, D.C.: Government Printing Office, 808-811.

The sources of U.S. foreign investment data are:

1950-1960 data: U.S. Department of Commerce, Office of Business Economics (1963) Balance of Payments of the United States, 1870-1961; A Statistical Supplement, rev. ed. Washington, D.C.: Government Printing Office, 210-215.

1950, 1957-1959 data: U.S. Department of Commerce, Office of Business Economics (1961) U.S. Business Investments in Foreign Countries [Supplement to the Survey of Current Business] by S. PIZER and F. CUTLER. Washington, D.C.: Government Printing Office, 89-91.

1965-1966 data: U.S. Department of Commerce, Bureau of Economic Analysis (1971) U.S. Direct Investments Abroad-1966. Part II. Investment Position, Financial and Operating Data. Group 1. Preliminary Report on Foreign Affiliates of the U.S. Petroleum Industry [Supplement to the Survey of Current Business]. Washington, D.C.: Government Printing Office, 23-24.

1965-1966 data: U.S. Department of Commerce, Bureau of Economic Analysis (1972) U.S. Direct Investments Abroad-1966. Part II. Investment Position, Financial and Operating Data. Group 2. Preliminary Report on Foreign Affiliates of U.S. Manufacturing Industries [Supplement to the Survey of Current Business]. Washington, D.C.: Government Printing Office, 22-23.

1965-1966 data: U.S. Department of Commerce, Bureau of Economic Analysis (1972) U.S. Direct Investments Abroad-1966. Part II. Investment Position, Financial and Operating Data. Group 2. Preliminary Report on Foreign Affiliates of U.S. Reporters in U.S. Industries other than Manufacturing and Petroleum [Supplement to the Survey of Current Business]. Washington, D.C.: Government Printing Office, 18.

3. The source for the size of U.S. diplomatic missions was: U.S. Department of State (1947-1968) Foreign Service List. Washington, D.C.: Government Printing Office.

4. The sources of U.S. military aid data are:

1945-1963 data: U.S. Department of State, Agency for International Development, Statistics and Reports Division (1965) U.S. Overseas Loans and Grants and Assistance from International Organizations, Obligations and Loan Authorizations, July 1, 1945-June 30, 1963 [Special Report prepared for the House Foreign Affairs Committee]. Washington, D.C.: Government Printing Office, 6-137.

1964 data: U.S. Department of State, Agency for International Development, and Department of Defense (1965) Proposed Mutual Defense and Development Programs FY 1966, Summary Presentation to Congress. Washington, D.C.: Government Printing Office, 226-228.

1965 data: U.S. Department of State, Agency for International Development (1966) Foreign Assistance Program, Annual Report to Congress, FY 1965. Washington, D.C.: Government Printing Office, 69-70.

1966 data: U.S. Department of State, Agency for International Development (1968) Foreign Assistance Program, Annual Report to Congress, FY 1966. Washington, D.C.: Government Printing Office, 69-70.

1967 data: U.S. Department of State, Agency for International Development (1968) Foreign Assistance Program, Annual Report to Congress, FY 1967. Washington, D.C.: Government Printing Office, 90-92.

1968 data: U.S. Department of State, Agency for International Development (1969) Foreign Assistance Program, Annual Report to Congress, FY 1968. Washington, D.C.: Government Printing Office, 77-78.

    5. Data on U.S. economic aid were obtained from CADY, R., F. MOGDIS, and K. TIDWELL (1973) Major Power Interactions with Less Developed Countries. Ann Arbor, Mich.: Inter-University Consortium for Political Research.

    6. Data on Communist Party membership in each state, percentage of each state's imports coming from the USSR, economic aid extended to state from the USSR, total imports of state from the USSR, total exports of state to the USSR, percentage of each state's imports coming from the PRC, economic aid extended to state from the PRC, total imports of state from PRC, and total exports of state to PRC, were obtained from: CADY, R., F. MOGDIS, and K. TIDWELL (1973) Major Power Interactions with Less Developed Countries. Ann Arbor, Mich.: Inter-University Consortium for Political Research.

    7. The source for data on armed attacks and deaths from domestic violence was: TAYLOR, C. L. and M. C. HUDSON (1972) World Handbook of Political and Social Indicators. New Haven: Yale University Press, 102-109. A previous study by the author found that armed attacks and deaths from domestic violence were two of the domestic conflict variables most associated with intervention (see Pearson, 1974b).

    8. For this reason, and because data on U.S. interventions in Europe (e.g., during the Berlin crises) are not yet complete, Europe is not included in this analysis.

    9. Trade data—i.e., combined imports and exports—are used because the U.S. Department of Commerce will not publish individual country investment data for certain regions in which operations of specific U.S. companies might be revealed.

    10. Both multiple regression and multiple discriminant analyses were used in trying to assess the impact of the independent variables in explaining U.S. interventions. However, neither technique showed any conclusive results. Although one particular regression accounted for a substantial amount of the total variance, it was mainly due to the large number of variables regressed against the intervention variable. A test for multicollinearity was performed by using a factor analysis and examining Pearson correlation coefficients, but the analysis showed that the independent variables were not highly related. Thus, the major reason for the inconclusive results seems to be a lack of variance in the dependent variable. Since there were only twenty-six interventions (as defined) during the total period, and since most countries were not intervention targets, it was very difficult for a regression or for a discriminant analysis to statistically detect the impact of the independent variables. A possible remedy for this problem may be to redefine the intervention variable such that duration, magnitude, and type of intervention could be accounted for. In future analyses, nonmilitary as well as military interventions could be used to construct a scale of intervention as the dependent variable.

REFERENCES

AAKER, D. A. (1971) Multivariate Analysis in Marketing: Theory and Application. Belmont, Calif.: Wadsworth.

BARNET, R. J. (1968) Intervention and Revolution: The United States in the Third World. New York: World.

BELOFF, M. (1968) "Reflection on intervention." Journal of International Affairs 22: 198-207.

GALTUNG, J. (1971) "A structural theory of imperialism." Journal of Peace Research 8: 81-117.

HAYS, W. L. (1963) Statistics for Psychologists. New York: Holt, Rinehart & Winston.

HOLSTI, O. R. (1972) Crisis, Escalation, War. Montreal: McGill-Queen's University Press.

KOHLER, G. (1974) "The imperialism/war hypothesis revisited." Presented at the annual convention of the International Studies Association, St. Louis, Missouri, March 1974.

KOLKO, G. (1969) The Roots of American Foreign Policy. Boston: Beacon Press.

KRAMER, H. and H. BAUER (1972) "Imperialism, intervention capacity, and foreign policy making." Journal of Peace Research 9: 285-302.

MAGDOFF, H. (1969) The Age of Imperialism. New York: Monthly Review Press.

MORRIS, B. S. (1973) Imperialism and Revolution: An Essay for Radicals. Bloomington: Indiana University Press.

PEARSON, F. S. (1974a) "A perceptual framework for analysis of international military intervention." Peace Research Reviews.

— — — (1974b) "Foreign military interventions and domestic disputes." International Studies Quarterly (September).

— — — (1974c) "Foreign military intervention by large and small powers." International Interactions.

— — — (1974d) "Geographic proximity and foreign military intervention: 1948-1967." Journal of Conflict Resolution (September).

ROSENAU, J. N. (1968) "The concept of intervention." Journal of International Affairs 22: 165-176.

— — — (1969) "Intervention as a scientific concept." Journal of Conflict Resolution 13: 149-171.

SULLIVAN, J. D. (1969) "International consequences of domestic violence: cross-national assessment." Presented to the annual meeting of the American Political Science Association, New York, September 1969.

TATSUOKA, M. M. (1970) Selected Topics in Advanced Statistics, An Elementary Approach, No. 6: Discriminant Analysis, The Study of Group Differences. Champaign, Ill.: Institute for Personality and Ability Testing.

TILLEMA, H. K. (1973) Appeal to Force: American Military Intervention in the Era of Containment. New York: Thomas Y. Crowell.

YOUNG, O. R. (1968) "Intervention and international systems." Journal of International Affairs 22: 177-187.

Chapter 3

ECONOMIC INTERESTS AND U.S. FOREIGN POLICY IN LATIN AMERICA: AN EMPIRICAL APPROACH

J O H N H. P E T E R S E N

Western Kentucky University

One of the dominant themes of inter-American relations has been the question of the motives and goals of the dominant power in the region, the United States, in the foreign policies it pursues vis-à-vis its neighbors in the hemisphere. A number of studies (Mecham, 1965; Perkins, 1955; Lieuwen, 1965; Williams, 1971; and many others) have appeared over the years which have assessed this question from historical, economic, strategic, and political points of view. Nevertheless, many of the central issues remain unresolved. Among these issues is the matter of the role of U.S. private economic interests in the policies followed by the U.S. government in Latin America. One goal to this paper is to explore this relationship further.

This study also represents one aspect of a larger project (Eley and Petersen, 1973) aimed at adapting some of the methods and techniques of contemporary comparative foreign policy research to an explanation of general U.S. foreign policy behavior. A central purpose of much of this research has been to provide statistical measures of relationships between indicators of foreign policy behavior and indicators of various clusters of independent variables in order to eventually develop generalizations which will account for variations in foreign policy behavior.[1] A corollary purpose of the present chapter will be to explore the utility of an empirically oriented approach to the study of U.S. policy in Latin America. Such an approach has rarely, if ever, been applied in a field which has been dominated by traditional, historical analyses or ideological polemics.

In the existing literature, there has been a diversity of positions taken on the role of private economic interests in U.S.-Latin American policy. For the purposes of this paper, these various positions have been combined into three basic categories. One is represented by the "neo-Marxist" interpretation, which ascribes central or causal importance to the role of private economic interests in U.S. policy. The other two categories, which I have labeled "strategic-defensive" and "paternalism-benevolence" represent views which emphasize other factors or variables in explaining U.S. foreign policy behavior and ascribe much less importance to the impact of private economic interests. In the sections which follow, each of these categories will be described and operationalized through the identification of empirical measures. The relationships between these measures and measures of U.S. foreign policy behavior will then be assessed.

SOME ALTERNATIVE EXPLANATIONS OF
U.S. POLICY IN LATIN AMERICA

NEO-MARXIST THEORIES

One of the dominant interpretations of the role of private economic interests in U.S. foreign policy can be placed under the general label of a neo-Marxist theory of imperialism. This theory, which makes a causal connection between the interests of the dominant corporate sector in the United States and American foreign policy behavior, has gained many supporters in recent years. As a general theory of U.S. foreign policy, it has a simplicity and directness that is very attractive.

This approach, based on the theory of imperialism developed by Lenin (1917) and others which linked capitalist economics with colonial foreign policies, asserts the existence of a new form of colonialism in contemporary international politics, or what has been called neo-colonialism. Neo-colonialism differs from classic colonialism in that the alleged pattern of imperial penetration and exploitation of the politics and economics of developing nations does not necessarily involve the imposition of direct rule by the dominant capitalist nation. Instead, various indirect and/or informal means of control are employed even though the purpose of the control remains the same.

Among the many contemporary adherents of this approach are Paul Baran, Heather Dean, Gabriel Kolko and Harry Magdoff. A quote from Magdoff (1969: 12) will indicate the thrust of this point of view.

> The resulting analysis of the available facts shows that there is a close parallel between, on the one hand, the aggressive United States foreign policy aimed at controlling (directly or indirectly) as much of the globe as possible, and, on the other hand, an energetic and expansionist policy of U.S. business.

Implicit in this theory is a model of foreign policy which describes behavioral outcomes as results of forces brought to bear on and through the political system. In this case, forces in the socio-economic environment are seen as shaping not only the outcomes, but the nature of the system itself.

In its general form, the theory is aimed at accounting for U.S. foreign policy activities throughout the world. However, it is particularly applied to the U.S. role in the developing nations. It is in this respect that its relevance to U.S.-Latin American policy has been developed. It is asserted that the determining factors in U.S. policy are the interests of private investors in maintaining profitable investments in Latin America, and for the corporations to have both protected sources of needed raw material imports and guaranteed markets for the export of production.

One of the more articulate representatives of this view among Latin Americanists has been Suzanne Bodenheimer. The following illustrates her perspective:

> In contrast to the above ['international relations' and other non-Marxist theories], a Marxist theory of imperialism addresses itself directly to the economic basis (as well as the political-military aspects) of American policies and to the causes of dependency and underdevelopment in Latin America. For our purposes the adoption of a Marxist framework implies

an integral relation between the actions of the U.S. government abroad and the structure of the American socio-economic system; it analyzes U.S. relations with Latin America as one aspect of American capitalism. . . . The nature of private corporate operations overseas is such that they require protection by the (imperialist) state. Thus the multinational corporation has an increasing stake in consolidating its influence over 'public' or (U.S.) government decisions [Bodenheimer, 1970: 172, 175].

Others who have written in this vein in recent years include John Gerassi (1965), Goff and Locker (1969), Cockcroft et al. (1972), and Miles Wolpin (1971). Edward J. Williams (1971: 8) summarizes their general point of view as follows:

The basic argument is that powerful nations control weak ones to insure a source of raw materials and a market for manufactured goods. The powerful nations also force the weak to sell cheap and buy dear. The strong nations are controlled (or greatly influenced) by powerful economic trusts that manipulate political policies for their own selfish ends. Thus, the argument goes, Wall Street, or the oil companies, or the sugar trusts, or the agri-business dictate Washington's imperialistic policy in Latin America. The purpose of that policy is to ensure economic domination.

Most exponents of the economic imperialism theory base their case largely on their acceptance of the logic of Marxist-Leninist doctrine. Often these arguments become polemical, with no more real support offered than the righteous indignation of the author. Some attempts at more careful, empirically based work by neo-Marxists have appeared in recent years, but for the most part the theory remains to be fully tested.

In sum, the neo-Marxist view is that U.S. private economic interests represent *the* dominant or controlling factor in the determination of patterns of U.S. foreign policy behavior, with other factors being of minor significance. In terms of a hypothesis, the view could be represented as asserting a very close relationship between measures of U.S. private economic interests in Latin America and U.S. foreign policy behavior in the region.

STRATEGIC-DEFENSIVE THEORIES

The major alternative to the neo-Marxist economic imperialism thesis, which is offered by many analysts of U.S.-Latin American relations, could be labeled the strategic-defensive theory. This approach, while not entirely rejecting private economic interest as a factor in foreign policy, argues that the major explanation for U.S. policy lies in the desire of political decision makers to protect the defensive and security interests of the country. Economic interests are seen as clearly minor in importance.

Most traditional international relations theory falls into this category. For example, the central thesis of Hans Morganthau (1967: 5) is that in the "real" world nations behave in terms of "interest defined as power." Among those who have taken a similar position in recent years with regard to the motives of U.S. foreign policy are John Spanier (1971), Robert Walters (1970), John Herz (1962), and many others. Even a major critic of recent U.S. foreign policy, Senator J. William Fulbright (1967: 3-15) ascribes the major motive in U.S. foreign policy, however misguided, to perceived security and international power considerations.

These authors regard the Cold War competition and the protection of American security to be the major factors in determining the foreign behavior of the United States. They ascribe no more than a secondary role to private economic interests in influencing such behavior.

Among scholars who have devoted primary attention to U.S.-Latin American relations, there are numerous adherents to this point of view. The work of J. Lloyd Mecham (1961), Samuel F. Bemis (1943), Norman Bailey (1967), William E. Kane (1972), and many others could be cited as representative. They assess U.S. policy in Latin America as reflecting the real and perceived security needs of the country in competition with other major powers in the world.

For example, throughout Mecham's work, it is emphasized that the dominant feature of U.S.-Latin American policy is the reaction to strategic threats posed by adversay nations—in recent years, mainly the Soviet Union.

> Since shortly after World War II, it became increasingly clear that overseas attack would probably come from but one source, that is, Soviet Russia; the inter-American security structure has been perfected and strengthened with this potential aggressor in view. More than overt military aggression must be reckoned with, however, for, by insidious and subversive undermining American governments can be toppled by the agents of international communism without the firing of a shot. [Mecham, 1961:424]

In a recent book by Norman Bailey (1967: 46), this point of view is central to his interpretation of U.S. foreign policy behavior in Latin America.

> The history of relations between the United States and Latin America from 1823 until the present can be considered as the history of the Monroe Doctrine. [Bailey interprets this as a claim to hemispheric hegemony by the U.S.]

Bailey (1967: 53, 52, 90) goes on to assert:

> It must first be said that there is no area of the world more strategically important to the United States than the Caribbean, if that term is used to include Colombia and Venezuela, as well as Mexico, Central America and the islands.

> The new era of international politics in the Western Hemisphere began as usual with an interpretation of the Monroe Doctrine, this time the Dulles Doctrine, and in a most unlikely spot, the tiny Central American republic of Guatemala. The Soviet Challenge has been, by far, the principal element in United States-Latin America relations since 1954. . . .

> Propaganda and subversion, then, are the strategies available to the Soviet Union that have the maximum likelihood of effectiveness. For this reason the local Communist parties in Latin America are of central importance to Soviet strategy in its Western Hemisphere struggle with the United States.

All of these scholars would place economic interests in a position far subordinate to security considerations (since World War II in the form of anti-communist and anti-Soviet activity) in the policies of the United States in Latin America. Edward J. Williams (1971: 22-23) sums it up as follows: "Security, not economic exploitation, primarily motivated Yankee imperialism. . . . In almost every instance of imperialism, genuine fear that failure to act defensively would result in a threat to American security seemed to motivate U.S. actions."

Thus, the strategic-defensive view is that security interests represent the dominant factor in the pattern of U.S. foreign policy behavior with economic interests and other factors of minor significance. In terms of a hypothesis, this view could be represented as asserting a close relationship between measures of U.S. security interests in Latin America and measures of U.S. foreign policy behavior, and little or no relationship between measures of private economic interests and U.S. foreign policy behavior.

THE PATERNALISM-BENEVOLENCE EXPLANATION

An alternative to each of the above theories is represented by the view that the major goal of U.S. foreign policy in Latin America is the promotion of improved social and economic conditions and the observation of democratic principles and practices in the region. This behavior is seen as stemming from either a sense of noblesse oblige or from a sense of genuine humanitarian good will which in the long run would serve U.S. interests. In either case, it leads to the assertion that U.S. policy in Latin America can be explained in terms of a developed, democratic nation attempting to aid its less fortunate neighboring nations achieve democratic government, economic development, and a better standard of living.

This characteristic of U.S. foreign policy has been frequently noted, beginning with the turn of the century administrations of Theodore Roosevelt and his commitment to maintaining the "ties of civilized society" in Latin America and of Woodrow Wilson and his desire to spread democracy through the hemisphere. Samuel Bemis (1943: 175-176) quotes Wilson regarding U.S. policy in Latin America as follows:

> We hold, as I am sure all thoughtful leaders of republican government everywhere hold, that just government rests always upon the consent of the governed, and that there can be no freedom without order based upon law and upon the public conscience and approval. We shall look to make these principles the basis of mutual intercourse, respect and helpfulness between our sister republics and ourselves. We shall lend our influence of every kind to the realization of these principles in fact and practice, knowing that disorder, personal intrigues, and defiance of constitutional rights weaken and discredit government and injure none so much as the people who are unfortunate enough to have their common life and their common affairs so tainted and disturbed.

During the Good Neighbor Era of Franklin Roosevelt, some elements of this general theme emerged in the form of non-intervention, mutual respect, and, in the words of Bryce Wood (1961), a "system of reciprocity." Shortly after World War II, U.S.

pro-democracy policies became more active, according to Yale Ferguson (1972: 351), in Ambassador Spruille Braden's attempt to make Juan Perón of Argentina the target of a "democratic crusade."

Again, during the Kennedy Administration, the themes of promoting democracy, development, and improved living standards were noted as important factors in the Latin American policy of the United States. In 1961, President Kennedy (cited in Levinson and de Onis, 1970: 334) asserted this position in a statement on U.S.-Latin American relations that represented the official philosophy of the Alliance for Progress.

> Our Hemisphere's mission is not yet complete. For our unfulfilled task is to demonstrate to the entire world that man's unsatisfied aspirations for economic progress and social justice can best be achieved by free men working within a framework of democratic institutions.

In his recent book, Robert Burr (1967: 46-47) supports a policy for the United States of promoting democracy in Latin America.

> Not only are arguments against a policy of promoting democracy in Latin America lacking in substance, but there are compelling positive reasons for supporting the adoption of such a program. The acts and outlook of a generally democratic rather than authoritarian Western Hemisphere community would be clearly more compatible with the style of the United States and its people.

Burr (1967: 45) goes on to cite several recent cases in which U.S. policy has been directed toward promoting democracy, at least insofar as economic assistance and diplomatic pressures were apparently exerted to this end in Peru, the Dominican Republic, El Salvador, Haiti, and Bolivia in the early 1960s. In an assessment of the early Alliance for Progress period, Yale Ferguson (1972: 351) says that "support for democracy was again a prominent feature of U.S. policies during the Kennedy years."

In sum, this view represents the argument that a major motivation for U.S. policy in Latin America is (or should be) the promotion of democracy, economic development, and the movement toward a higher standard of living in Latin America. In terms of a hypothesis, it asserts a close relationship between measures of these paternalistic-benevolent objectives and U.S. policy behavior in Latin America, and little or no relationship between private economic interests and foreign policy behavior.

OPERATIONALIZING VARIABLES

Each of the three explanations identified above represents different interpretations of the role of private economic interests in U.S.-Latin American policy. They are not necessarily mutually exclusive categories but have been divided in this manner for the purpose of analysis. The goal here is to subject each of the defined hypotheses to empirical testing in order to shed further light on the central issue of the paper—namely, the relationship of economic interests to U.S. foreign policy and the relative impact of this variable compared to other possible independent variables.

One of the more difficult tasks in any empirically based research project is bridging the gap between theoretically and operationally defined variables. The central variables of this study have been operationalized in the following manner. (Further information on the data used for these variables is found in the Appendix.)

FOREIGN POLICY VARIABLES

The foreign policy of the United States constitutes the dependent variable(s) of this analysis. The focus is on measurable foreign policy outputs, or concrete behaviors of the United States in Latin America.[2] The measures employed include:

(1) Economic assistance, measured in terms of total Agency for International Development commitments to each country for each year. This includes the total of development loans and grants, supporting and technical assistance, and contingency funds.

(2) Military assistance, measured in terms of the total value of funds committed by the United States to each country under the military assistance program for each year.

(3) Diplomatic personnel, measured in terms of the number of official representatives stationed by the United States in each country of Latin America. This total includes both regular foreign service personnel attached to the State Department and U.S. Information Agency personnel.

These indicators are widely recognized as important dimensions of U.S. foreign policy. Each represents resources which are allocated by the government in response to the interests and objectives which shape foreign policy.

Since shortly after World War II, the transfer of monetary and material goods in the form of economic and military assistance has been a principal means utilized by the United States to accomplish foreign policy objectives. These programs have been called one of the most important components of U.S. policy by representatives of both the Kennedy and Johnson Administrations during the 1960s. The allocation of these important resources reflects the interests and goals toward which foreign policy is directed.

In order to maintain communications and attempt to accomplish certain foreign policy objectives in other nations, the United States dispatches regular diplomatic representatives to these nations. Within some limits, the allocation of diplomatic personnel among foreign nations will reflect the interest and importance that the United States attaches to each target nation. As with economic and military assistance, diplomatic personnel represents a finite foreign policy resource that decision makers allocate in terms of the dominant values and factors shaping U.S. policy outputs.

These measures have two other virtues which are important to this analysis. Each can be measured in aggregate form with comparable data available for all Latin American nations, and the method of reporting data on these indicators provides substantial confidence in their reliability.

ECONOMIC INTEREST VARIABLES

According to the neo-Marxists, the most important factors determining U.S. foreign policy are one or all of the following: the need to maintain access to imported raw materials, the need to maximize foreign markets for the production of U.S. business, and the need to promote and protect private foreign investments. In accord with this, the economic interest variables have been operationalized as follows:

(1) Exports, measured as the total value of exports sent from the United States to each Latin American country each year.
(2) Imports, measured as the total value of imports received by the United States from each Latin American country each year.

(3) Investments, measured as the total book value at year end of U.S. foreign direct investments in each Latin American country.

These measures, taken separately or combined, give a good indication of the economic importance of each Latin American country to the United States.

STRATEGIC-DEFENSIVE VARIABLES

Operationalizing strategic-defensive variables involves identifying measurable dimensions of national security factors. For the purposes of this paper, strategic considerations will be defined in terms of five measures. Each has the virtue of being quantifiable. They include:

(1) Proximity to the United States, measured in terms of air miles between the U.S. capital and the capitals of each Latin American country. Proximity is a frequently cited strategic consideration. As Edward J. Williams (1971: 21) points out, "The overriding opinion [of strategic analysts] does indeed envisage distance as an important criterion in a strategy of national security."

(2) Size, measured in terms of total population. Although population size might be viewed as a separate variable, for the purpose of this analysis it is included as a measure of the strategic-defensive dimension. This is based on the assertion that larger countries are strategically more important in international politics than small countries so that if strategic considerations dominate U.S. policy in Latin America this will be reflected in relatively greater attention being given to countries of greater size.

(3) Domestic instability, measured in terms of the level of internal civil strife experienced in each Latin American nation. Presumably, U.S. strategic interests favor order and stability inasmuch as internal instability may be perceived as offering opportunities for unfriendly regimes to come to power.

(4) Size of Communist Party, measured in terms of U.S. government estimates of Communist Party membership in each Latin American country. The Communist Party in the region is looked upon by most in this school (strategic-defensive) as an agent of the Soviet Union (and possibly China) and hence constituting a strategic threat to the United States.

(5) Diplomatic relations with the Soviet Union, measured by dividing the Latin American countries into those having full relations with the Soviet Union, those having formal relations but no diplomats ex-

changed, and those having no diplomatic relations. Since the establishment of Soviet diplomatic relations is seen in both Latin America and the United States as a gain in influence for the Soviets, this is also a measure of perceived strategic threat to the United States.

PATERNALISTIC-BENEVOLENCE VARIABLES

For the purposes of this paper, this dimension has been operationalized through three measures of social and political characteristics of Latin American countries. In order to study the "promotion of democracy" theme two measures have been employed:

(1) Level of democratic development, measured by the well-known Russell Fitzgibbon scale based on the ratings of Latin American countries along several aspects of democratization by a panel of specialists in the area.

(2) Military involvement in politics, based on a rating scale developed by Robert Putnam on which each Latin American country was annually ranked in terms of the degree of military control over the domestic political system.

(3) Social and economic need, measured in terms of the per capita gross national product reported annually for each Latin American country. This measure is used to indicate an estimate of the relative degree of development and prosperity of each country and hence their relative need for a U.S. foreign policy response.

THE ALTERNATIVE HYPOTHESES RESTATED

NEO-MARXIST

There will be a very strong positive relationship between the measures of U.S. private economic interests (exports, imports, investments) and measures of U.S. foreign policy output in Latin America and little or no relationship between the latter and strategic or paternalistic variables.

STRATEGIC-DEFENSIVE

There will be a strong positive relationship between measures of U.S. strategic interests (proximity, size, instability, size of Communist Party, diplomatic relations with the Soviet Union) and measures of U.S. foreign policy outputs in Latin America and little relationship between the latter and private economic interests.

PATERNALISTIC-BENEVOLENCE

There will be a strong positive relationship between both democratization and economic need and foreign policy outputs and a strong negative relationship between degree of military intervention in politics and foreign policy outputs.

AN EXAMINATION OF RELATIONSHIPS

In order to test these relationships, data have been gathered on each of the operational measures for U.S. relations with twenty-four Latin American countries for the ten-year period 1960 to 1969. Correlation coefficients, as measured by the Pearson Product-Moment Statistic, were derived for each of the relationships between the dependent foreign policy output variables and the alternative independent variable clusters for each year in the period. The correlation statistics presented are intended to indicate the extent of covariance among the variables tested rather than the statistical significance of the relationships. The results are presented in Tables 1, 2, and 3.

In Table 1, the correlations between private economic interest measures and foreign policy outputs reveal a pattern of generally substantial relationships over the decade. Support is thus lent to the neo-Marxist theory and the hypotheses derived from it. The relationship between exports and diplomatic personnel is consistently very close, with a decade mean correlation of .90, a finding consistent with that of Louis M. Terrell (1972: 170) that "trade and the flag go hand in hand." Lower, but still very strong, relationships are found between imports and diplomatic personnel (decade mean .55).

Both economic and military assistance are moderately to substantially related to the three measures of economic interest (decade mean correlations of .30, .37, .38, .44, .44). Although these correlations are lower than those discussed above, they still demonstrate a notable degree of covariance among variables, particularly in the early years of the decade. Clearly, private economic interest, as defined here, is related to U.S. foreign policy behavior in Latin

TABLE 1

Economic Interests and Foreign Policy Output Correlations

	1960	1961	1962	1963	1964	1965	1966	1967	1968	1969	Decade Mean
				Economic Assistance							
Exports	.60*	.57*	.64*	.45*	.45*	.64*	.26	.24	.30	.24	.44*
Imports	.40*	.68*	.59*	.48*	.55*	.57*	.30	.29	.32	.23	.44*
Investments	.38*	.57*	.50*	.45*	.38*	.43*	.24	.27	.30	.27	.38*
				Military Assistance							
Exports	.48*	.46*	.50*	.40*	.32	.39*	.29	.12	.11	−.04	.30
Imports	.64*	.51*	.43*	.54*	.57*	.59*	.30	.15	.15	.03	.39*
Investments	.50*	.42*	.48*	.50*	.50*	.61*	.35	.17	.17	−.01	.37*
				Diplomatic Personnel							
Exports	.92*	.90*	.91*	.91*	.91*	.87*	.90*	.88*	.90*	.90*	.90*
Imports	.62*	.68*	.67*	.70*	.71*	.67*	.71*	.70*	.78*	.79*	.70*
Investment	.42*	.43*	.48*	.54*	.58*	.57*	.59*	.61*	.63*	.66*	.55*

*significant at the .05 level

America. In other words, the pattern of distribution of private U.S. economic interests among Latin American countries is closely matched by the allocation of the U.S. government's foreign policy resources. On the other hand, the economic monocausality implicit or explicit in neo-Marxist theories is not necessarily demonstrated here. Economic interests are an important, but not the sole, factor in the explanation of these foreign policy outputs.

An examination of trends in these relationships over the course of the decade reveals some interesting changes. Only the export-diplomatic personnel relationships remained constant over the period. Both the import-diplomatic personnel and investment-diplomatic personnel correlations gradually increased in magnitude. Significantly, there is a noticeable decline in the strength of relationships between private economic interests and both economic and military assistance, which is particularly marked in the latter case. Evidently, while the economic interest factor became more important in the allocation of diplomatic resources from the early to the late 1960s, it became less important during that time in the allocation of the other foreign policy measures.

STRATEGIC-DEFENSIVE INTERESTS AND FOREIGN POLICY OUTPUT

The relationships among the measures of strategic-defensive interests and foreign policy outputs present a very mixed picture as shown in Table 2. Size is most consistently related to the three foreign policy measures (decade means of .82, .74, and .56) confirming the commonsense notion that larger nations receive more foreign policy attention and resources than small nations.

The perceived strategic threat posed by Latin American communist parties and diplomatic advances by the Soviet Union demonstrated a pattern of moderate relationships (decade means of .28, .21, .21, .13, .53, and .36) with foreign policy allocations over the course of the decade. These factors are obviously of some importance in foreign policy, but do not dominate as suggested by the relevant hypothesis.

Proximity (measured in terms of distance from the United States) exhibits a consistently moderate relationship with economic assistance. Decade means for these two sets of relationships are - .30 and

TABLE 2

Strategic Defensive Interests and Foreign Policy Output Correlations

	1960	1961	1962	1963	1964	1965	1966	1967	1968	1969	Decade Mean
Economic Assistance											
Proximity	−.30	−.39*	−.36*	−.45*	−.31	−.14	−.28	−.21	−.27	−.30	−.30
Size	.43*	.81*	.75*	.70*	.90*	.87*	.74*	.77*	.77*	.69*	.74*
Communist Party	.47*	.44*	.46*	.43*	.31	.43*	.06	−.02	.12	.08	.28
Dip. Re.-USSR	.16	−.24	.15	.30	.23	.45*	.03	.17	.42*	.39*	.21
Dom. Instability	.25	.06	−.09	.17	−.09	−.12	.09	.13	.02	.05	.05
Military Assistance											
Proximity	−.27	−.52*	−.53*	−.48*	−.48*	−.53*	−.58*	−.50*	−.43*	−.31	−.46*
Size	.87*	.63*	.78*	.54*	.65*	.59*	.68*	.51*	.33	.06	.56*
Communist Party	.41*	.34	.50*	.17	.16	.22	.23	.06	.13	−.09	.21
Dip. Rel.-USSR	−.20	−.19	.34	.01	.04	.25	.00	.27	.49*	.28	.13
Dom. Instability	.01	.16	.07	.20	.15	.16	.16	.31	.50*	.56*	.23
Diplomatic Personnel											
Proximity	.00	−.10	−.09	−.15	−.17	−.16	−.16	−.16	−.16	−.20	−.14
Size	.75*	.78*	.80*	.81*	.80*	.83*	.85*	.86*	.84*	.84*	.82*
Communist Party	.84*	.76*	.65*	.64*	.64*	.60*	.57*	.50*	.07	.07	.53*
Dip. Rel.-USSR	.27	.15	.38*	.42*	.40*	.45*	.10	.47*	.48*	.49*	.36*
Dom. Instability	−.11	−.13	−.13	−.06	−.06	−.06	−.04	−.02	−.02	−.06	−.07

*significant at the .05 level

-.46 with a range of -.14 to -.58. The indicated relationship lends support to the hypothesis of the strategic-defense view of U.S. policy. In other words, as distance from the United States increases, allocations of foreign policy resources tend to go down. For the Latin American region, then, proximity is a factor of some importance in U.S. foreign policy attention. This was true in spite of the influence of Cuba, a close neighbor which received little measured foreign policy allocations after 1960.

The fifth measure in this category, domestic instability, is not significantly related (decade means of .05, .23, -.07) to foreign policy outputs over the decade as a whole. Although the existence of domestic instability may be perceived as a potential strategic threat, it was not apparently of major importance in the allocation of foreign policy resources.

Changes in relationships during the decade showed some trends worth noting. The size of communist party measure became less closely associated with foreign policy outputs during the course of the period under study. Domestic instability became significantly more important in military assistance allocations. This combination of trends suggests that U.S. foreign policy attention during the decade gradually was transferred from concern with communist parties to concern with threats of insurgency.

The other relationships either remained constant during the decade or exhibited no clear pattern of change.

The hypothesis derived from the strategic-defensive theories is only partly supported by these relationships. With the exception of size, the measures used here are generally less closely related to foreign policy than are the private economic interest measures. Proximity proved to be moderately related to U.S. foreign policy allocations, at least within this region.

PATERNALISM-BENEVOLENCE INTERESTS AND FOREIGN POLICY OUTPUT

In Table 3, the relationships between certain "paternalism-benevolence" measures and U.S. foreign policy are presented. They show that, on the whole, these relationships demonstrate substantially less covariance with foreign policy than the private economic interest measures. As such, the hypotheses based on this viewpoint are not confirmed.

The highest correlations in this group are the moderate relation-

TABLE 3

Paternalistic-Benevolent Interests and Foreign Policy Output Correlations

	1960	1961	1962	1963	1964	1965	1966	1967	1968	1969	Decade Mean
Economic Assistance											
Economic Need	-.05	-.03	.06	.01	.13	.06	.24	.29	.19	.34	.12
Dem. Devel.	.48*	.26	.36*	.25	.24	.30	.03	-.06	.06	-.06	-.03
Mil. Int.	-.12	.14	.08	.15	.23	.16	.28	.31	.24	.24	.16
Military Assistance											
Economic Need	-.04	.07	-.14	.15	.06	-.20	.09	.32	.35	.40*	.11
Dem. Devel.	.24	.26	.39*	.22	.24	.36*	.16	-.08	-.15	-.20	.14
Mil. Int.	.16	.19	.29	.18	.29	.23	.29	.53*	.34	.37*	.29
Diplomatic Personnel											
Economic Need	-.19	-.08	-.10	-.06	-.10	-.13	-.06	-.07	-.08	-.11	-.10
Dem. Devel.	.34	.34	.34	.36*	.38*	.38*	.36*	.35	.35	.42*	.36*
Mil. Int.	-.22	-.10	-.08	.06	.11	.22	.25	.30	.28	.23	.11

*significant at the .05 level

ships between level of democratic development and diplomatic personnel (decade mean of .36 with a range of .34 to .42) and between degree of military intervention in politics and military assistance (decade mean of .29 with a range of .16 to .53). The remaining correlations between economic need, democratic development and military involvement and the foreign policy measures show that only slight relationships (decade means ranging from .19 to -.10) exist over the course of the decade.

Even though the decade mean relationships are not strong, some interesting trends are evident. Over the years of the period there is an increasingly close relationship between economic need and both economic and military assistance. A similar trend occurs in the relationships between military involvement and all three measures of foreign policy output. On the other hand, there is a trend of declining relationships between democratic development and both economic and military assistance. This would suggest that in the early years of the decade relatively more foreign policy attention was devoted to democratic regimes, but that this attention waned over time and was replaced by growing attention to military regimes and to countries with lower per capita incomes. This may reflect the loss of enthusiasm for Alliance for Progress "democratic" goals during the Johnson and Nixon Administrations as well as the rise in the number of military governments in the region. In any case, the overall relationships of these measures are of relatively minor importance.

To summarize the above sections, we can conclude that, as a group, the private economic interest measures are most closely associated with foreign policy outputs by comparison with the other variables examined. Several strategic measures are of some importance, while paternalism-benevolence indicators are of little significance. Based on a distribution comparison, over half the economic interest relationships examined could be considered substantial compared to about one-fourth of the strategic-defensive relationships and only about one percent of the paternalism-benevolence group.

SUMMARY AND CONCLUSION

The purpose of this chapter was twofold: first, to shed further light on the role of private economic interest in inter-American relations; second, to suggest a research strategy for dealing with problems of this type which employs the statistical analysis of empirical data. New dimensions can be added to the discussion of highly controversial issues, such as the one considered here, through the application of some of the newer tools of social science research.

What can be concluded from these data about the central questions of the study? First, private economic interest appears to be the most important factor in U.S. foreign policy behavior in Latin America. That is, among the measures examined, the distribution of this factor covaries significantly with the distribution of measured foreign policy resources in both a relative and an absolute sense. Strategic and "benevolent" factors were less closely related over the course of the decade studied. Trends during the period suggest that some changes in these relationships may be taking place, but the tentative conclusion from the dataset as a whole must remain as stated.

Regarding the three alternative hypotheses posited earlier in the chapter, the following conclusions are reached. The paternalism-benevolence hypothesis is not supported by these data. There is no evidence that support for democracy, opposition to military regimes, or concern for economic need were central factors in the distribution of foreign policy resources. Within this context it is interesting to note that, apparently, support for democracy became relatively less important over the decade and economic need and accommodation with military regimes relatively more important.

The strategic-defensive hypothesis that placed security and strategic considerations above other factors in explaining U.S. policy is not confirmed by the data studied here. On the other hand, this factor clearly is of some importance in foreign policy allocations. Any explanation of U.S. foreign policy behavior in the region must take it into account. Among the measures used for this dimension, population size, proximity, the size of the local community party and type of diplomatic relations the country had with the Soviet Union were most consistently related to foreign policy outputs. The hypothesized relationship between proximity and foreign policy output was given some support, although not to the extent suggested by many "strategic" theorists. This relationship emerged in spite of the existence of Cuba, which is a close neighbor to the United States but received little measured foreign policy output during this period.

The neo-Marxist hypothesis is given support by the data developed here, although the strong version of this thesis, which posits a monocausal relationship between private corporate economic interests and the foreign policy of capitalist nations like the United States, is not confirmed. Economic interests are very important, but they do not nearly account for all the variation in foreign policy allocations. A weaker version of the thesis, however, which simply places primary importance on private economic interests in a multivariate framework is supported by the results of this research. It would suggest that explanations of U.S. foreign policy behavior in Latin America need to give central attention to the distribution of U.S. private economic interests in the region, though not to the exclusion of other factors.

The study demonstrates that concepts and theories that have been dealt with mostly through historical analyses or ideological rhetoric can be assessed quantitatively within a framework of the empirical study of foreign policy. The conclusions that have been reached are only tentative. Additional research will be needed before stable underlying relationships are fully identified. Specifically, additional research should take the direction of both expanding the data period to see if relationships hold over time (there is some indication that change was occurring during the 1960s) and the development of other measures of relevant dimensions, particularly aspects of foreign policy output behavior not included in the present study. Hopefully, however, some of the groundwork has been laid for new approaches to these and similar issues in inter-American relations.

NOTES

1. The growing interest in quantitative approaches to the comparative study of foreign policy is reflected in the work of James Rosenau, Charles Hermann, Rudolph Rummel, Raymond Tanter, Steven Salmore, Jonathan Wilkenfield, Ivo and Rosalind Feierabend, and others.

2. There is no suggestion here that these are the only indicators of foreign policy behavior that might have been used. Activities such as deployments of troops in foreign bases, communications (protests, threats, warnings, agreements, etc.) and specific acts (embargos, interventions, boycotts, etc.) could also be appropriate indicators of foreign policy interest and attention. They have not been included here primarily because of concern over accessibility and reliability of data on these activities. In future research, it may be possible to include these, and other measures of foreign policy behavior.

REFERENCES

AGUILAR, L. E. (1968) "Diplomatic relations of the independent Latin American states with the USSR," in L. E. Aguilar (ed.) Marxism in Latin America. New York: Alfred A. Knopf.

BAILEY, N. A. (1967) Latin America in World Politics. New York: Walker.

BEMIS, S. F. (1943) The Latin American Policy of the United States. New York: Harcourt, Brace.

BODENHEIMER, S. (1970) "Dependency and imperialism: the roots of Latin American underdevelopment," in K. T. Fann and S. C. Hodges (eds.) Readings in American Imperialism. Boston: Porter Sargent.

BURR, R. N. (1967) Our Troubled Hemisphere: Perspectives on United States-Latin American Relations. Washington, D.C.: Brookings Institution.

COCKCROFT, J. D., A. G. FRANK, and D. L. JOHNSON (1972) Dependence and Underdevelopment: Latin America's Political Economy. Garden City, N.Y.: Doubleday Anchor.

ELEY, J. D. and J. H. PETERSEN (1973) "Economic interests and American foreign policy allocations, 1960-1969," pp. 161-187 in P. J. McGowan (ed.) Sage International Year-book of Foreign Policy Studies I. Beverly Hills: Sage Publications.

FERGUSON, Y. (1972) "The United States and political· development in Latin America," pp. 348-390 in Contemporary Inter-American Relations. Englewood Cliffs, N.J.: Prentice-Hall.

FITZGIBBON, R. (1967) "Measuring democratic change in Latin America." Journal of Politics 29 (February): 129-166.

——— and K. F. JOHNSON (1961) "Measurement of Latin American political change." American Political Science Review 55 (September): 515-526.

FULBRIGHT, J. W. (1967) The Arrogance of Power. New York: Vintage.

GERASSI, J. (1965) The Great Fear in Latin America. New York: Collier.

GOFF, R. and M. LOCKER (1969) "The violence of domination: U.S. power and the Dominican Republic," pp. 249-291 in I. L. Horowitz et al. (eds.) Latin American Radicalism. New York: Vintage.

GURR, T. R. and C. RUTTENBERG (1971) "The conditions of civil violence: first tests of a causal model," in J. V. Gillespie and B. Nesvold (eds.) Macro-Quantitative Analysis. Beverly Hills: Sage Publications.

HERZ, J. H. (1962) International Politics in the Atomic Age. New York: Columbia University Press.

KANE, W. E. (1972) Civil Strife in Latin America: A Legal History of U.S. Involvement. Baltimore, Maryland: Johns Hopkins.

LENIN, V. I. (1917) Imperialism: The Highest Stage of Capitalism. New York: International.

LEVINSON, J. and J. deONIS (1970) The alliance that Lost Its Way. Chicago: Quadrangle.

MAGDOFF, H. (1969) The Age of Imperialism: The Economics of U.S. Foreign Policy. New York: Modern Reader Paperback.

MECHAM, J. L. (1961) The United States and Inter-American Security 1889-1960. Austin: University of Texas Press.

——— (1965) A Survey of United States-Latin American Relations. Boston: Houghton Mifflin.

MORGANTHAU, H. (1967) Politics Among Nations. New York: Alfred A. Knopf.

PERKINS, D. (1955) A History of the Monroe Doctrine. Boston: Little, Brown.

PUTNAM, R. D. (1967) "Toward explaining military intervention in Latin American politics." World Politics 20 (October): 102-125.

SPANIER, J. (1971) American Foreign Policy Since World War II. New York: Praeger.

Statistical Office of the United Nations (1960-1970) United Nations Statistical Yearbook. New York.

TERRELL, L. M. (1972) "Patterns of international involvement and international violence." International Studies Quarterly 16 (June).

UCLA Latin American Center (1962-1969) Statistical Abstract of Latin America. Los Angeles: University of California Press.

U.S. Department of Commerce, Bureau of the Census (1960-1969) Foreign Commerce and Navigation of the United States. Washington, D.C.: Government Printing Office.

——— Office of Business Economics (1960-1969) Survey of Current Business. Washington, D.C.: Government Printing Office.

U.S. Department of State (1960-1969) Foreign Service List. Washington, D.C.: Government Printing Office.

——— Agency for International Development (1960-1969) Foreign Assistance Program. Washington, D.C.: Government Printing Office.

——— Bureau of Intelligence and Research (1960-1969) World Strength of Communist Party Organization. Washington, D.C.: Government Printing Office.

WALTERS, R. (1970) Soviet and American Aid. Pittsburgh: University of Pittsburgh Press.
WILLIAMS, E. J. (1971) The Political Themes of Inter-American Relations. Belmont, Calif.:
    Duxbury.
WOLPIN, M. (1971) "Latin American studies: for a radical approach." Journal of Develop-
    ing Areas 5 (April): 321-329.
WOOD, B. (1961) The Making of the Good Neighbor Policy. New York: Columbia
    University Press.

APPENDIX ON SOURCES

Data used in this study were drawn from a collection of sources
covering the years 1960 through 1969. The empirical measures
include the following:

ECONOMIC INTEREST MEASURES

Exports and Imports: Data on these measures are based on annual
totals of trade between the United States and each Latin American
country. Totals for 1960 through 1969 were drawn from publications of the U.S. Department of Commerce, Bureau of the Census
(1960-1969).

Investments: This measure is based on the total book value at year
end of U.S. foreign direct investments in each Latin American
country for the years 1960 through 1969. Data were drawn from
both unpublished compilations and publications of the U.S. Department of Commerce, Office of Business Economics (1960-1969).

STRATEGIC-DEFENSIVE MEASURES

Proximity: This measure is based on the air distance between
Washington, D.C., and the capitals of each Latin American country.
Data were drawn from the World Almanac (1965) and additional
measurements by the author.

Size: Based on estimated annual population totals for 1960
through 1969 as reported by the Statistical Office of the United
Nations (1960-1970).

Size of Communist Party: Based on data collected for the years
1960 through 1969 for each Latin American country. These totals
are official U.S. government estimates and hence reflect their per-

ceptions of this strategic "threat" as reported by the U.S. Department of State, Bureau of Intelligence and Research (1960-1969).

Diplomatic Relations with the Soviet Union: Based on a three-category compilation: full relations, relations but no diplomats exchanged, and no relations, drawn and updated from Aguilar (1968).

Domestic Political Instability: Based on a ranking (Gurr and Ruttenberg, 1971) of all nations of the world for the years 1961 through 1963 on several measures of the types and intensity of civil strife.

PATERNALISTIC-BENEVOLENCE MEASURES

Level of Democratic Development: This measure is based on the scaling of Latin American nations on a number of dimensions of democracy published in 1960 by Russell Fitzgibbon and Kenneth F. Johnson (1961) and then again in 1965 by Fitzgibbon (1967) alone. Although this scale is subject to criticism for both its methodology and its content, it has been employed as one of the only available measures of this factor.

Military Involvement in Politics: Based on Robert Putnam's (1967) annual ranking of Latin American countries on a scale of 0 through 3 in terms of the character and types of military-political relationships. The Putnam scalings of 1961 through 1965 were extended to 1969 by the author.

Economic Need: Based on annual measures of per capita gross national product for each of the Latin American countries for the years 1960 through 1969 as reported by the UCLA Latin American Center (1962-1969) and the Statistical Office of the United Nations (1961-1970).

FOREIGN POLICY OUTPUT MEASURES

Economic Assistance: Based on the total value of technical, grant, loan, and commodity assistance granted annually by the U.S. to each Latin American country.

Military Assistance: Based on the total annual value of military aid and equipment supplied by the United States to Latin American countries under the Military Assistance Program as reported by the

U.S. Department of State, Agency for International Development (1960-1969).

Diplomatic Personnel: Measured by the total number of Foreign Service and U.S. Information Agency personnel stationed annually in each Latin American country as reported on the Foreign Service List of the U.S. Department of State (1960-1969).

Chapter 4

POLITICAL ALLEGIANCE AS A DETERMINANT OF MULTILATERAL AID IN LATIN AMERICA

JAMES T. BENNETT

George Mason University

and

MIGUEL A. GUZMAN

Inter-American Development Bank

INTRODUCTION

The purpose of this chapter is to test hypotheses regarding the determinants of the allocation of development assistance funds provided by multilateral aid organizations to less developed countries. More specifically, we will test the extent to which objective measures of economic performance, need, and creditworthiness explain the allocation of aid funds in 1971 among twenty-two Latin American countries that are members of both the World Bank and the Inter-American Development Bank. Because voting rights in these two multilateral aid agencies are allocated in proportion to capital subscriptions, the United States has the largest number of votes in both organizations. It has been suggested that aid allocations are influenced by the political allegiance demonstrated by the recipient country toward the donor. Therefore, a test is also provided of whether allegiance of the Latin American countries toward the United States has influenced the amount of aid received.[1]

In the second section, a brief overview is given of the relevant literature on foreign economic assistance; the third section contains a discussion of the aid allocation model used in this chapter and the empirical results. The last section contains a summary and the conclusions.

MULTILATERAL AID: AN OVERVIEW OF THE LITERATURE

Although considerable attention has been given to the role of economic assistance in the development of LDCs, there are no rigorous theoretical or empirical treatments of the allocation of multilateral aid funds among countries. Indeed, aside from the issue of how aid is allocated, the justifications of why aid is provided at all are, at best, vague (Chenery, 1964; Higgins, 1968: 575-576). Obviously, the allocation criteria vary, depending upon the objectives pursued. According to Chenery and Carter (1973: 466), the 1960s were an era during which "the donors were primarily concerned with (a) the efficiency of use of capital, (b) the risk of loss, and (c) intercountry equity."

Other writers have suggested different, though related, aid allocation criteria. Higgins (1968: 576-577) seems to favor economic growth, whereas Seers (1964: 480) emphasizes that "the main criterion in the long run should be the simple one of economic need, measured for example by per capita income." Although Harberger (1972: 637) asserts that economic need is a criterion, he adds the dimension of "self-help"—i.e., "more aid per capita should be given to poorer countries than to richer countries, and . . . more should be given to those making strong as against weak or negligible self-help efforts."

In addition to these economic factors, the political dimension of aid has more recently been advanced as a basis for allocating aid. Griffin and Enos (1970: 315), for example, have stated that the amount of economic aid provided to a country is not "determined by its need, or its potential, or its past economic performance, good or bad, or its virtue, but by the benefits it yields in terms of political support." In a similar vein, Chenery (1964: 81), as an official of the Agency for International Development, asserted that "the main objective of foreign assistance . . . is to produce the kind of political and economic environment in the world in which the United States can pursue its own social goals." Enke (1963: 12) refers to a school of thought which believes that "the U.S. can help to maintain friendly . . . governments in office by extending economic aid to their countries." Most of the criticisms of the political rationale for providing economic aid to LDCs has been directed toward bilateral assistance. It is generally believed that multilateral organizations are largely insulated from noneconomic considerations such as political allegiance. However, whether or not this is the case is subject to empirical investigation.

Based upon the statements in the literature, it is reasonable to postulate that the principal determinants of the amount of multilateral aid per capita received by a country are economic need, past performance of the economy, creditworthiness, and political orientation. It is well known that bilateral aid between nations is often based on political considerations; thus, arguments in favor of multilateral aid as opposed to bilateral assistance must rest upon the assumption that the allocation of multilateral aid is free of political bias. Because most of the bilateral assistance is provided by the United States, and given that the United States is the largest contributor to the multilateral organizations included in this analysis, the political attitude of the recipient countries toward the United States is employed to test the hypothesis that the allocation of aid to Latin American countries by the World Bank and Inter-American Development Bank during 1971 was free of political considerations.

THE MULTILATERAL AID ALLOCATION MODEL AND THE FINDINGS

Based upon the discussion above of the aid allocation criteria, the aid allocation model can be stated as

$$(C/Pop)_i = \alpha + \beta_1 (Y/Pop)_i + \beta_2 G_i + \beta_3 D_i + \beta_4 P_i + u_i \qquad [1]$$

where

$(C/Pop)_i$ = the dollar value per capita of assistance committed to the ith Latin American country (i = 1,

    2, . . . , 22) during 1971 by the World Bank and
the Inter-American Development Bank;

$(Y/Pop)_i$ = the income per capita in 1970 which is a measure of economic need;[2]

G_i = the average annual rate of growth of gross domestic product for the five-year period 1966-1970. This is an indicator of economic performance;

D_i = the debt service ratio (the total debt service charges divided by total export proceeds) in 1970. This is employed as a measure of creditworthiness;[3]

P_i = an indicator of political allegiance of country i to the United States; and

u_i = a random disturbance.

The value of the political allegiance variable was based on the assumption that "the United States should support any government that will support us, as for instance by . . . voting with us in international organizations" (Enke, 1963: 13). The voting record of each country in the General Assembly of the Organization of American States was examined for the years 1969 and 1970 and P_i is the percentage of the votes in which country i voted in the same manner as the United States. P takes on values from zero to one hundred. A value for P of one hundred implies complete allegiance to the United States; total opposition to U.S. policy results in a zero value for P. If multilateral aid allocation is independent of political considerations, the estimated coefficient of the political allegiance variable should not be significantly different from zero. If the coefficient β_4 is positive and significant, this implies that more aid is given to countries that demonstrate political allegiance to the United States than to those which do not. On the other hand, if this coefficient is negative and statistically significant, it would imply that the United States may be favoring its "enemies" with aid in an attempt to secure them as friends.

With regard to the a priori signs of the other explanatory variables, one would expect the coefficient of the per capita income variable to be negative, indicating that, if economic need is a criterion, countries with a low per capita income receive more aid. The coefficient of G, the rate of growth, is anticipated to be positive, reflecting that countries with good economic performance receive more aid.[4] With other variables held constant, the expectation is that the coefficient of the creditworthiness variable will be negative, for as the ability of a country to repay loans declines, less aid is granted. All coefficients should be significantly different from zero. Multiple regression was employed to estimate the coefficients of equation 1, and the results are shown below.

$$C/Pop = -4.061 + .0012 (Y/Pop) + 1.691G - .036D - 6.061P \quad [2]$$

$$(.0004)^* \qquad\qquad (.064)^* \quad (.016)^* \quad (4.240)$$

$$R^2 = .4828 \qquad \bar{R}^2 = .3612 \qquad F_{4,17} = 3.968 \qquad N = 22$$

Below each estimated coefficient, the standard error is shown in parentheses. The level of statistical significance is indicated by an asterisk, denoting those coefficients that are statistically different from zero at the 0.05 level or better according to the usual t-statistic.

The summary statistics for the regression below the estimated equation itself indicate that the four independent variables explain forty-eight percent of the variance in the committed aid per capita among countries. The predictive power of the regression is significantly different from zero. (The F-statistic is significant at the 0.02 level.) All coefficients are significantly different from zero at the 0.05 level or better, except for the political variable. With regard to per capita income, one notes that, although significant, it has a theoretically inappropriate sign. For each $100 increase in per capita income, aid committed increases by $.12, holding other variables constant. Thus, the positive sign implies that as a country becomes richer, larger amounts of development assistance are provided. Although this finding appears to be contrary to the concept of need as a determinant of aid, Harberger (1972: 637), who has obtained a similar result, has argued that "it is a sad commentary that the distribution of per capita . . . aid in the past has probably been negatively correlated . . . with the level of the recipient countries' per capita incomes." It could also be suggested that multilateral agencies consciously favor countries which are further along the road to development in order to get the richer countries to "graduate" from aid and perhaps join the ranks of the donor countries.

Both the performance and creditworthiness variables have the anticipated sign and are significantly different from zero. For each one percentage point change in the average rate of growth in GDP over the past five years, aid per capita during 1971 increased by $1.69, other variables held constant. Similarly, each unit increase in the debt service ratio, D, resulted in a decline of $.36 per capita in aid. The estimated coefficient of the political variable is not significantly different from zero even at the 0.15 percent level. From these results, one can reject the hypothesis that the allocation of development assistance through the multilateral aid agencies to these Latin American countries is affected by the political stance of the recipient toward the United States.

Some authors have asserted that aid per capita may not be an appropriate measure of effective aid, because it shows a bias in favor of the smaller-sized nations as measured by population (Strout and Clark, 1969). Although there may be some substance to this argument, the issue is not settled. Furthermore, the rationale for using development assistance deflated by imports rather than by population (Isawi, Kellerman, and Rottenberg, 1971) is not at all clear. To determine the effect that population may have had in influencing the results, a second regression was estimated which incorporated a size variable. The results are given as equation 3.

$$C/Pop = -5.285 + .0020(Y/Pop) + 1.722G - .329D - 6.172P + .0979S \qquad [3]$$

$$(.0005)^* \qquad (.665)^* \quad (.181) \quad (4.365) \quad (2.785)$$

$$R^2 = .4868 \qquad \overline{R}^2 = .3264 \qquad F_{5,16} = 6.819 \qquad N = 22$$

The variables C/Pop, Y/Pop, G, D, and P have the same definition as in equation 2, and the size variable, S, is given a value of 1 if country i has a population of less than ten million inhabitants and a value of zero if country i has more than ten million population. The coefficient of S indicates whether there is a significant difference in the per capita amount of aid given to countries with less than ten million inhabitants relative to the amount provided to countries with larger populations. As before, the standard error of each coefficient is given in parentheses and the level of significance is denoted by an asterisk.

From equation 3, it is evident that the estimated coefficient of S is not significantly different from zero, even at the twenty percent level. In addition, a comparison of equations 2 and 3 indicates that the improvement in R^2 is minimal after adding the size variable; i.e., R^2 increases from .4828 to .4868 after including the size variable. Therefore, the increase in the predictive power of the model is negligible. After correcting for the loss in the degrees of freedom by adding the size variable, the adjusted coefficient of determination, $\bar{R}^2$, falls from .3612 in equation 2 to .3264 in 3. Moreover, there are only small changes in the magnitudes of the coefficients of the other variables when S is added. All remain with the same sign and significance, except for the coefficient of the debt service ratio which becomes insignificant at the 0.05 level. This implies a relationship between the size of a country and its credit (or debt) position. In fact, the determinants of a country's debt service ratio are the size of its debt service charges and the value of its exports of goods and services. Because smaller countries are more reliant on trade than larger ones, it is likely that the value of exports per capita of the former will be greater than for the latter. Smaller nations, then, are likely to have a smaller debt service ratio, and, therefore, the introduction of size in the regression reduces the significance of the creditworthiness variable. (Size and debt service are negatively correlated; the simple correlation coefficient between these two variables, $r_{SD} = -.557$.) Thus, there is no evidence of a significant difference between the average allocation of development aid per capita to countries with less than ten million inhabitants relative to those with larger populations.

SUMMARY AND CONCLUSIONS

The findings discussed in the previous section support the conclusion that the allocation of development aid among Latin American countries by multilateral agencies is related to economic need, performance, and creditworthiness of the recipients. The political orientation of the recipients, however, does not appear to be a significant determinant of the amount of development funds committed. Nor does it seem that the size of the country as measured by population influences the amount of per capita aid received, because there was no significant difference in aid per capita for countries with less than ten million inhabitants relative to those with larger populations.

Although these findings are in agreement with views expressed in the literature, the results of this study should be considered suggestive rather than exhaustive. The sample, though relatively homogeneous, is limited to Latin America and therefore not representative of all aid-receiving countries. A larger study is currently under way which includes all LDCs.

NOTES

1. Aid, in this study, refers to the nominal amounts distributed among countries. No attempt has been made to determine the "grant component" of the loans which depends on the amortization period, the effective interest rate charged, and the grace period which may vary for each loan.

2. For the independent variables, data for 1970 or earlier were employed in order to incorporate a "recognition lag" on the part of the aid authorities.

3. There are cases in which this variable may not be the most desirable indicator of creditworthiness. Panama, for example, has a unique monetary system in which the U.S. dollar is legal tender. In this case, the ratio of debt service charges to government revenues may provide a better indicator of creditworthiness.

5. Griffin and Enos (1970) advance the hypothesis that foreign aid may be inversely correlated with the rate of growth; i.e., they believe that aid deters growth. A different line of reasoning is suggested here—namely, that foreign aid in year t is positively associated with the average rate of growth during the preceding five-year period.

REFERENCES

BALOGH, T. (1967) "Multilateral vs. bilateral aid." Oxford Economic Papers 19 (November): 328-344.

CHENERY, H. B. (1964) "Objectives and criteria of foreign assistance," in G. Ranis (ed.) The United States and Developing Economies. New York: W. W. Norton.

――― and N. CARTER (1973) "Foreign assistance and development performance, 1960-1970." American Economic Review Papers and Proceedings 63 (May): 459-468.

ENKE, S. (1963) Economics for Development. Englewood Cliffs, N.J.: Prentice-Hall.

GRIFFIN, K. B. and J. L. ENOS (1970) "Foreign assistance: objectives and consequences." Economic Development and Cultural Change 18 (April): 313-327.

HARBERGER, A. (1972) "Issues concerning capital assistance to LDCs." Economic Development and Cultural Change 20 (July): 631-640.

HIGGINS, B. (1968) Economic Development. New York: W. W. Norton.

ISAWI, C., M. KELLERMAN and S. ROTTENBERG (1971) "Foreign assistance: objectives and consequences: comment." Economic Development and Cultural Change 20 (October): 142-154.

SEERS, D. (1964) "International aid: the next steps." Journal of Modern African Studies 2: 471-489.

STROUT, A. and P. G. CLARK (1969) "Aid, performance, self-help, and need." Agency for International Development Discussion Papers 20.

Chapter 5

U.S. DIRECT FOREIGN MANUFACTURING INVESTMENT
IN THIRD WORLD COUNTRIES, 1962-1966:
IMPLICATIONS FOR U.S. FOREIGN AID POLICY

MICHAEL ROCK

Bennington College

and

University of Denver

INTRODUCTION

Historically, U.S. direct foreign investment has followed a pattern typical of other industrializing nations. The United States remained an international net debtor; that is, foreign investments into the United States exceeded U.S. foreign investments in other countries until after World War I. Toward the end of the nineteenth century, concomitantly with rapid economic growth and industrialization, the United States began to invest abroad in considerable volume. Through the end of World War I, the majority (61%) of American foreign investment was geographically concentrated in the Third World. Its sectoral concentration was in raw material investment, with less than twenty-four percent of the total in manufacturing.

Since World War II, the United States has become a mature creditor, this development being accompanied by shifts in both the geographical and the sectoral patterns of U.S. direct foreign investment. The Third World share of this investment declined from forty-two percent in 1945 to thirty-one percent in 1966, while U.S. direct foreign investment in manufacturing increased from thirty-one percent of total U.S. direct foreign investment in 1945 to forty-one percent in 1966 (see Table 1).

Yet the recent shift into manufacturing investment has not been concentrated solely in the developed countries. Although the Third World share of total U.S. direct foreign investment has been declining, U.S. direct foreign investment in manufacturing to these countries has been increasing. From 1957 to 1966, manufacturing investment in less developed countries increased from sixteen percent to twenty-three percent of all the U.S. foreign investment in less developed countries. Currently this investment is geographically concentrated. Nine countries—seven in Latin America and two in Asia—attract approximately eighty percent of the total U.S. direct foreign investment in manufactures in less developed countries, and Western Hemisphere less developed countries receive about eighty-five percent of this investment, but both the country and geographic concentrations have been declining. Between 1957 and 1966, the Latin American share of this investment has fallen from ninety-one

TABLE 1

Distribution of U.S. Direct Foreign Investment 1919-1966
(book value in billions, various years)

	All Areas			Less Developed Countries			Less Developed Countries	
	Total	Mfg.	Mfgd. %	Total	Mfg.	Mfgd. %	LDC % Total U.S. Investment	LDC % Total Mfgd. Investment
1919	3.9	.8	20	2.4	n.a.		61	
1929	7.7	1.9	25	4.1	n.a.		53	
1945	8.4	2.7	32	3.6	n.a.		43	
1957	23.24	7.89	33	10.99	1.84	16	47	23
1961	34.68	11.93	34	13.37	1.89	14	39	16
1966	54.71	22.05	40	17.92	3.95	22	33	18

Source: Survey of Current Business, various years.

percent to eighty-five percent, the Asian share has increased from eight percent to thirteen percent, while the African share has increased slightly from less than one percent to about two percent (see Table 2). These developments reopen an old and unresolved argument within the U.S. government as to the role of private capital flows in U.S. development assistance policy.[1]

Since the establishment of the Economic Cooperation Administration there have been those in the U.S. government (mainly in the Treasury and Commerce Departments) who have consistently maintained that private capital, rather than public aid should be the

TABLE 2

Geographic Distribution of U.S. Direct Foreign Investment in
Manufacturing to Less Developed Countries
(book value in millions)

	1966		Percentages of Total		1957	Percentages of Total
Latin America						
Argentina	656		16.5		256	1.0
Brazil	846		21.0		659	36.0
Chile	51		1.0		39	2.0
Colombia	190		4.7		62	3.3
Mexico	802		20.0		363	19.6
Peru	93		2.3		33	1.7
Venezuela	291		7.3		97	5.2
Other	388		9.7		166	8.9
Total—Latin America	3,317		84.0		1,675	91.1
Africa		62	1.6		18	1.0
Middle East		51	1.2		34	1.8
Asia						
India	119		3.0		36	1.9
Philippines	180		4.5		42	2.2
Other	233		5.8		40	2.1
Total—Asia		532	13.4		118	6.3
Total—All Less Developed Countries		3,962	100.0[a]		1,845	100.0[a]

a. Totals may not add to 100% due to rounding errors.

Source: Survey of Current Business, various years.

means of offering economic assistance to other nations. These private flow proponents have not shunned the use of foreign aid, but rather they hope the government's foreign aid program will be a catalyst for an increased flow of private capital since "private foreign investment is generally held to carry . . . greater 'fringe benefits' than public lending, in the form of the . . . whole ethical-cultural complex of ground rules which are essential to the development of an economy on a private enterprise . . . basis" (Whitman, 1964: 2). This perspective has been stated by a number of presidential commissions, including the 1948 Herter Commission on Foreign Aid, the 1950 Gray Report, the 1951 Rockefeller Report, the 1952 Paley Commission Report, and the 1954 Randall Report, and is reflected in the Foreign Assistance Acts of 1961 and 1963.

This trend has been reinforced by U.S. balance of payments deficits and domestic opposition to foreign aid, both of which have led officials to ask whether private flows (direct foreign investment) can replace public flows as the primary way in which resources will be transferred from the developed world to the underdeveloped world.

These views proposing an expanded role for private capital in U.S. development assistance have not gone unchallenged in government. The post-World War II neo-nationalism of the newly emerging nations of the Third World has caused State Department officials to ask whether the political price of reliance on private capital flows is too high. The recent experience of many of these countries with European colonialism and/or American dollar diplomacy makes it difficult for leaders in these nations to separate foreign investment from political domination. Officials in the State Department fear that policies which tend to tie public flows to private flows or which place private flows in a prominent position in development assistance policy make it more difficult to allay the fears of aid/private investment recipient countries in this respect. This is particularly true of such programs as the U.S. Investment Guarantee Program. This program is designed to reduce the political risks associated with investment in less developed countries, but the program, by making the U.S. government a party in the settlement of claims between private U.S. firms and host governments, unnecessarily complicates already difficult foreign policy problems in these areas, especially in an era of anti-Americanism (Chadwin, 1972: 97-105, 147-156). To ameliorate the political entanglements of public/private capital flows, State Department officials desire to shift responsibility of development assistance from bilateral to multilateral agencies.

As the outline of the above dialogue within government makes clear, there has been much discussion over the last few years concerning various approaches to development assistance. Although much of this literature has been concerned with the role of private capital in development assistance policy, little of it has approached this issue from a theoretical understanding of the foreign investment process. There have been a number of recurrent, government-sponsored survey-research-interview studies of international investors (U.S. Department of Commerce, 1953, 1954, 1960, 1970), but few have relied on theoretical analyses of foreign investment. This paper will attempt to begin to fill that gap by (1) analyzing the theoretical determinants of U.S. direct foreign investment in manufacturing in sixty-five less developed countries in 1962-1966, and (2) using that analysis to draw some tentative conclusions about the impact of various aid policies on foreign investment.

THEORIES OF DIRECT FOREIGN INVESTMENT

Attempts to explain the size distribution of U.S. direct foreign investment by appealing to the "theory" of direct foreign investment is limited by the paucity of theory in this area. Perhaps no other aspect of international economics is in such a state of flux as is the theory of international capital movements. Furthermore, attempts to discriminate among the various approaches now taken are frustrated by an appalling lack of data. A dearth of published micro data has forced researchers to work with very aggregate data, making empirical testing difficult. This has been alleviated to some extent by some researchers gaining access to unpublished micro (firm level) data, but these kinds of data have not been and are not likely to become available to most researchers in the field.

In part, this lack of theory reflects the fact that, until recently foreign trade was the primary way in which firms serviced foreign markets and, in part, the long-held assumption of trade economists regarding factor immobility among nations.

Despite these problems, the last few years have witnessed the development of two alternative paradigms of the direct foreign investment process. Researchers in this field can be classified into (1) those who see foreign investment as capital expenditure, and (2) those who see it as part of the international trade process. Those who view foreign investment as a form of capital formation believe the key to understanding direct foreign investment lies in the theory of investment. Consequently, these researchers utilize developments in investment theory to explain direct foreign investment. Those who see foreign investment as related to international trade attempt to focus on the processes the firm engages in as it decides how best to service a foreign market. Here the obvious focus is on both the timing of foreign investment and its relationship to other means of servicing foreign markets, especially exports, but also, to a lesser extent, licensing.

INVESTMENT THEORIES OF DIRECT FOREIGN INVESTMENT

As Fisher, Keynes, and others have argued, the decision to invest depends on whether the discounted expected rate of return on any investment is greater than the cost of borrowing or, if the firm is using internal funds, on whether the return is greater than the cost of earnings foregone in the firm's next best alternative. The investment decision is seen to hinge on identifying that interest rate which equates the discounted value of all expected future earnings to the cost of the investment. If that rate equals the rate of interest at which money can be borrowed, the investor will either lend the money or invest it in capital; but if the rate is greater than the rate at which money can be borrowed, the present value of future earnings will exceed the present value of the alternative investment, and the firm will invest in capital. The firm then ranks investment projects in order of decreasing profitability, and it carries out those projects for which the rate of return is greater than or equal to the market rate of interest (Dernburg and McDougal, 1968: 125).

This rate of return approach to the theory of capital accumulation has come under fire by Jorgenson (1963). Although the theory is sound, he believes that attempts to test the theory have been less than successful because of poor empirical specification. He reconstructs the theory by specifying those factors which influence the rate of return.

In Jorgenson's model, the rate of return is influenced by the firm's discounted net revenues—that is, its sales minus its costs. Thus, the basic determinants of investment are demand for the firm's output, the prices of its inputs, and the supplies of its inputs.

As could be expected, a number of researchers have utilized these developments in their theoretical and empirical analyses of the foreign investment process. Stevens (1969), in his examination of the foreign investment behavior of seventy-one foreign subsidiaries of U.S. firms, discovered that the important determinants of plant and equipment expenditures of those subsidiaries were the subsidiaries' sales (demand for its output), its factor costs, and the parent firm's alternative investment opportunities. Severn (1970) provided additional support for investment theory approaches to foreign investment when he determined that the foreign investment of sixty-three U.S. firms, accounting for approximately fifty percent of U.S. direct foreign investment in manufacturing between 1961 and 1966, was influenced by the firm's foreign sales and its cost of funds.[2]

TRADE THEORY APPROACHES TO FOREIGN INVESTMENT

Researchers who take a trade theory approach to foreign investment argue that, in viewing direct foreign investment as capital formation, investment theory analysts of foreign investment face serious problems. Investment theories have traditionally attempted to explain the determinants of plant and equipment expenditures, but the U.S. Department of Commerce (1960), Richardson (1971), and Mikesell (1967) believe this variable is an inadequate measure of foreign investment. The Department of Commerce defines direct foreign investment "to include all foreign business organizations in which a U.S. . . . organization owns an interest of 10% or more" (1960: 2). The obvious emphasis is on the ownership of assets, not plant and equipment expenditures. Richardson presses this distinction further:

> Direct investment flows represent the investor's share in the change in the book value of all foreign assets, including inventory . . . financial capital . . . takeovers and sales of existing operations in all of which no new capital formation is involved. This would not be a serious objection, however, if some rough proportionality existed between plant and equipment expenditures and direct investment flows. In fact, this is not a reliable assumption [Richardson, 1971: 8].

If researchers decide to utilize plant and equipment as their measure, they must realize they are ignoring the crucial ownership dimension; on the other hand, if they decide to use book value as their measure, they must realize the inadequacy of investment theory approaches.

At some point, it is necessary to ask whether the variables affecting plant and equipment expenditures are the same as those affecting the investor's desire to own productive assets in a foreign country. This question ultimately introduces space into the analysis and further illuminates the inadequacy of investment theory. Investment theory models of foreign investment may define the optimal capital stock, but they say nothing about the location of that stock in space. The introduction of space changes the nature of the investment decision as it forces the investor to evaluate forces affecting how and from where any market will be serviced. Unlike the plant and equipment expenditures decision, here the investor must decide whether to export to a market, or to produce locally in that market. Furthermore, if the firm decides to produce locally, it must decide whether to maintain a wholly owned subsidiary, to enter a joint partnership, or to lease a patent. This process is described by Barlow and Wender: "If a company starts selling in a particular country through exports . . . one might assume that the natural progression [as sales expand] . . . would be . . . local assembly [foreign investment]" (1955: 147). Furthermore, the shift to local production (direct foreign investment) is often the result of outside pressure which forces the firm to invest if it wishes to maintain its market. This outside pressure usually takes the form of host government activity such as the deliberate policy of import substitution.

This argument by Barlow and Wender encompasses a number of interesting hypotheses about direct foreign investment. It suggests that one factor limiting foreign investment may be the lack of awareness on the part of many firms of the investment opportunity, and this lack of knowledge about profitable investment opportunities is primarily overcome by contact with (exports to) the foreign market. Second, it implies that the motive for investment in many cases is defensive. The firm must either invest abroad or lose the market.

Horst (1970) provides the first micro-level theoretical and empirical arguments which support the trade-related view of the foreign investment process. In examining the behavior of seventeen

SIC two-digit U.S. manufacturing industries and the form of their participation in Canadian markets (whether they exported to the market or produced locally), he discovered that differences in the form of participation were significantly related to Canadian tariff rates. The higher the tariff, the more likely the firm was to service the market with local production. At an aggregate level, Scaperlanda and Mauer (1969) relate the growth of U.S. direct foreign investment in the EEC to the common tariff barrier of that market. They argue that, with the establishment of the EEC, U.S. firms were faced with the decision of either foregoing the market within the EEC or establishing foreign subsidiaries, and that they chose to circumvent the tariff barrier rather than forego the market because of the market's size. Finally, Grueber, Vernon, and Mehta (1967) offer further empirical support for the defensive nature of U.S. foreign investment in their test of the "product cycle" hypothesis. They determined that U.S. foreign investment was positively related with the size of the foreign market firms were exporting to, and with the shift in comparative advantage to foreign host countries that tended to occur as product standardization occurred.

A TAXONOMIC FRAMEWORK

These differences in approach to foreign investment (trade-related versus investment theory) are closely related to the distinction between initial foreign investment and expansion foreign investment. All researchers now recognize the theoretical importance of this difference. Expansion investment appears to be determined by the same set of factors which affects domestic investment expenditures (e.g., factor costs, tax rates, and sales), whereas initial investment is influenced by those variables affecting the firm's locational decisions (e.g., tariff rates, the nature of U.S. comparative advantage, information barriers). Researchers now believe that once the initial investment is made, strategic spatial variables (trade variables) become less important and the more traditional (investment theory) variables dominate. This is not to say the strategic factors disappear from expansion considerations. Changes in the strategic factors may affect the firm's desire to expand or cause it to liquidate its capital in any given country.

To carry out a cross-country analysis of the determinants of U.S.

direct foreign investment in manufacturing in less developed countries in a way reflecting both aspects of the foreign investment
decision, this analysis will follow Richardson's (1971) taxonomy of
the theoretical relationships between initial and expansion investment. Most of what follows is adopted from his work.

$$\text{Let } K^* = (K_1{}^*, \ldots, K_i{}^*, \ldots, K_p{}^*)^T$$

be a column vector of optimal capital stocks in the p areas in which
the firm invests. The pth area is the parent country. Then let $X = (X_1,
\ldots, X_i, \ldots X_p)^T$ be a column vector of the determinants of the
optimal capital stocks, where each element x_i is a row vector of
components $X_i = (I_i, S_i)$. The components of this vector represent
traditional investment variables, I_i, and strategic (trade, information)
variables, S_i. In turn, each of these components may be a row vector.
For example, the investment theory variable I_i may be a vector of
factor costs and demand variables, and the strategic variable S_i may
be a vector of tariff rates and firm exports to a given market. Finally,
let the optimal capital stock $K^* = AX$ where

$$A = a_{ij} = \begin{bmatrix} a_{11} \cdots a_{1p} \\ a_{p1} \cdots a_{pp} \end{bmatrix} \qquad \text{where } a_{ij} = (a_{ij}{}^I, a_{ij}{}^S).$$

Utilizing this framework, one can test the alternative theories either
singly or jointly. For example, to test the investment theory approach to foreign investment, the specification of the optimal capital
stock is given by

$$K^*{}_i = {}_j\sum a_{ij}{}^I I_j.$$

If, on the other hand, the investment is new investment, the
strategic factors may dominate the traditional investment factors. As
suggested earlier, new investment involves a consideration of a spatial
preference which will be affected by such factors as information and
tariffs. In this case, only the strategic factors matter such that the
optimal capital stock would be determined by

$$K^*{}_i = {}_j\sum a_{ij}^S S_j.$$

Finally, to test a joint theory reflecting the complexity and
interdependence of the trade and investment process the optimal
capital stock would be given by

$$K^*{}_i = {}_j\sum (a_{ij} I_j + a_{ij}{}^S S_j).$$

The theoretical frameworks provided by these two paradigms will be used to analyze the size distribution of U.S. direct foreign investment in manufacturing. The paradigms will be tested singly and then jointly, and it is expected that the joint model will provide a better understanding of the investment process, particularly since it more accurately characterizes the complexity and the interdependence of the trade and investment decision.

STATISTICAL ANALYSIS

WHY A CROSS-NATIONAL APPROACH?

To focus the analysis on location factors between nations dictates the use of a cross-national approach. Critics of such a cross-section approach to foreign investment might argue that there may be few or no common variables entering the investment decision in different countries, or that the same or similar configurations of given variables in different countries may affect the investment differently. This may lead them to argue that the only way to explain the intercountry distribution of foreign investment (or why Bolivia gets foreign investment and Uganda does not) is to analyze Bolivia and Uganda case by case. The theoretical and statistical approach offered here does not deny that "special" factors may enter the investment decision with respect to any given country, but this analysis does maintain that useful cross-country generalizations can be made. In statistical terms, the cross-country approach may explain X percent of the cross-country variation in foreign investment, while the residual or unexplained variation will include, among other things, the influence of the "special" factors. If the cross-section critics are correct, the approach will have low explanatory power, but this remains an empirical question.

Further, several characteristics of the phenomenon under examination support the use of cross-section analysis. First, it is reasonable to assume the firms involved are long-run profit maximizers (this assumption does not rule out maximizing other objectives such as sales or the firm pursuing a satisficing behavior), and that the same or similar variables affect long-run profitability. This implies different firms will consider many of the same variables when facing a foreign investment decision. Second, the relatively small number of firms involved, fifty, account for approximately sixty percent of U.S.

direct foreign investment in manufacturing, and the similar characteristics of these firms limit interfirm differences in behavior (Severn, 1970: 1).

DEPENDENT VARIABLES

The dependent variable is the book value of direct foreign investment in manufacturing per capita in the host country. Book value was chosen since the alternative variable, plant and equipment expenditures, is inadequate. As already noted, direct foreign investment involves much more than capital expenditures. The Department of Commerce defines direct foreign investment to include

> all foreign organizations in which a U.S. person, organization, or affiliated group owns an interest of 10% or more. In addition, a foreign business organization in which 50% or more of the voting stock is owned by U.S. residents is counted . . . even though no single U.S. group owns as much as 10% [U.S. Department of Commerce, 1970: 2] .

Thus, direct investment is defined as the ownership of assets which include inventory, financial capital, and the sales and takeovers of existing assets in which no new capital formation takes place. The ownership dimension is crucial. This variable enables one to ask not what is the optimal capital stock (a question that can be answered, at least theoretically, without reference to the spatial dimension of foreign investment), but rather to ask what factors affect the desire of firms to own the means or production in different countries. Ownership of the means of production most likely will depend on the strategic variables affecting foreign investment. The firm owns capital or desires to own capital in a foreign country to protect its market. Plant and equipment expenditures are likely to be affected by more traditional variables such as firm sales.

Since the Department of Commerce does not publish country-by-country information on U.S. direct foreign manufacturing investment, the data were estimated by piecing together information supplied in a series of Commerce Department publications (its "Establishing a Business in . . .," "Market Profiles of . . .," and the *Survey of Current Business)*. Utilizing these sources, two measures of U.S. direct foreign investment in manufacturing in Third World countries were devised. The first measure is the average book value of investment in the country in the period, a measure of the stock value of the investor's assets. Although this variable reflects investment outside the period of analysis, it does represent the amount the investor stands to lose if the assets are expropriated. The second measure is the average change in book value over the period, a representation of the flows over the period of analysis.[3]

INDEPENDENT VARIABLES

The choice of indicators was guided by, among other factors, the results of a number of surveys on the factors limiting U.S. investment abroad, as well as by recent theoretical advances in investment theory, especially the theory of foreign investment. As was shown above, there is a multiplicity of theories of direct foreign investment, most of which focus on one aspect of foreign investment, ignoring others. For example, Vernon, Horst, Keesing, and others relate foreign investment to the problem of from where a market should be serviced while Stevens, Severn, and others deal with foreign investment as an investment theory problem. Variables were chosen which best reflect these different approaches.[4]

INVESTMENT THEORY VARIABLES

These variables are designed to capture aspects of the host country which at an aggregate level represent the neoclassical considerations of investment. The dimensions chosen range from measures of basic infrastructure (the supply of ancillary facilities necessary for manufacturing to exist) to measures of factor costs (supply), to measures of market size (demand). They include the following variables:

Basic Economic Infrastructure—Physical Infrastructure per Capita and Human Capital Infrastructure per Capita: A 1953 survey of the U.S. Department of Commerce on factors impeding foreign investment argues, "The relatively low level of economic development . . . is reflected in the lack of adequate transportation, sufficient power facilities, and skilled labor, all of which are prerequisites" for foreign investment (U.S. Department of Commerce, 1953: 75). Furthermore, Jorgenson's analysis of investment suggests that factor supplies are crucial determinants of investment. These two variables attempt to measure the availability of such necessary inputs.

Because of the wide variety of data available on infrastructure, no single piece of which adequately represents the notion of infrastructure, factor analysis was used to detect any underlying pattern in the data. The variables used in the factor analysis to reflect physical infrastructure include energy production (kilowatt hours) per capita, number of commercial vehicles per capita, and number of telephones per capita, while the variables used to measure labor force skills were the number of teachers per capita and the number of students per capita. These data were gathered from Banks (1971).

FACTOR LOADINGS

VARIABLE	FACTOR 1	FACTOR 2
(1) Energy production per capita	.802	.363
(2) Commercial vehicles per capita	.902	.154
(3) Telephones per capita	.874	.316
(4) Teachers per capita	.453	.831
(5) Total students per capita	.170	.950

The factor loadings represent the relative importance of each factor in each variable. Because of the factor loads on F_1 (note the heavy loading of energy production, commercial vehicles, and telephones), the variable was named physical infrastructure. The heavy loading of students and teachers on F_2 suggests that this factor reflects human capital infrastructure, and F_2 was so named. Factor scores for each country were calculated for F_1 and F_2.

Gross National Product: The inability of the data to support a rate of return hypothesis for foreign investment has led economists to utilize various alternative variables which are more precise than the rate of return. The most commonly used variable is some measure of market size (sales), the most frequent of these being GNP per capita. The argument for the use of this variable is that the market size reflects long-run profitability of the investment—i.e., that the firm is more concerned with the volume of sales than with rates of return. Initially it was felt that in a cross-country study one would have to focus on GNP per capita as one would need to deal with a standardized variable, but the interpretation of the impact of this variable on foreign investment can lead to very odd conclusions. For example, it implies that a one-person country with a high GNP/N would attract more investment than a more populous country with a lower GNP/N. Furthermore, the variable reveals little about the distribution of income within the country and, hence, it fails to reflect whether demand in the country is adequate to permit efficient production. Finally, development economists usually define economic development, which implies a structural transformation of an economy, as an increase in GNP/N. This relationship between GNP/N and industrial structure has been statistically analyzed by Chenery and Taylor (1968). Their work suggests that cross-country differences in GNP/N are highly correlated with differences in industrial structure as measured by the percentages of primary production and manufacturing production to GNP.

Unstandardized GNP was adopted for several reasons. The distribution of U.S. manufacturing investment in less developed countries covers a wide span of manufactured goods. These goods range from those with very low income elasticities of demand (food and beverages, and textiles with income elasticities of demand in the range 1.2 to 1.5), to those with relatively high income elasticities of demand (primary and fabricated metals, and nonelectrical machinery with income elasticities of demand in the range of 1.96 or greater) (Maizels, 1963: 46). Data on the breakdown of the book value of direct foreign investment by regions and by SIC two-digit industrial categories reveal that approximately twenty percent of U.S. foreign investment in manufacturing in less developed countries consists of low income elasticity of demand goods (food and textiles); approximately forty-two percent consists of middle income elasticity of demand goods (chemicals and chemical products, and rubber and rubber products), while the remainder, thirty-eight percent represents high income elasticity demand goods (fabricated metals and electrical and nonelectrical machinery) (Pizer and Cutler, 1960: 22).

To test a market size hypothesis with such a broad aggregation of goods, a variable is needed which reflects a demand for output of both low and high income elasticity of demand goods. GNP meets this requirement. A high GNP may reflect either a small country with a relatively high GNP per capita, thus reflecting a market size capable of demanding goods with relatively high income elasticity of demand, or it may reflect a large country with a relatively small GNP per capita, thus mirroring a demand for goods that have relatively

low income elasticity of demand. This variable is the only independent variable capable of reflecting the size dimension associated with
foreign investment. The other independent variables that are used
have all been standardized so as to reflect the relative importance of
a dimension rather than an absolute dimension. [This variable was
gathered from Banks (1971).]

TRADE THEORY VARIABLES

The trade theory approach to foreign investment is tested by
capturing dimensions of the host country which reflect information
available to American investors, threats to a given market, and,
finally, net exports to that market (the host country's net imports).

*Trade with the United States as a Percentage of the Host
Country's Total Trade:* A common thread running through many of
the analyses of direct foreign investment suggests that foreign investment may be the last stage of a process that begins with the firm
exporting to the foreign market. This view is an integral part of both
the tariff factory hypothesis and Vernon's product cycle hypothesis.
Furthermore, a U.S. Department of Commerce study of the factors
limiting U.S. investment abroad concludes, "The limited knowledge . . . on the part of many American businessmen . . . has increased the hesitancy to invest" (U.S. Department of Commerce,
1953: 101). This variable reflects the relative amount of information
available to foreign investors on opportunities in host countries. The
hypothesis is that contact with a market (trade in the market)
increases information available to the foreign investor, and the more
trade the host country has with the United States, the more aware
U.S. firms will be of opportunities in the host country. This variable
was collected from the IMF's *Direction of Trade Annuals*
(1962-1966) and is defined as U.S. exports plus U.S. imports with a
given country as a percentage of the host country's total trade
(exports plus imports).

Net Imports: The trade theory models of foreign investment
offered by Barlow and Wender (1955), Vernon (1966), Grueber,
Vernon, and Mehta (1967), Keesing (1967), and Horst (1970) all
suggest that foreign investment is the last stage of a process that
begins with exports to a foreign market. These models suggest—for
various reasons such as (1) getting around tariff barriers, (2) protect-

ing a foreign market when comparative advantage in production shifts from the domestic (U.S.) market to the foreign market, or (3) protecting a developed market when the foreign market reaches some threshold size—that firms will replace exports to a market with foreign production (investment). The common element in these approaches is that exports to a market and local production in a market (foreign investment) are close substitutes. The substitution relationship between exports and foreign investment is tested by examining the relationship between a country's net imports (imports − exports), and foreign investment. If the hypothesis is correct, there should be a negative relationship between net imports and foreign investment. It was decided to use net imports as opposed to gross imports as a measure of a country's demand satisfaction through imports because in less developed countries the ability to satisfy demand through imports is integrally related to the ability to export. Most less developed countries find themselves in the position of having overvalued currencies, and a relatively large demand for imports, and they are often forced to limit the value of imports to the value of their exports. As exports rise and fall, so do imports. Given this, it is necessary to remove the influence of exports from a country's ability to import, and thus to focus on demand for foreign goods that is being satisfied irrespective of the level of a country's exports. A country's excess demand for imported goods (net imports) should be negatively related to foreign investment. A high excess demand for imports suggests the country is relatively open with respect to imports and that foreign investors in this case will satisfy that demand with exports, whereas a country with negative net imports (negative excess demand for foreign goods) must be either limiting imports to export earnings or alternatively, that excess foreign demand is being met by foreign investment (local production) of the previously imported good.

STATISTICAL TESTS AND RESULTS

To test the investment theory model of foreign investment, the following equations were estimated:

$$K_i = a + b \, PKI_i + c \, HKI_i + d \, GNP_i \qquad [1]$$

$$\Delta K_i = a + b_i \, PHI_i + c \, HKI_i + d \, GNP_i \text{ where} \qquad [2]$$

K_i = the average book value of investment (capital stock) in country i

ΔK_i = the average change in book value (capital stock) in country i

PKI$_i$ = the physical infrastructure of country i (supply of infrastructure)

HKI$_i$ = the human infrastructure in country i (supply of trained labor)

GNP$_i$ = gross national product in country i (market size-demand)

To test the trade theory approach to foreign investment, the following equations were estimated:

$$K_i = a + b \, TUS_i + c \, NETIMP_i \qquad [3]$$

$$\Delta K_i = a + b \, TUS_i + c \, NETIMP_i \qquad [4]$$

where K_i and ΔK_i are defined as in equation 1 and 2 above and

TUS$_i$ = % of country i's total trade with the U.S. (information by U.S. firms about i)

NETIMP$_i$ = demand for foreign goods in country i that are satisfied via imports

Finally, to test a joint theory of foreign investment which combines the trade theory approach with the investment theory analysis of foreign investment, the following equations were estimated:

$$K_i = a + b \, PHI_i + c \, HKI_i + d \, GNP_i + e \, TUS_i + f \, NETIMP_i \qquad [5]$$

$$\Delta K_i = a + b \, PHI_i + c \, HKI_i + d \, GNP_i + e \, TUS_i + f \, NETIMP_i \qquad [6]$$

The results of these tests appear in Table 3.

The results of the estimations for all three models were statistically significant. Model 1, the investment theory model (equations 1 and 2) explains more of the cross-country variation in U.S. direct foreign manufacturing investment to Third World countries than model 2, the trade theory model (equations 3 and 4), while as expected, model 3, the joint theory (equations 5 and 6) explains more than either single hypothesis. Additionally, it is interesting to note that the relative contribution of the independent variables in

TABLE 3

Regression Equations Testing Three Models of Foreign Investment
Across 54 Less Developed Countries for the Period 1962-1966

Model 1

(1) $K_i = .75 \, PKI_i{}^a + .25 \, HKI_i + .15 \, GNP_i$ $R^2 = .64$
      (89.9)   (10.4) $(4.21)^b$

(2) $\Delta \, K_i = .66 \, PKI_i + .30 \, HKI_i + .13 \, GNP_i$ $R^2 = .58$
      (63.77)   (12.80) $(2.51)^c$

Model 2

(3) $K_i =$ $.39 \, TUS_i - .40 \, NETIMP_i$ $R^2 = .31$
                               (14.75)   (13.9)

(4) $\Delta \, K_i =$ $.44 \, TUS_i - .24 \, NETIMP_i$ $R^2 = .26$
                               (16.72)   (4.96)

Model 3

(5) $K_i = .59 \, PKI_i + .14 \, HKI_i + .39 \, GNP_i + .28 \, TUS_i - .42 \, NETIMP_i$ $R^2 = .83$
      (99.6)   (5.83)   (27.9)   (21.83)   (31.7)

(6) $\Delta \, K_i = .63 \, PKI_i + .17 \, HKI_i + .14 \, GNP_i + .35 \, TUS_i - .13 \, NETIMP_i$ $R^2 = .71$
      (70.71)   (5.18)   (2.97)   (21.63)   (2.57)

a. Because of the differences in the units of measurement of the independent variables the regression coefficients presented above are normalized regression coefficients. Normalized coefficients permit comparability with respect to the relative importance of the independent variables (Johnson, 1972).

b. Figures in parentheses are F values.

c. These variables are statistically insignificant at the .10 level.

explaining the size distribution of this investment in model 3 further suggests that profitability variables are more important determinants of this investment than the trade variables.[5] (In the joint tests, equations 5 and 6, the physical infrastructure variable [with a normalized regression coefficient in the range of .59 to .63] is more important than either of the trade variables [the highest normalized regression coefficient being .42 for net imports in equation 5].) Furthermore, of the profitability variables, it is interesting to note that the infrastructure variables are more important than market size (demand for the firm's output). Note that in equations 1, 2, and 6 physical infrastructure is more important than human infrastructure, which in turn is more important than market size. The obvious implication of this ordering of normalized regression coefficients is that the availability (supply) of ancillary facilities (communication, transportation, skilled labor) necessary to carry out manufacturing production is more important to foreign investors than demand for the firm's output in potential host countries. The policy implication of these results suggests that if either host governments or the U.S. government wish to increase the flow of private manufacturing investment to Third World countries, they can expect some success by fostering policies which increase infrastructure development.

Perhaps the most important finding here is that the trade theory and investment theory explanations of foreign investment are complementary hypotheses (as reflected by the greater explanatory power of the joint tests) rather than competing hypotheses. Furthermore, the complementary nature of the results suggests the following interpretation of the foreign investment decision.

The statistical significance of the information variable (trade with the United States) and the foreign demand variable (net imports) implies, as Barlow and Wender (1955) argue, that foreign investment is closely related to exports. That is, initially firms service foreign markets with exports, but either when the market (GNP) reaches a critical size or when threats to the market arise (due to tariffs, nontariff barriers, or changes in comparative costs), the firm decides it may be necessary to invest in the local market to protect that market. The significance of these two variables suggests that foreign investment is the last stage of a process that begins with exports.

But this view of direct foreign investment is incomplete; the other side of the picture is profitability. When faced with the loss of a market, the firm must decide whether it is profitable to invest in the threatened market or to forego that market. This profitability calculation ultimately focuses on some form of rate of return analysis. In evaluating profitability, the firm must estimate potential demand (market size as measured by GNP), as well as the availability (supply and cost) of necessary inputs for the production process. Since the firm is investing in less developed countries, this evaluation must include an evaluation of the supply of ancillary facilities (power, transportation, and communication) necessary to engage in manufacturing production. Other aspects of supply (cost) considerations include the availability of labor. These variables in an interaction with the trade variables suggest that when threats to markets serviced by exports arise, the firm evaluates the profitability of foreign investment. If these profitability calculations show local production to be unprofitable, no investment follows, but if they show investment to be profitable, the firm will usually invest.

Finally, it should be mentioned that the stock equations (equations 1, 3, and 5 in Table 3) for all three models "fit" better than the corresponding flow equations (equations 2, 4, and 6). What is the difference between the stock measure and the flow measure which might account for this disparity? It may be because the stock variable, unlike the flow measure, includes investment in a country accumulated before and during the period of analysis, whereas the flow measure includes only new net investment made during the period of analysis (1962-1966). The importance of this difference lies in the fact that the stock measure reflects the responsiveness of foreign investments to long-run structural trends in the host country, whereas the flow measure is more reflective of short-run changes in those trends. Two kinds of problems, both of which may contribute to a poorer fit for the flow equations, emerge from this basic difference between stocks and flows.

First, the flow variable may raise critical "timing" problems which cannot be adequately dealt with cross-sectionally. The existence of a timing problem suggests that the flow over the period may be responding to the independent variables with a lag, and unless the time lag is one of instantaneous adjustment (which is obviously unlikely) cross-section regressions which assume instantaneous (time-less) adjustment are likely to result in poorer fits where timing issues are important.

Second, conceptual analysis of flows raises questions as to whether flows respond to flow variables or to stock (level) variables. If the flow of investment is more responsive to changes in the levels (flows) of the independent variables, then it might make sense to re-estimate equations 2, 4, and 6 by regressing flows on flows. But the question is whether it is reasonable to do this in a cross-section analysis. In this case (foreign investment), it is clear, for example, that for some countries (particularly the EEC countries), the high *level* of trade barriers stimulates the flow of investment, whereas for other countries this is accomplished by a change in those barriers. In a cross-section analysis, there is no way of determining whether the level of a variable encourages a flow or whether a change in the level encourages a flow. The multivariate nature of this analysis further complicates the picture. High levels of one variable (trade with the United States) and changes in the level of another (net imports) may stimulate flows to one country, while changes in the level of the first variable (trade with the United States) and the level of the second (net imports) are stimulating the flows to another. Since it is impossible, a priori, to specify in a cross-section analysis whether the independent variables should be in stock or flow form, it was decided to use stock measures, realizing that the equations of stocks on flows were likely to have a poorer "fit."

CONCLUSIONS

All that remains is to draw inferences from this analysis about the role of public capital (foreign aid) in stimulating U.S. private foreign investment in Third World countries.

The strength of the trade and information variables implies that a primary impediment to foreign investment in less developed countries, particularly in Africa and Asia, is the lack of information by potential investors about profitable opportunities in those countries. Consequently, U.S. government efforts to increase the flow of information to investors might have some positive effect in fostering foreign investment. The United States has increasingly been attempting to provide such information through a series of information pamphlets such as "Basic Data on the Economy of . . .," "Market Profiles of . . .," "Foreign Investment Laws of . . ." No attempt was made here to assess the impact of this process, but other characteristics of the foreign investment decision suggest this approach may not be very productive. For an information series approach to stimulate private capital flows, it will either have to work through exports, or the information made available will have to be of a sufficient character as to entice firms to skip the trade stage. The latter prospect appears quite unlikely if foreign investment, as the last stage of a process beginning with exports, tends to occur when markets are threatened. Before trade, there is no market to be threatened and, hence, there should be no investment. If it proves impossible to skip the export stage of foreign investment, there is little reason to expect foreign investment to flow to countries which have few trade ties to the United States. Furthermore, if foreign investment is to increase in the near future, it can be expected to flow to those countries with the greatest trade ties to the United States—the very countries which currently receive the bulk of this investment.

If the analysis is correct, increasing capital flows to countries with which the United States has little trade ties can only be achieved by increasing the flow of trade with these countries. Thus, any foreign aid policy (such as aid tying) which increases the trade flows between the United States and Third World countries (Cooper, 1972) can be expected to lead to a long-run increase in the flow of private capital to those countries. This places policy makers in a difficult position. They know tied aid reduces the net resource transfer to the aid recipient and, hence, the economic development impact of a given dollar of aid. Since it is in the U.S. interest to identify with the development interests of aid recipient countries, it could achieve greater influence (through the impact on development) if aid were not tied. This reduction in grant equivalence of tied aid is acutely recognized by decision makers, and many have suggested the United States reduce the amount of its tied aid to less developed countries to increase the productivity (economic as well as political) of a dollar's worth of aid. So far, U.S. balance of payments constraints have kept policy makers from moving from tied aid. If the above argument is correct, another argument can be added for the retention of tied aid. If tied aid increases trade flows to less developed country recipients of aid, and if this aid/trade link becomes the first stage of a process leading to foreign investment in aid recipient countries, aid officials wishing to stimulate the flow of private investment to aid recipient countries ought to increase rather than reduce the amount of tied aid the United States allocates.

In addition to trade and information variables, economic infrastructure variables (physical as well as human) are crucial determinants in the cross-country distribution of U.S. direct foreign investment in manufacturing. To the extent foreign aid (loans and grants) fosters infrastructure development, it should provide some impetus for foreign investment by increasing profitability in aid recipient countries. But just as with the trade and information aspect of foreign investment, infrastructure development is a long-run process. Consequently, increasing aid for this purpose in the short run is not likely to have much effect on either the cross-country distribution of U.S. direct foreign investment in manufacturing or the amount of investment.

Finally, the influence of both infrastructure development and of the aid/trade link on foreign investment has important implications for the way in which aid is disbursed. Some within the U.S. government have been calling for the gradual replacement of bilateral aid with multilateral aid. This, it is hoped, will reduce somewhat the onerous political burdens attached to bilateral aid. This analysis suggests that there may be important political and economic consequences associated with such a move. Multilateralizing U.S. aid is likely to influence U.S. trade with Third World countries, and this impact on trade will undoubtedly have some effect on U.S. private capital flows to aid recipients. For example, a reallocation of U.S. aid from tied bilateral aid to untied multilateral aid might reduce trade between U.S. firms and aid recipient countries, causing a reduction in private capital flows to these countries. This would tend to impede the development process by denying these countries needed capital and technology unless public flows are increased to make up for this loss or unless private flows from other countries are increased. But domestic pressures within donor countries mitigate against the first possibility, while the paucity of private flows from most of the rest of the developed world offers little hope regarding the second. Thus, the multilateralization of U.S. aid could well reduce the volume of private capital flows to Third World countries. Although it is impossible to predict a priori what the impact of the multilateralization of aid would be on U.S. private capital flows to Third World countries, policy makers must gauge the impact before multilateralizing aid. At the very least, multilateralizing U.S. aid will lead to a different cross-country distribution of aid, which will lead in all likelihood to a different pattern of trade with Third World countries, and, ultimately, to a different pattern (cross-country distribution) of foreign investment. Decision makers thus must take into account not only whether the different pattern of aid which flows from aid multilateralization is desirable in terms of U.S. foreign policy objectives, but also whether the resulting influence on the distribution of private capital flows to these countries is consistent with those objectives.

Additionally, if multilateralizing aid leads to a reduction of trade between U.S. firms and aid recipient countries, the influence of infrastructure aid on foreign private capital will diminish. This analysis of the foreign investment process suggests that infrastructure development will lead to foreign investment only if firms are aware of the enhanced profitability of investment opportunities resulting from infrastructure aid. But this awareness seems to turn on the amount of trade between U.S. firms and the aid recipient country. Consequently, policies which reduce trade and, hence, information to potential investors are also likely to reduce the flow of private capital associated with infrastructure development.

In conclusion, this paper has attempted to illuminate the nature of the interrelationships between U.S. foreign aid and U.S. direct foreign investment to less developed countries by focusing on the empirical determinants of U.S. foreign investment to those countries. Since the postwar period, U.S. government policy regarding the role of private capital in development assistance policy has been characterized by ambiguity and uncertainty. There have always been those who have argued that aid must stimulate private investment, as well as those who have realized that such an emphasis on private enterprise extracts a high political price, particularly in an era of anti-Americanism. This analysis has attempted to demonstrate how various aspects of aid policy influence the flow of private capital to Third World countries as well as indicate the likely impact of changes in various aspects of aid policy (particularly aid tying and multi-lateralizing aid) on the flow of private capital to the Third World.

It appears that if a basic objective of aid is to foster development through capital inflows, this can best be achieved by the United States continuing to grant tied aid on a bilateral basis. But if policy makers decide to attempt to reduce the political costs of bilateral aid by multilateralizing U.S. aid, they should realize that such a process is likely to reduce the transfer of private capital from the United States to less developed countries.

NOTES

1. For an excellent discussion of this argument see Whitman (1964: ch. 2).

2. Additional support for investment theory hypotheses of foreign investment have been provided by Scaperlanda and Mauer (1969), Mikesell (1967), Balassa (1966).

3. The *Survey of Current Business* provided data in the period on regional groupings of countries, and the publication identified the countries in each regional grouping. Along with this information, the department's other publications provided country-by-country data on many of the countries in the regional groups. We took the data provided by "Establishing a Business in . . ." and "Market Profiles of . . ." and used it to allocate the more complete SCB data to the various countries.

Caution must be exercised in interpreting the relationship between the stock and the flow variable. Theoretically, a change in the stock value between two periods is equal to the flow over the period, but certain valuation changes during a period may alter this relationship. The Department of Commerce measures the change in the book value (stock) of direct foreign investment by adding to the stock at the beginning of the year and the capital outflow, recorded in the balance of payments under direct foreign investment, and reinvested earnings by U.S. subsidiaries abroad. To this basic adjustment of real flows, price valuation adjustments can be made. These price adjustments are usually minor, but in 1959 and 1960 exchange rate changes in a number of Latin American countries (Brazil, Chile, Costa Rica, Dominican Republic, Ecuador, Guatamala, and Paraguay) caused these adjustments to overshadow the real flows to these countries (Pizer and Cutler, 1960: 20).

4. Regarding the procedures utilized in obtaining data, only one needs clarification. To obtain meaningful measures of certain parameters for host countries, factor analysis was employed. Although this statistical procedure has a number of uses, it is used here to detect underlying regularities in certain data such that composite measures of these data which are more meaningful and complete than single variables could be used to test various hypotheses. The procedure involves reducing a number of original explanatory variables into a smaller number of factors in terms of which the whole set of variables can be characterized. Besides providing us with more meaningful indicators of certain characteristics, factor analysis yields an important statistical advantage—it saves degrees of freedom. For a more detailed discussion of factor analysis, see Rummel, 1967.

5. Because of differences in the units of measurement of the independent variables, the regression coefficients presented below are normalized coefficients. Normalized regression coefficients permit comparability with respect to the relative importance of the independent variables (Johnston, 1972).

REFERENCES

BALASSA, B. (1966) "American direct investment in the Common Market." Bonca Naz Lavonis Quarterly (June): 121-146.

BANKS, A. (1971) Cross Polity Time Series Data. Cambridge, Mass.: MIT Press.

BARLOW, E. R. and I. T. WENDER (1955) Foreign Investment and Taxation. Englewood Cliffs, N.J.: Prentice-Hall.

CHADWIN, M. (1972) "Foreign policy report/Nixon Administration debates new position paper on Latin America." National Journal (January 15): 97-105, 147-156.

CHENERY, H. and L. TAYLOR (1968) "Development patterns: among countries and over time." Review of Economics and Statistics 50, 4: 391-417.

COOPER, R. (1972) "The additionality factor in tied U.S. development assistance." A Rand Corporation Report for the Agency for International Development, July.

DERNBERG, T. and D. McDOUGALL (1968) Macroeconomics. New York: McGraw-Hill.

GRUEBER, W., R. VERNON, and P. MEHTA (1967) "The R & D factor in international trade and international investment of U.S. industries." Journal of Political Economy (February): 20-37.

HORST, T. (1970) "American participation in Canadian markets: a multinational firm approach." Harvard Institute of Economic Research Discussion Paper 104.

JOHNSTON, J. (1972) Econometric Methods. New York: McGraw-Hill.

JORGENSEN, D. (1963) "Capital theory and investment behavior." American Economic Review: Papers and Proceedings 53, 2: 252.

KEESING, D. (1967) "The impact of R & D on U.S. trade." Journal of Political Economy (February): 138-148.

MAIZELS, A. (1963) Industrial Growth and World Trade. Cambridge, Mass.: Harvard University Press.

MIKESELL, R. (1967) "Decisive factors in the flow of American investment into Europe." Economia Internazionale (August): 413-453.

PIZER, S. and F. CUTLER (1960) "U.S. direct foreign investment: measures of growth and economic effects." Survey of Current Business. Washington, D.C.: U.S. Department of Commerce, 20.

RICHARDSON, D. (1971) "Theoretical considerations in the analysis of direct foreign investment." Western Economic Journal (March): 96.

RUMMEL, R. (1967) "Understanding factor analysis." Journal of Conflict Resolution: 444-480.

SCAPERLANDA, A. and L. MAUER (1969) "The determinants of U.S. direct investment in the E.E.C." American Economic Review (September): 558-568.

SEVERN, A. K. (1970) "Investment and financial behavior of American direct investors in manufacturing." Presented at the Conference on International Mobility and Movement of Capital at the Brookings Institute, January.

STEVENS, G. (1969) "Fixed investment expenditures of foreign manufacturing affiliates of U.S. firms: theoretical models and empirical evidence." Yale Economic Essays 9 (Spring): 137-198.

U.S. Department of Commerce (1953) Factors Limiting U.S. Investment Abroad: Part I. Survey of Factors in Foreign Countries. Washington, D.C.

––– (1954) Factors Limiting U.S. Investments Abroad: Part II. Business Views on the U.S. Government's Role. Washington, D.C.

––– (1960) U.S. Business Investments in Foreign Countries: Supplement to the Survey of Current Business. Washington, D.C.

––– (1970) U.S. Direct Investment Abroad, Part I: Balance of Payments Data: Supplement to the Survey of Current Business. Washington, D.C.

VERNON, R. (1966) "International trade and international investment in the product cycle." Quarterly Journal of Economics (May): 190-207.

WHITMAN, M. (1964) Government Risk Sharing in Foreign Investment. Princeton: Princeton University Press.

Chapter 6

ECONOMIC AND POLITICAL
ASPECTS OF U.S. MULTILATERAL AID

G. R O B E R T F R A N C O

International Monetary Fund

and

University of Maryland

President Nixon's message to Congress on September 15, 1970, contained the seeds of a new program that would channel U.S. foreign aid through multilateral organizations. This new policy would permit recipient countries to purchase goods and services with Agency for International Development (AID) dollars anywhere they desire. The purpose of this chapter is to examine the economic impact of such a policy. The chapter is divided into five sections. The first section discusses the trends in the U.S. foreign assistance program from the start of the Marshall Plan in 1948 to 1973. The second section traces the development of the idea of untied aid.

AUTHOR'S NOTE: This paper was written while the author was a Senior Research Associate at CACI, Inc., Arlington, Virginia. He is presently an economist with the International Monetary Fund and a lecturer at the University of Maryland. Special assistance was given by Mr. Donald Krysakowski in the preparation of this chapter.

Special attention is given to the work of the Organization for Economic Cooperation and Development (OECD) in this area. The third section examines the position of U.S. labor and industry on untied aid, with particular emphasis on the maritime and fertilizer industries. The fourth section develops a simple stochastic model to discover whether the major donor nations would benefit from a system of untied aid. Finally, the last section summarizes the chapter and discusses the future prospects of such a system from the point of view of the developing as well as the developed countries.

TRENDS IN THE U.S. FOREIGN ASSISTANCE PROGRAM: 1948-1972

Since 1961, the U.S. official foreign assistance program has been administered by three agencies: the Agency for International Development (AID),[1] the Export-Import Bank (EXIMBANK), and the International Operations Branch of Action. A fourth channel of aid is the Food for Peace program administered on an interagency basis. AID and its predecessor agencies were specifically designed to provide development assistance on concessional terms. EXIMBANK, on the other hand, is motivated primarily by commercial considerations; but its official long-term export credits to developing countries nonetheless contain concessional elements.[2] The Peace Corps, an officially sponsored volunteer scheme, has supplied middle-level manpower to developing countries in all areas of the globe since 1961. In 1971, the Peace Corps merged with domestic volunteer programs into one agency called Action. The foreign activities of Action are part of the International Operations Branch which has assumed all of the responsibilities of the Peace Corps. Finally, considerable quantities of aid in the form of food are transferred to Third World countries through the Food for Peace program which is administered jointly by AID and the Department of Agriculture.

From 1948 through 1972, U.S. overseas loans and grants amounted to $125 billion, of which $85 billion was given to developing countries and the balance to developed countries. Aid to less developed countries was allocated as follows: military programs received $24.3 billion, Food for Peace received $14.6 billion, and regular economic programs totalled $56.1 billion of which $8.7 billion was channeled through EXIMBANK, $20.5 billion through AID, and $26.9 billion through AID's predecessor agencies. Of the total $85 billion given to developing countries, about $16 billion was channeled through the World Bank. The developed countries received a total of $40 billion over the same period. This sum was allocated as follows: $12.3 billion for military programs, $11.5 billion for Marshall Plan aid, $6.6 billion for postwar relief, $3.8 billion for EXIM-BANK distribution, and $5.8 billion for AID distribution.

Table 1 presents the U.S. official and private net flows to developing countries from 1948 to 1972. Official development assistance is a concept introduced by the Development Assistance Committee (DAC) of the OECD. It includes all contributions on concessional terms that promote the economic development and welfare of developing countries. Total official assistance ranges from a high of

TABLE 1

**U.S. Official and Private Net
Flows to Developing Countries, 1948-1972
(in billions of U.S. dollars)**

Year	Official	Private	Total
1948	3.240	1.953	5.193
1949	3.211	2.452	5.663
1950	3.020	1.134	4.154
1951	3.461	1.173	4.634
1952	3.642	1.399	5.041
1953	4.118	2.231	6.349
1954	3.858	0.886	4.744
1955	3.311	0.906	4.217
1956	3.168	1.171	4.339
1957	2.091	2.008	4.099
1958	2.410	1.275	3.685
1959	2.322	0.954	3.276
1960	2.776	1.042	3.818
1961	3.447	1.102	4.549
1962	3.535	0.819	4.354
1963	3.699	0.880	4.579
1964	3.445	1.326	4.771
1965	3.627	1.897	5.524
1966	3.660	1.360	5.020
1967	3.723	1.922	5.645
1968	3.605	2.204	5.809
1969	3.092	1.733	4.825
1970	3.050	3.204	6.254
1971	3.324	3.727	7.051
1972	3.545	3.809	7.354

Source: OECD, 1973.

$7.4 billion in 1972 to a low of $3.3 billion in 1959. From the aid procurement program perspective, the U.S. postwar foreign assistance programs can be divided into three periods: 1948 to 1959, 1960 to 1969, and 1970 to date.

THE 1948-1959 PERIOD

From the beginning of the Marshall Plan in 1948 to 1959, the total U.S. aid bill amounted to $55 billion for economic and military support. Approximately $26 billion represented economic disbursements for Europe. Most of these monies went to the United Kingdom, France, Germany, Italy, and the Netherlands. During the same period, Latin America received $1.2 billion while the Mideast, Southeast Asia, India, and Africa together accounted for $1.9 billion. With the success of the Marshall Plan and the recovery of Europe, the United States shifted its aid program from Europe to the poorer countries of Asia and Africa. From 1948 to 1959, the average yearly contributions (both private and official) of the United States amounted to $4.62 billion. About three-fifths of this aid was in the form of grants, one-fifth was in loans, and the other one-fifth financed net sales of surplus agricultural commodities.

By and large, foreign aid in this period was not tied to domestic procurement. In the early postwar period, however, most of the recipients of U.S. aid spent their dollars in the United States to purchase capital equipment required for the European postwar recovery. The United States at that time was the only country where these goods could have been procured. By the mid-fifties, however, the European economies and Japan were well on their way to recovery and began to compete with the United States for world markets. As a result, a growing portion of U.S. foreign assistance dollars was not used to purchase goods and services in the United States, but elsewhere. With increased deficits in the U.S. balance of payments and with employment opportunities dwindling in the domestic economy, there was increased pressure in Congress to tie U.S. foreign assistance to domestic procurement.

THE 1960-1969 PERIOD OR THE EISENHOWER PROCUREMENT POLICY

In this period, the total U.S. aid package amounted to $48.89 billion, of which $14.29 billion was in disbursements by the private sector. The foreign assistance program in the sixties differed from the one in the fifties in several respects. First, greater emphasis was placed on loans rather than on grants. Long-term loans became especially important; these were usually given at low interest to be repaid in hard currency. Second, there were renewed attempts to provide technical assistance with greater focus on health and education and less attention given to industrial know-how. Third, the programs strove to encourage private domestic participation in the foreign assistance programs through export-loss guarantees and private-investment surveys.

The Eisenhower procurement policy was the basic U.S. foreign aid policy throughout the sixties under four presidents. Beginning in late 1960, with a directive from President Eisenhower, U.S. foreign assistance was progressively tied to U.S. purchases so that procurement in the United States increased from forty-seven percent of all AID-financed commodities in 1959 to ninety-nine percent in 1969. This action by President Eisenhower was one policy in a move to strengthen the U.S. economy by easing pressures on the balance of payments and helping retard trends toward further disequilibrium in the U.S. trade balance. The results of the Eisenhower policy were evident in the steady upward trend of procurement in the United States during the 1960-1969 decade in relation to procurement in third countries.

Table 2 shows a breakdown, by standard industrial trade classification (SITC), of total U.S. aid and the proportion expended in the United States in the 1960-1969 period. Over the whole period, eighty-one percent of U.S. aid was used to purchase commodities in the United States. The percentage ranged from a low of fifty-three percent for stone, clay, and glass products to ninety-seven percent for miscellaneous manufactures. Over the entire period, $8.2 billion or approximately three percent of annual U.S. exports were the result of the Eisenhower procurement policy. If one limits the observations to the 1965-1971 data after tied procurement had been fully implemented, the picture is more dramatic with more than ninety-six percent of U.S. AID dollars tied to domestic procurement. Table 3 presents a yearly breakdown of the percentage of AID dollars used by developing countries to procure commodities in the United States.

The Eisenhower procurement policy came under heavy criticism at the first United Nations Conference on Trade and Development (UNCTAD)[3] that took place in 1964. One of the recommendations that emerged from the conference was that donor countries should,

TABLE 2

Proportion of Aid Loans Spent in the United States
by Major Industrial Groups, 1960-1969
(in millions of U.S. dollars)

Major Industry Group (SITC Categories)	Total Aid 1	Amount Spent in U.S. 2	Percent 2:1
Machinery (excluding electrical) (35)	2,197	1,911	0.87
Primary Metal—Fab. & Metal Products (33-34)	1,968	1,611	0.82
Chemicals (28)	1,785	1,513	0.85
Transportation Equip. (37)	1,105	972	0.88
Petroleum Refining (29)	686	375	0.55
Electrical Machinery (36)	620	481	0.76
Food Products (20)	516	415	0.80
Rubber Products (30)	290	205	0.71
Textile Mill Products (22)	287	199	0.69
Paper (26)	268	232	0.87
Stone, Clay, Glass (32)	156	82	0.53
Misc. Manufactures (39)	117	114	0.97
Prof. Scientific (38)	64	57	0.89
Total	10,059	8,167	0.81

Source: AID, 1961-1970.

whenever possible, channel external resources through multilateral institutions. On the domestic front, development economists argued that with increased opposition from Congress to grant aid appropriations and a shrinking aid package, available aid dollars should be maximized by allowing aid-recipient countries to spend these funds where they will get maximum usage. Thus, there was increased pressure for foreign aid dollars to be stretched to allow purchases of goods and services at lowest world prices, regardless of source or nationality of contractor.

THE NIXON PROCUREMENT POLICY

In his "Foreign Assistance Program for the Seventies" delivered to Congress on September 15, 1970, President Nixon stated that the

TABLE 3

Percentage of Aid Commodity Expenditures
(by source of purchase)

| | | | Offshore | |
| | | | Developed | Developing |
Year	USA	Total	Countries	Countries
1959	47.4	52.6	42.1	10.5
1960	40.6	59.4	49.4	10.0
1961	44.2	55.8	47.1	8.7
1962	66.3	33.7	15.8	17.9
1963	79.4	20.6	6.7	13.9
1964	86.6	13.4	3.3	10.1
1965	92.1	7.9	1.7	6.2
1966	90.2	9.8	0.9	8.9
1967	96.2	3.8	0.5	3.3
1968	98.4	1.6	0.7	0.9
1969	98.9	1.1	0.2	0.9
1970	98.0	2.0	0.1	1.9
1971	99.7	0.3	0.1	0.2
1972	95.5	4.5	0.0	4.5
1973	94.1	5.9	0.0	5.9

Source: AID, 1974.

United States would untie its foreign assistance program from domestic procurement, provided the other industrialized Western countries follow suit. This new policy would result in AID dollars losing their donor identity except at the funding stage, and, more importantly, in the loss of donor identity for the commodities and services provided by the foreign assistance program based on tied procurement as developed by President Eisenhower.

The administration's new aid policy was based principally on four sets of policy recommendations. The first was generated by the so-called Rockefeller Report on Latin America (1969); the second by guidelines of a U.S. government-sponsored study entitled "U.S. Foreign Assistance in the 1970s: A New Approach" headed by Rudolph Peterson (1970); the third by the outcome of a meeting of the OECD's (1971) DAC which met in Tokyo in the summer of 1970; and the fourth by the Pearson Commission on International Development (1969), a World Bank-sponsored study. The Rockefeller Report argues:

The United States assistance program has become increasingly encumbered with conditions and restrictions which seriously reduce the effectiveness of

our assistance. These include requirements to ship half the goods purchased with assistance loans on United States freighters; provision that all
imports be purchased in the United States no matter how much more
expensive; earmarking of funds contrary to the particular needs of a
country; threats to withhold aid if United States investments are expropriated without appropriate payment, if a nation purchases "sophisticated" weapons, or if United States commercial fishing boats are taken
into custody and fined [Rockefeller, 1969: 81].

Similarly, the Peterson Report states that

the United States proposes that all industrial countries agree to untie their
bilateral development lending permitting the developing countries to use
these loans for procurement from the cheapest source on a competitive bid
basis [Peterson, 1970: 32].

The untying process began with great momentum but slowed as
implementation of legislation became more difficult and other donor
countries failed to untie substantially their foreign assistance programs. On November 1, 1969, the United States acted unilateraly by
untying procurements of AID loan dollars to the Latin American
countries. On September 15, 1970, the untying process was expanded to include most lower-income countries.[4] These actions
permitted Latin American and lower-income countries to procure
commodities in any country of the world except the recipient
country, the Socialist countries, and the following forty-one
countries:

Algeria, Andorra, Australia, Austria, Belgium, Canada, Cyprus, Denmark,
Finland, France, Federal Republic of Germany, Greece, Hong Kong,
Iceland, Iraq, Ireland, Israel, Italy, Japan, Kuwait, Liechtenstein,
Luxembourg, Malta, Monaco, Netherlands, New Zealand, Norway,
Portugal, Rhodesia, San Marino, Somalia, South Africa, Spain, Sudan,
Syria, Sweden, Switzerland, Arab Republic of Egypt, the United Kingdom,
Yemen, and Yugoslavia.[5]

Further untying legislation that would allow procurement in any
one of the aforementioned countries was to proceed as these countries also untied their foreign assistance programs. On December 6,
1972, Sudan and Yemen were removed from the list, but Libya,

Qatar, South Yemen, and the United Arab Emirates were added. By late 1973, there was little change in the U.S. untying regulations. AID loan dollars were untied only with respect to developing countries; yet general restrictions on where these funds could be spent were retained. None of the Western European countries or Japan chose to follow the U.S. example; thus commodities could not be purchased in those countries with U.S. aid dollars.

Furthermore, only AID loan dollars are untied. This does not apply to AID grants. U.S. aid dollars that are channeled through the Food for Peace program and EXIMBANK are not covered by the untying legislation. The very nature of these programs makes untying impossible under existing laws governing Public Law 480 and the EXIMBANK. In summary, out of the total U.S. foreign assistance program, only loans channeled through AID and contributions to multilateral organizations are untied. AID loans can generate procurements in any country of the world except the recipient country, the Socialist countries, and any of the countries in the aforementioned list. Contributions to multilateral organizations are usually under the control of the multilateral organizations and procurement rules are set by these organizations. In reality, most of these contributions are totally untied.

An important new regulation in U.S. policy that will benefit developing countries concerns a change in the component rules of aid commodities. Traditionally, no more than ten percent of the component cost of a commodity, measured as a percentage of price, could be obtained outside the country of production. Thus, under the tied system, where the United States was the only eligible source, U.S. commodities could not contain more than ten percent in foreign components. With the untying process, AID realized that if the ten percent rule were to apply to lower-income countries, those with low-cost labor could not take full advantage of the untying rules. These countries traditionally import components for domestically produced items. The ten percent rule would make too many of their products ineligible for AID financing. The Agency, therefore, changed the rule to provide for a fifty percent limitation. Now a Korean product may be eligible for AID financing even though it contains fifty percent Japanese components. This radical change in AID policy will undoubtedly help shift buying patterns by aid-recipient countries toward other developing countries.

BILATERAL VERSUS MULTILATERAL AID

Bilateralism, or tied aid, is defined as a condition in which the recipient country is compelled to spend the aid dollars it receives in the donor country. Multilateralism, or untied aid, on the other hand, is defined as a condition in which the recipient country can procure aid commodities anywhere it desires. Bilateral aid does not always involve tied conditions. In the early postwar period, the largest proportion of U.S. aid was bilateral, but was untied. In actuality, those aid dollars were used to procure commodities in the United States, where they were available. Similarly, multilateral aid may, in certain instances, have conditions imposed on its usage. Recently, Arab donor countries have exerted pressure on world institutions to withhold the use of Arab resources by Israel. Nevertheless, tied aid is usually transferred directly from the donor country to the recipient country on a bilateral basis, while untied aid is transferred from the donor country to the recipient country via some international agency. As a rule, bilateral aid is tied at both ends. This means that the aid given is specified for particular projects and involves the purchase of goods and services in the donor country. Multilateral aid, on the other hand, is only tied at one end. This implies that aid is given for a specific project, but the inputs for the project can be purchased anywhere the recipient country chooses.

The objectives of tied aid are mostly political and economic. The latter permit the donor country to make fuller use of idle domestic resources, including industrial capacity, thus expanding domestic employment opportunities. Tied aid can also be used to expand exports and alleviate pressures on the balance of payments of the donor country. The political objectives involve the desire by the donor nations to be recognized as the initiator of particular projects and to receive credit which generates spillovers into political alignment or UN voting patterns that support the donor country. Furthermore, under a tied system, appropriations for aid can be more easily justified by the legislative branches of the donor countries.

The objections against tied aid are basically threefold. First, tied aid may constitute a disguised subsidy by the developing country to the noncompetitive industries of the donor country. This is especially true when prices in the donor country are not competitive internationally. This, in turn, diminishes the value of a given quantity of aid when compared to the quantity received under a system of untied aid. Second, tied aid may hamper the expansion of trade among developing countries by compelling them to purchase aid-financed goods and services in donor countries. Third, multilateral aid is preferred by many developing countries because it is received without any special obligations to the donor countries. Many developing countries have reservations about accepting aid directly from a particular developed country. Bilateral programs are objectionable because they are apt to exert undue political influence on the recipient.

The Peterson Report (1970) estimates that bilateralism has reduced the value of aid to developing countries by about fifteen percent. In 1969, this figure represented $300 million worth of goods and services that the developing countries would have received had the foreign assistance programs of all donor countries been untied. For the United States, Mikesell (1969: 242) estimates that the price of U.S. aid-generated export commodities is about fifteen to twenty percent higher than world market prices. This figure, however, is based on the pre-devaluation value of the dollar; the gap between U.S. prices and world prices has undoubtedly narrowed since then as the value of the dollar has fallen.[6]

The idea of untied aid was first discussed in detail in the first and second UNCTAD conferences. These were massive and very political affairs in which numerous disagreements among the participants emerged. Two important recommendations, however, did obtain general consent. The first was that a larger proportion of foreign assistance be channeled through multilateral organizations, preferably the United Nations; the second was that developed countries pledge one percent of their GNP annually to development assistance. Both of these proposals received some attention by the developed countries but in varying degrees. Of the sixteen member countries of the DAC, only seven contributed more than one percent of their GNP to development assistance in 1971.[7] Nevertheless, the untying proposals suggested by UNCTAD have received considerable attention by the OECD and its member governments. At the DAC meeting of September 1970, held in Tokyo, member countries agreed that their contributions to multilateral institutions should not be tied to domestic procurement (OECD, 1971). Furthermore, the great majority of member countries agreed that regular bilateral development loans should be untied, provided arrangements are made to insure that such funds are used by the developing countries on the basis of truly competitive international bidding. These OECD proposals were put forth quite independently of the two U.S. government-sponsored studies and of the Pearson Report sponsored by the World Bank. Despite all these recommendations, bilateral tied aid remains the most important mechanism by which donor countries transfer resources to developing countries. There are indications, however, that multilateral aid is slowly becoming increasingly important in transferring resources. This is especially true for the United States, as will be discussed in the forthcoming sections.

THE RISE OF MULTILATERALISM

International organizations have become, over the last two decades, increasingly important in the development business. In the previous section, some of the reasons for multilateral aid were discussed. Of great importance are the mounting pressures from the developing countries that are striving to channel political and economic decisions into international bodies where each country is represented and can take a position and vote. Furthermore, multilateralism has been backed by smaller donor countries because they cannot, by themselves, put together comprehensive bilateral programs. These donor countries usually contribute the highest percentage of their aid through international organizations. Multilateralism has also been popular in intellectual circles since it contributes to the process of building an international community and, hence, enhances world peace.

Basically, there are three sets of multilateral organizations through which aid funds can be channeled—the World Bank Group, the regional development banks and funds, and various UN agencies.[8] It is important to point out that the World Bank is technically part of the United Nations. In actuality, however, the responsibilities of operations of both groups are quite distinct.

The World Bank Group is composed of three organizations—the International Bank for Reconstruction and Development (IBRD), the International Finance Corporation (IFC), and the International Development Association (IDA). IBRD is the most important of all multilateral agencies. It was established, together with the International Monetary Fund (IMF),[9] as a result of the Bretton Woods Conference held in New Hampshire in 1944. The Bank's principal function has been to lend subscribed capital to governments for development projects. The Bank has also, in certain instances, borrowed directly from donor countries and has also issued its own bonds. These transactions are possible since many member countries permit their financial institutions to purchase IBRD bonds for trust accounts. IFC was created in 1956 to finance undertakings outside the responsibilities of IBRD. The main scope of IFC's work is in making loans to private enterprise in the developing countries. Since 1961, IFC has been able to purchase equity shares as well as bond obligations of private corporations. Under its charter, it is permitted to finance local currency costs as well as the foreign exchange components of approved undertakings.

IDA was created in 1960 to help the least developed countries.[10] For that reason, IDA's loans consist of soft, long-term loans at extremely low interest rates. The average length of the loans is fifty years.

The regional development banks are the latest trend in multilateral organizations. The number of such banks has mushroomed recently. The oldest and most famous of the banks is the Inter-American Development Bank (IDB) which was founded in 1958. Newer additions include the Asian Development Bank (ADB), the Andean Development Corporation, the African Development Bank, the East African Development Bank, and the Caribbean Development Bank which was created in 1970 with an initial capital of $50 million. The most important development funds are the European Development Fund and the Arab Fund for Economic and Social Development. The former channels European Economic Community aid to developing countries, mostly to ex-colonies of the member countries. The European Development Fund and the European Investment Bank have contributed $1.5 billion in foreign assistance in the sixties. The Arab Fund for Economic and Social Development, which had a total capacity of $300 million in 1972, channels most of its aid to Moslem and African countries.

The UN development system is very complex and multifaceted. It was last examined in 1969 by Sir Robert Jackson (1969) of Australia. He concluded that, if the system were to carry any greater load, it would have to be redesigned. At that time, the UN system was under the control of at least thirty separate governing bodies. Jackson discovered that the various programs were fragmented and that they had no comprehensive development policy. UN agencies were also fragmented geographically, without an adequate central policy structure, and were slow and often incapable of reacting to new situations and opportunities. Many examples describing these inadequacies are available. They range from the incapacity of the Food and Agricultural Organization (FAO) to react to current food shortages, to the unsuccessful attempts by the World Health Organization (WHO) to develop comprehensive family-planning schemes. To correct these shortcomings, the activities of the United Nations and its specialized agencies were reorganized in 1967, with the creation of the United Nations Development Program (UNDP). This program replaced all existing programs and placed them under a separate unit created within the Secretariat. The unit is financed through the regular annual budget of the United Nations, and its activities deal principally with economic development, social welfare, and public administration. It is through the technical assistance programs that the United Nations provides direct material contributions to the development process of developing countries.

In 1973, the UNDP became the world's largest source of multilateral technical and investment assistance. Furthermore, in that year, a decisive shift in emphasis to the world's poor countries took place, with an eighteen percent increase in the number of field projects in these countries jointly administered by the UNDP and donor countries. The total financial support for development under the program for 1973 amounted to $600 million, of which $269 million was provided by the United Nations and $331 million by individual governments. These figures brought the cumulative expenditures for technical cooperation of UNDP (1974: 21) and its predecessor agencies to $5 billion from 1950 through 1973. The majority of UNDP contributions are not tied to procurement in any one country.

Table 4 presents UNDP expenditures through the United Nations and its specialized agencies for 1973. It can be seen that the largest proportion of the funds was channeled through the FAO with 29.3 percent of total expenditures. Over 16 percent of the funds were channeled directly through the United Nations itself. It should be pointed out, however, that these funds do not represent the actual

TABLE 4

UNDP Project Expenditures in 1973 by Agency
(in millions of U.S. dollars)

Agency	Expenditure	Percent of Total
FAO	78.7	29.3
IBRD	15.2	5.7
UNDP (direct)	3.8	1.4
UNCTAD	3.9	1.5
UPU	1.4	0.1
ITU	10.0	3.7
IAEA	2.0	0.1
IMCO	1.4	0.1
WHO	14.1	5.3
ICAO	7.3	2.7
IDB	0.4	0.0[a]
UNIDO	16.9	6.3
WMO	5.3	2.0
ILO	27.2	10.1
UNESCO	36.4	13.6
U.N. (direct)	44.2	16.5
Total	268.2	100.00[b]

a. Less than 0.05 percent.

b. Does not add to 100 percent because of rounding errors.

Source: UNDP, 1973.

UPU = Universal Postal Union; ITU = International Telecommunication Union; IAEA = International Atomic Energy Agency; IMCO = Inter-Governmental Maritime Consultive Organization; ICAO = International Civil Service Organization; IDB = Inter-American Development Bank; UNIDO = United Nations Industrial Development Organization; WMO = World Meteorological Organization; ILO = International Labor Organization; UNESCO = United Nations Educational Scientific and Cultural Organization.

yearly expenditures of each agency, but only the portion that comes from UNDP. Over the last few years, UNDP resources have expanded more rapidly than the total official development assistance of the OECD. On both a long-term basis (1960-1972) and a medium-term basis (1968-1972), the growth in UNDP contributions has been twice the average growth rate of the DAC flows. While DAC flows have declined as a share of the total GNP of DAC countries (from 0.52

percent of GNP in 1960 to 0.34 percent in 1972), the expansion of UNDP resources from these same countries has kept pace with their GNP growth rates. Similarly, UNDP resources have expanded at a substantially faster rate than the bilateral technical assistance programs of the DAC countries. Although DAC members have increasingly emphasized technical cooperation in their bilateral programs (which averaged 19.1 percent of total bilateral aid in 1965 and rose to 27.2 percent in 1972), UNDP financial support for technical cooperation and pre-investment work grew more than 50 percent faster than the growth rate of the DAC bilateral technical assistance over the same period.

Table 5 presents the bilateral and multilateral contributions of all DAC member countries to the developing countries from 1961 to 1971. The percentage of multilateral contributions out of total contributions fluctuated from a low of 3.3 percent in 1966 to a high of 7.6 percent in 1969. While there was some increase in the late sixties and early seventies when multilateral contributions rose above 7 percent, over the entire period there was no marked increase in the proportion of multilateral assistance despite the general untying

TABLE 5

**Bilateral and Multilateral Contributions
by DAC Member Countries 1961-1971
(in millions of U.S. dollars)**

Year	Bilateral 1	Multilateral 2	Total 3	Percent 2:3
1961	8,728	521	9,249	5.6
1962	7,926	511	8,437	6.1
1963	8,204	368	8,572	4.3
1964	9,240	405	9,645	4.2
1965	9,972	348	10,320	3.4
1966	9,984	336	10,320	3.3
1967	10,699	736	11,435	6.4
1968	12,826	683	13,509	5.1
1969	12,728	1,050	13,778	7.6
1970	14,667	1,124	15,791	7.1
1971	16,819	1,339	18,158	7.4

Source: OECD, 1973.

recommendations of UNCTAD, the OECD, and the Rockefeller, Peterson, and Pearson reports.

U.S. MULTILATERAL ASSISTANCE

The flow of U.S. resources to multilateral organizations consists of: (1) contributions to international organizations such as the United Nations and its specialized agencies, and (2) contributions or capital subscriptions to multilateral financial institutions such as the World Bank Group and regional banks.

Table 6 presents U.S. official and private contributions to multilateral organizations. These have risen from $200 million in 1961 to $1.026 billion in 1972. The percentage of multilateral contributions out of total flows has risen from 4.4 percent in 1961 to 14.0 percent in 1972. Contributions to UN agencies are in the form of grants that are financed out of the AID budget except for donations under Public Law 480 and certain contributions to specific UN programs. These grants are extended to support technical and humanitarian assistance programs which are implemented by these organizations. Various UN agencies are the recipients of this assistance, including the United Nations Children's Fund (UNICEF), WHO, the United Nations Relief and Works Agency for Palestine Refugees (UNRWA), the FAO World Food Program, and the United Nations Fund for Population Activities (UNFPA). Of these agencies, the main recipients are UNDP, UNFPA, UNRWA, and UNICEF. The U.S. contribution to UNDP has been limited by a statute to forty percent of all voluntary contributions and assessed local costs of the program in any one year. In recent years, the U.S. share tended to be below the statutory maximum owing to increases in the voluntary contributions of other donors. In 1971, total U.S. contributions to UNDP totaled $107 million. Starting with an initial contribution of $500,000 in 1968, the U.S. pledge to UNFPA rose to $14.5 million in 1971. The U.S. pledge was on a 50/50 matching basis for 1970 and 1971; that is to say, the United States agreed to match contributions made by all other donors. In subsequent years, the U.S. percentage share declined to forty-eight percent in 1972 and to forty-five percent in 1973. For UNRWA, the statutory limit to U.S. contributions was set at seventy percent of the total UNRWA budget; but in 1971 disbursements of $38 million represented only fifty-five percent of total contributions by all countries. Total U.S. contributions to UNICEF totaled $21 million in 1971 and represented approximately one-third of the official contributions to the Fund. Other UN programs assisted by the United States include the FAO World Food Program where the share of the United States is set at forty percent of the total commodity contributions by all countries and the programs of the UN High Commission for Refugees. Finally, grant assistance to non-UN programs includes contributions to the Organization of American States, the Pan-American Health Organization, and various other bodies.

U.S. contributions to international financial institutions are the responsibility of the Treasury Department. The most important contributions have been given to the following institutions: the World Bank Group, IDB, and the ADB. As of June 30, 1970, IBRD had total subscriptions amounting to $23.2 billion with $2.3 billion actually paid in and the remainder callable when and if needed to back the bonded obligations of the Bank (IBRD, 1972: 51). The United States has contributed twenty-seven percent ($6.26 billion) of the total subscriptions and thirty-six percent ($8.28 million) of the paid-in capital. In December 1970, the International Financial Institutions Bill (HR 18306) passed the Congress. This bill increased U.S. subscriptions by $246.1 million which is part of a $3 billion additional capitalization of the Bank. Thus, the United States will have contributed about twenty-five percent of the total Bank subscriptions and paid-in capital. The charter of IBRD stipulates: "The Bank share imposes no conditions that the proceeds of a loan shall be spent in the territories of any particular member or members" (IBRD, Article III, Section 5a). This means that despite the Bank's ability to borrow dollars in the U.S. marketplace (using their callable capital as a guarantee for the bonds), there is no way to assure that any part of the Bank's funds is used to purchase commodities in the United States. Thus, all U.S. contributions to IBRD are essentially untied.

The IDA has total subscriptions of $1.01 billion and supplementary resources which are additional monies pledged by developed countries of $1.95 billion or a grand total of $2.96 billion. The United States contributed $1.11 billion of this total divided into subscriptions of $321 million and supplementary resources of $792 million (World Bank/IDA, 1971). Supplementary resource contributions by developed countries may have conditions placed upon their use by the donor nation, but subscriptions may not according to Article V (f) of the Articles of Agreement. In any event, the United States contributes 37.5 percent of IDA's total funds; yet IDA's procurement in the United States amounted to $269 million or 15.9 percent of total IDA credit disbursements as of December 31, 1969. Japan, on the other hand, supplies 5.1 percent of IDA's funds and received 9 percent of the IDA's generated exports. Similar figures for the United Kingdom were 14.1 and 19.2 percent, respectively. For Germany, they were 8.6 and 12.6 percent.

The IDB has currently used windows in which subscriptions of participating governments are made. Two such windows exist; one handles ordinary capital—the Social Progress Trust Fund (SPTF)—and the other handles funds for special operations—the Fund for Special Operations (FSO). In 1961, the SPTF was set up by the United States to be administered by the Bank for the U.S. government. The United States provided the initial capital, which amounted to $394 million. In 1964, the contribution was raised by $134 million. In 1971, the IDB had a total subscribed ordinary capital of $2.27 billion, with the U.S. share amounting to $968 million. Of the total subscribed ordinary capital, $1.89 billion was callable and $388.5 million actually paid in. The U.S. share of callable capital was $817.6 million and of paid-in capital $150 million. The IDB charter forbids tying procurement to any particular member country; the procurement rules allow for the purchase of products in non-IDB countries to the extent of Bank financing in the country's market. If Japan, for example, allows a Bank security issue to be floated in its home market, it may supply goods paid for by IDB money.

The second window of IDB is FSO. This fund is used for soft, low-interest loans and has a total authorized capital of $2.32 billion, with the U.S. share being $1.8 billion, representing 77.6 percent of the FSO capital resources. Actual total contributions received thus far amount to $329.3 million, with the U.S. share equaling $294 million or 89.3 percent. All procurement by regulations must be in IDB member countries excluding the country where the project is taking place (IDB, 1971).

The ADB is a relatively new international institution having its first year of operation in 1967. The total bank subscription amounts to $978 million, with a U.S. share of $200 million or 20.5 percent. The total paid-in capital of the bank equals $489 million with the U.S. contribution to $100 million or 20.5 percent. This makes the

United States the largest contributor to the Bank, with Japan a close second. In the coming years, the institution will undoubtedly become larger as the U.S. role in Asia changes from a military to an economic one. The ADB possesses a Technical Assistance Special Fund to which the United States contributes $1.25 million or 19 percent of the Fund's resources. The United States has not, as of this time, contributed to other special funds of the ADB.

The United States has also extended assistance to regional development banks of which it is not a member. The Central American Bank for Economic Integration, for example, has received a grant of $2 million and concessional loans amounting to $142.5 million. By and large, U.S. contributions to multilateral organizations are untied. The largest proportion of these contributions are grants given to these organizations to cover daily operation costs of the organizations and distributed to recipients with no procurements tied to any particular country or set of countries. As Table 6 indicates, over the 1961-1972 period there was a marked increase in the proportion of U.S. aid that

TABLE 6

U.S. Allocations to Multilateral Agencies
1961-1972
(in millions of U.S. dollars)

Year	Official 1	Private 2	Total 3	Total U.S. Aid (Official & Private) 4	Percentage of U.S. Aid Channeled Through Multilateral Agencies 3:4
1961	202	−2	200	4,549	4.4
1962	138	160	298	4,354	6.8
1963	142	5	147	4,579	3.2
1964	204	131	335	4,771	7.0
1965	164	152	316	5,524	5.7
1966	112	1	113	5,020	2.3
1967	310	256	566	5,645	10.0
1968	251	255	506	5,809	8.7
1969	330	39	369	4,825	7.7
1970	393	372	765	6,254	12.2
1971	431	322	753	7,045	10.7
1972	625	401	1,026	7,354	14.0

Source: OECD, 1973.

was channeled through international organizations, and this upward trend is likely to continue.

THE REACTION OF U.S. LABOR AND INDUSTRY TO PRESIDENT NIXON'S PROPOSALS TO UNTIE AID

The proposals and initial policy implementations to untie the U.S. foreign assistance program and channel U.S. aid through world institutions has received great opposition from the AFL-CIO and from certain domestic industrial sectors. In this section, the nature of this opposition will be examined. The opposition was particularly pronounced in the AFL-CIO Maritime Trades Department, [11] in the maritime industry, and in the fertilizer industry.

THE POSITION OF LABOR

American labor has been at the forefront in its criticism of the proposal to channel U.S. aid dollars through multilateral organizations. A research memorandum of the Maritime Trades Department of the AFL-CIO on the subject summarizes the union's position:

> When we look at jobs, when we look at specific industries, when we look at our balance of payments, when we look at our balance of trade—in other words, when we look at the welfare of the United States—we are left with one conclusion. There should be no "untying" of United States aid, now, or in the immediate future [Transportation Institute, 1971: 6-7].

An empirical study undertaken by the Washington-based Transportation Institute, the research arm of the Maritime Trades Department, indicates that over 169,700 jobs would be lost per year if the United States totally unties its foreign assistance programs (Transportation Institute, 1971). Table 7 breaks down the institute's estimates by SITC category. The table is self-explanatory and there is no need to discuss it here. What is important, however, is to discuss the assumptions and methodology used to derive those estimates. First, the study assumes that U.S. aid-generated exports would go to zero under untied conditions. Second, it assumes that, in the future, the 1960-1969 market basket of commodities would be purchased in the United States by recipient countries if aid were untied. The first assumption is clearly unrealistic, as it is inconceivable that the United States would not provide some quantity of aid-generated commodities to aid-receiving countries under a totally untied system. [12] It is very likely that, in the late seventies and eighties, food produce would become a major source of imports of the developing countries. Clearly, the United States, one of the surplus countries in this area, would become an important exporter of these goods. The second assumption of the Transportation Institute study is also unrealistic, since it is very likely that the composition of U.S. aid-generated exports will be different in the future from what it was in the sixties. Table 2 indicates that in the sixties machinery, metal products, and chemicals were the main AID-generated exports to developing countries. This export mix will undoubtedly change in favor of food and fertilizer exports, the demand for which will rise in view of the forecast food shortages over the next decade and a half.

The methodology used by the Transportation Institute to calculate job-loss estimates consisted of calculating output per person for major industrial groups and using these productivity indices to extrapolate job losses. The productivity estimates which were derived from 1960-1969 data ignore any technological change which may affect the value of output per person differently across industries. Thus, job losses may be overstated in some sectors and understated in others. Moreover, the job-loss estimates of 169,700 represent the upper limit since they are based on zero aid-generated U.S. exports under untied conditions. A more precise set of estimates would have been based on the predicted level of U.S. exports which would be generated with untied aid. Estimates of such expected values of exports are made in the fourth section of this chapter.

THE MARITIME AND FERTILIZER INDUSTRIES

American industry, particularly the maritime and fertilizer industries, has also opposed the untying of aid. Great disapproval of channeling U.S. foreign assistance through multilateral institutions was voiced by spokespeople of the U.S. maritime industry. The American maritime industry is perhaps the most subsidized industry in the United States. [13] Decades ago, it became clear that without assistance from the federal government the industry would go bankrupt. The subsidy program is administered by two important acts— the Merchant Marine Acts of 1936 and of 1970. Both Acts provided

TABLE 7

Estimated U.S. Job Loss Per Year with United Aid
(by major industry groups)

Major Industry Group (SITC Category)	Direct Job Loss in Each Industry per Year	Total Job Loss—Direct and Indirect in Each Industry per Year
Machinery (excluding electrical) (35)	16,000	48,000
Primary Metal—Fab. & Metal Products (33-34)	13,000	29,000
Chemicals (28)	6,300	19,000
Transportation Equip. (37)	6,400	21,000
Petroleum Refining (29)	1,400	4,300
Electrical Machinery (36)	4,200	13,000
Food Products (20)	3,100	9,300
Rubber Products (30)	1,600	5,500
Textile Mill Products (22)	2,800	8,400
Paper (26)	1,800	5,500
Stone, Clay, Glass (32)	650	2,000
Misc. Manufactures (39)	1,100	3,400
Prof. Scientific (38)	430	1,300
Total	58,780	169,700

Source: Transportation Institute, 1971.

for the use of subsidies to make the industry competitive in the international economy. These subsidies may be direct—such as the operation and construction subsidies—or indirect—such as the Cargo Preference Regulations.[14] The issue of untied aid became important to the industry in the context of indirect subsidies.

The part of the Cargo Preference Regulations relevant to untied aid is contained in the following excerpts from Public Law 664:

Whenever the United States shall procure, contract for or otherwise obtain for its own account, or shall furnish to or for the account of any foreign nation without provisions for reimbursement, any equipment, materials, or commodities, within or without the United States, or shall advance funds or credits or guarantee the convertibility of foreign currencies in connection with the furnishing of such equipment, materials, or commodities, the appropriate agency or agencies shall take such steps as may be necessary and practicable to assure that at least 50 per centum of the gross tonnage of such equipment, materials or commodities (computed separately for dry bulk carriers, dry cargo liners, and tankers), which may be transported on privately owned United States-flag commercial vessels, to the extent such vessels are available at fair and reasonable rates for United States-flag commercial vessels, in such manner as will insure a fair and reasonable participation of United States-flag commercial vessels in such cargoes by geographic areas [U.S. Congress, 1970].

The Cargo Preference Regulations state that no less than fifty percent of the U.S. government-generated cargo be transported on U.S. bottoms. The impact of these regulations on a system that channels U.S. aid through multilateral organizations becomes self-evident when aid is untied. There is no guarantee that a recipient country would expend aid funds in the United States, and thus there is no guarantee that cargo would become available to the merchant marine. The Labor-Management Maritime Committee,[15] a maritime lobby, argues that any attempt to untie aid is a violation of U.S. legislations, since it prevents the functioning of the Cargo Preference Regulations. At the present time, a good deal of the domestic fleet's cargo is generated by the foreign assistance program, especially Public Law 480. At least fifty percent of the cargo movements generated under this law is transported by U.S. flag vessels. Moreover, the act specifies that this minimum is to be maintained for dry bulk carriers, dry cargo liners, and tankers separately.[16] The vast majority of cargo generated under Public Law 480 is from the Agriculture Department. Under this agency's regulations, the procedure works as follows. In the first instance, an agreement is reached with a foreign government to purchase (with U.S. AID dollars) a certain amount of agricultural produce. Once the price for the commodity is established, it is then left to the purchasing party to make arrangements for the transportation, provided fifty percent of the commodity is carried on U.S. vessels. The purchaser then invites bids from both U.S. and foreign carriers. After the bids are received, a decision is made, subject to the approval of the Agriculture Department. Since U.S. shipping rates are fifteen to thirty percent above world rates, the purchaser pays the foreign cost and the difference between the U.S. and the foreign rates is made up by the Department of Agriculture. Under a system of untied aid, aid dollars do not necessarily have to be spent in the donor country, and this neutralizes the protection the U.S. maritime industry enjoys under the Cargo Preference Rules.

The U.S. fertilizer industry, similarly to the maritime industry, has been at the forefront in its criticism of untied aid. In 1973, the United States was the world's largest producer of fertilizer with a total output of over $4 billion. During this same period, U.S. fertilizer exports amounted to $468 million or 11.7 percent of domestic output. The fertilizer industry has undergone remarkable changes since the late sixties. World fertilizer prices bottomed out in 1969 and 1970 at abnormally low levels. Prices began to recover, however, in the early seventies, reaching record high levels in 1973 and early 1974. The U.S. price of urea and phosphates tripled in a two-year period. In the same two-year period, world fertilizer prices doubled; thus, the gap between U.S. domestic prices and foreign prices has widened (TVA, 1974). The current world fertilizer situation is characterized by extreme tightness with positive excess demand for nitrogen and phosphates. With a large part of the productive capacity in North America, the United States has been a major source of fertilizer exported to developing countries. In 1964, AID began large-scale financing of U.S. fertilizer exports, and thus the proposals by President Nixon to untie aid have brought substantial opposition by the fertilizer industry.

Table 8 presents U.S. exports of selected fertilizer products and their relative proportions financed by AID. In 1972, 14.42 percent of total U.S. fertilizer exports was financed by AID. In 1973, this percentage rose to 19.90 percent. In 1972, AID funds provided 100 percent of the exports of mixed fertilizer and 69 percent of the exports of urea. In 1973, these percentages rose to 100 percent for both products. The untying proposals which have thus far been implemented have had very little effect on the fertilizer industry. As was pointed out in the previous sections, present untying regulations do not permit AID dollars to procure commodities in the industrialized or Socialist countries where most of the world's fertilizer output is produced. Thus, for all practical purposes, all AID fertilizer aid remains tied to procurement in the United States. This situation is likely to remain unchanged until aid becomes totally untied or the developing countries become net exporters of fertilizer. This is becoming increasingly possible, however, as large deposits of natural gas and phosphates, both inputs required for the production of some fertilizers, have been discovered in certain developing countries.

To rally support against the untying forces, the Maritime Trades Department of the AFL-CIO organized a conference in December

TABLE 8

Total Fertilizer Exports and Proportions Financed by Aid
(in millions of U.S. dollars)

Fertilizer	1972		1973	
	Total Exports	AID Financed	Total Exports	AID Financed
Urea	21.40	14.80	32.00	32.00
Ammonium Sulphate	9.80	0.39	13.40	0.44
Ammonium Phosphate	9.60	0.02	157.40	0.00
Potassium Chloride	28.10	0.24	40.70	0.43
Mixed Fertilizer	9.20	9.20	11.20	11.20
Concentrated Superphosphates	33.10	3.12	52.40	6.19
Others	227.10	21.10	161.10	42.92
Total	338.90	48.87	468.20	93.18

Source: U.S. Department of Agriculture, 1974.

1970 which was attended by representatives of various industries and labor unions. The conference focused on the economic impact of the untying legislations on the domestic economy. Spokespeople of the U.S. maritime and fertilizer industries were among the principal critics of the untying proposals that were put forth by Dr. John Hannah, then with AID. The Maritime Trades Department also tried to exert pressure on the House Merchant Marine and Fisheries Committee to introduce legislation to prevent further untying. By and large, these efforts have been unsuccessful and have slowed down as the untying momentum diminished. While the opposition to untying has been concentrated in the aforementioned industries, it has been expounded by other sectors of the economy, as well as by certain government agencies. In general, this opposition has tended to increase in periods of economic difficulty and to diminish in periods of economic prosperity.

A STOCHASTIC MODEL TO EXAMINE THE IMPACT OF UNTIED AID ON EXPORTS

In this section, some aggregated estimates to determine the number of donor countries that would benefit from a multilateral system of foreign assistance will be generated. The following DAC countries are considered in the analysis: the United States, Japan, France, West Germany, Great Britain, Canada, the Netherlands, Italy, Australia, Belgium, Sweden, Switzerland, Portugal, Denmark, Austria, and Norway. A simple stochastic model is used to calculate the expected value of aid-generated exports for each of these countries. Under a system of aid tied to domestic procurement in which 100 percent of the funds are spent by the recipient country in the donor country, the latter's exports include commodities whose demand was generated by the foreign assistance program. Under a totally untied system, the level of aid-generated exports for a particular donor country depends on the probability that a dollar of export demand would go to that country. This probability value could be estimated and used to calculate value of the expected aid-generated export demand for that donor country's goods. This value could then be compared to aid-generated exports under a system of tied aid. The donor country would benefit if the expected value of export demand under a system of untied aid is greater than the value of export demand under a system of tied aid.

THE STRUCTURE OF THE MODEL

The aforementioned can be expressed symbolically as follows. Let N be the number of countries in the world, and n be the number of aid-giving countries, where $N > n$. Then, $N - n$ represents the number of aid-receiving countries.[17]

Let Y_j be a vector of aid dollars that the aid-receiving countries obtain from the aid-giving countries $(j = 1, \ldots, n)$. T represents the total aid bill per time period given to the recipient countries by the donor countries; or

$$\sum_{j=1}^{n} Y_j = T$$

Under a bilateral system where aid is 100 percent tied to domestic procurement for all donor countries, aid-generated exports of the jth country are equal to y_j, that is, the total aid package of the jth country. Under a system of totally untied procurement for all donor countries, the probability that the jth country will receive one dollar of aid-generated exports is equal to:

$$\frac{1}{n}$$

This probability value assumes that only aid-giving countries can provide the goods and services demanded by the aid-receiving countries; moreover, it assumes that all donor countries produce the same commodities which have identical prices, and that the donor countries cannot influence the magnitude of the probability. Alternatively, this probability value assumes that the process is totally random, in which free trade and zero transportation costs are present. Under this system, the expected value of aid-generated exports for the jth aid-giving country is given as follows:[18]

$$\left[\frac{1}{n}\right]\left[\sum_{j=1}^{n} Y_j\right]$$

The jth donor will prefer a system of multilateral aid with an untied procurement system if

$$Y_j < \left[\frac{1}{n}\right]\left[\sum_{j=1}^{n} Y_j\right]$$

If the inequality sign is reversed, then the country will prefer a bilateral system with tied aid. Finally, if both sides of equation are equal, the jth aid-giving country will be indifferent to either system.

The aforementioned assumption which determines the probability value $\frac{1}{n}$ is very crucial to the foregoing discussion and must be examined in greater detail. It contains three parts. The first assumes that only donor countries produce commodities demanded by recipient countries. It would be conceivable, however, for a recipient country under a system of untied aid to want to purchase commodities from another recipient country. In this instance the probability value that the jth donor country receives one dollar of aid-generated exports would not equal $\frac{1}{n}$ but some smaller number. The second part of the assumption states that all donor countries produce similar goods, equally priced. Once again, it is very possible that a recipient country wishes to use aid funds to purchase large quantities of some commodity—wheat, for example—which may only be available in the United States, Canada, or Australia. In this instance, the probability that the United States, Canada, or Australia receives a dollar's worth of export demand for wheat rises substantially, but the probability value for the other donor countries goes to zero. The third part of the assumption concerns the size of the donor country which undoubtedly influences the value of the probability. Under a system of untied aid, the United States would, for example, be more likely than Austria to sell a hydroelectric plant to Togo even if the latter were equally efficient in the production of such plants as the former. This likelihood would be a function of the mere size of the United States, which enables it to exert pressure on Togo to purchase the American plant. Furthermore, the United States would possess more sophisticated public relations procedures, advertising personnel, overseas trading bureaus, and so forth, which would raise the probability of the American sale.

The most difficult aspects of the analysis lie in determining the magnitude of the probability value. If the process is totally random and if all foreign assistance funds can only go to the sixteen DAC countries, then the probability that one dollar of aid-generated exports goes to any one donor county is 1/16. This probability value, however, has to be modified to account for the realities of the international economy. The modification procedure employed in this paper assumes that certain countries have a comparative advantage in certain areas of production. Thus, in agricultural production, the United States, Australia, and Canada are more efficient than is Austria. Technical assistance, on the other hand, can probably be provided equally well by the four aforementioned countries. Furthermore, the probability estimate for each country must be based on the premise that aid dollars can be used to procure commodities in countries other than the sixteen DAC members, such as, for example, some developing countries.

EMPIRICAL RESULTS

The probability value that any particular country gets one dollar of aid-generated exports will be modified as follows. First, total aid-generated exports will be divided into eighteen aggregate commodity categories. Second, the proportion of each category out of total aid-generated exports will be calculated for the 1971 period. Third, a list of countries that could have provided each group of commodities will be devised; and, fourth, probabilities for each category will be calculated. There are eighteen commodity groups that will be considered in the following analysis. Table 9 lists the commodity groups as well as the percentage, for each commodity, purchased by the developing countries in 1971 with DAC funds. Thus, for example, iron and steel products accounted for twelve percent of total purchases by recipient countries from the DAC countries with DAC funds. Throughout the analysis, the following two assumptions are made. First, the eighteen commodity groups are assumed distinct and independent; that is to say, a given quantity of aid for the purchase of motor vehicles does not generate aid in the form of spare parts. This differentiation may be somewhat unrealistic since aid to purchase the former commodity may eventually generate demand for the latter commodity. It is reasonable to assume, however, that some cancelling out between various sectors will occur and it will tend to reduce any double counting. Second, DAC aid dollars are assumed not to flow to the Socialist countries and generate exports to Third World countries.

Table 10 presents the list of countries that could provide the developing countries with the commodities presented in Table 9. This list was derived by looking at the composition of exports for each country by commodity and their proportion to total world exports of each commodity. In 1971 the DAC countries contributed approximately ninety-five percent of the total resources supplied from abroad to developing countries. This includes resources channeled through international organizations and through bilateral programs. A total of $18 billion was transferred in 1971 from the DAC countries to the developing countries in the form of official and private aid. Given the breakdown in the aforementioned percentages by commodity group, the total quantity of each commodity purchased by the developing countries with DAC aid can be calculated. These quantities are presented in Table 9. Thus, in 1971, aid-receiving countries purchased $2.16 billion of iron and steel products from the DAC countries with DAC dollars.

The probability that a dollar's worth of aid goes to any one country can now be calculated for each commodity group. Table 10 indicates that iron and steel products could be purchased by aid-receiving countries in any one of six countries. In this instance, the probability that a dollar of iron and steel products is purchased from the United States by the developing countries is one-sixth. For New Zealand, on the other hand, which does not produce iron and steel, the probability equals zero. In this same manner, the probabilities for various commodity groups are estimated. They are presented in the

TABLE 9

Developing Countries' Purchases with DAC Funds for 1971
(by commodity groups)

Commodity	Percent	Quantity (in billions of U.S. dollars)
Iron & Steel Products	12.0	2.16
Chemicals (except medicinal)	6.1	1.10
Plastics & Related Products	2.1	0.38
Medicinal & Pharmaceutical	1.5	0.27
Pulp & Paper	2.7	0.49
Fertilizer	7.1	1.28
Petroleum Products	2.7	0.49
Agricultural Products	6.8	1.22
Motor Vehicles, Engines & Parts	8.5	1.53
Miscellaneous Industrial Machinery	8.5	1.53
Electrical Machinery & Appliances	6.1	1.10
Engines & Turbines	2.9	0.52
Construction & Mining Equipment	4.5	0.81
Tractors & Agricultural Equipment	2.4	0.43
Textile Machinery	1.6	0.29
Rubber Products	1.0	0.18
Scientific Equipment	0.9	0.16
Miscellaneous	22.6	4.06
Total	100.0	18.00

Source: OECD, 1972.

last column of Table 10. Given these probability values, the expected value of a donor country's aid-generated exports under a system of tied aid can be calculated. This value can then be compared to aid-generated exports under a system of tied aid to determine whether the donor country would tend to benefit from a system of multilateral untied aid.

Table 11 indicates that all the DAC countries except the United States would have benefited if aid had been untied in 1971. Under the bilateral tied system, $2.8 billion of U.S. exports were generated by U.S. aid in that year. If aid had been untied, however, only $1.9 billion would have been generated. This loss in U.S. exports appears

TABLE 10

List of Countries that Could Provide Selected Aid-Generated Export Commodities to Developing Countries

Commodity Group	US	J	FR	G	UK	I	B	SW	NO	C	NZ	AUS	P	ST	D	AUT	N	IS	AR	FN	SA	BR	YU	T	Probability
Iron & Steel Products	x	x	x	x				x		x															1/6
Chemicals (export medicinal)	x	x	x	x	x	x	x		x	x								x							1/10
Plastics & Related Products	x	x	x	x	x	x			x	x															1/8
Medicinal & Pharmaceutical	x	x	x	x	x	x	x	x	x					x											1/10
Pulp & Paper	x							x	x	x							x			x		x			1/7
Fertilizer	x	x	x	x	x				x	x							x		x			x			1/10
Petroleum Products	x								x	x		x					x		x	x					1/7
Agricultural Products	x		x							x	x	x							x						1/6
Motor Vehicles, Engines & Parts	x	x	x	x	x	x	x	x		x															1/9
Miscellaneous Industrial Machinery	x	x	x	x	x	x	x	x	x	x		x				x									1/12
Electrical Machinery & Appliances	x	x	x	x	x	x	x	x	x	x				x										x	1/12
Engines & Turbines	x	x	x	x	x	x	x		x																1/8
Construction & Mining Equipment	x	x	x	x	x					x															1/6
Tractors & Agricultural Equipment	x	x	x	x	x	x				x															1/7
Textile Machinery				x													x								1/2
Rubber Products	x	x	x	x	x	x			x									x							1/8
Scientific Equipment	x	x	x	x	x	x	x	x	x	x		x					x	x			x	x	x		1/16
Miscellaneous	x	x	x	x	x	x	x	x	x	x	x	x	x	x	x	x	x	x	x	x	x	x	x	x	1/24

This table was prepared by looking at each country's commodity group exports as a proportion of total world exports of the same commodity group. If this proportion represented more than 5 percent in 1971 for any one commodity, then the country was assumed capable of providing the developing countries with that commodity.

The following abbreviations for country names have been employed: United States (US), Japan (J), France (FR), W. Germany (G), United Kingdom (UK), Italy (I), Belgium (B), Sweden (SW), Norway (NO), Canada (C), New Zealand (NZ), Australia (AUS), Portugal (P), Switzerland (ST), Denmark (D), Austria (AUT), Netherlands (N), Israel (IS), Argentina (AR), Finland (FN), South Africa (SA), Brazil (BR), Yugoslavia (YU), and Taiwan (T).

to have been transformed into increases in the exports of the other fifteen DAC countries and into exports of non-DAC members if DAC aid dollars were used to procure commodities in those countries. In 1971, the DAC countries contributed $18 billion to the developing countries; of this total, only $14.8 billion was used to procure commodities in the DAC countries. The rest was used by the developing countries to procure commodities outside the DAC. The second country presented in Table 11 is Japan. The calculations showed that it would have benefited if aid had been totally untied in 1971, since its expected exports equalled $1.6 billion, while the actual value of its aid-generated exports equalled $434 million. Similarly, the other DAC countries would have exported larger quantities of goods and services under untied conditions as the table indicates.

This section has attempted to determine which countries, that are members of the OECD's DAC, would benefit from a totally untied system of administering aid. In this context, a country benefits when it experiences an increase in the value of its aid-generated exports. Expected values of aid-generated exports under an untied system were calculated for each DAC country and compared to actual aid-generated exports. A country was said to benefit from a system of untied aid if its value of aid-generated exports was smaller under a system of tied aid than under untied conditions. It was shown that fifteen of the sixteen DAC countries would have benefited from a system of untied aid. The United States, however, would have exported less aid-generated commodities under untied conditions. These calculations applied to 1971; nevertheless, under certain assumptions, inferences about the short-range future impact of tied versus untied aid can be made for the DAC countries. The afore-mentioned conclusion will hold in the future if: (1) the proportion of each commodity group purchased with aid dollars by developing countries remains constant, and (2) the probability value that any one country exports a dollar of a particular commodity does not change. The first condition may hold in the short run, but will undoubtedly change in the long run as the composition of import demand by developing countries changes. It is expected, for example, that developing countries will become net importers of agricultural produce in the 1980s. This will negate the first assumption. The second, on the other hand, is somewhat more realistic since the

TABLE 11

Actual Versus Expected Values of Aid-Generated Exports, 1971
(by DAC countries in millions of U.S. dollars)

Country	Expected Values[a]	Actual Values[b]
United States	1,868	2,825
Japan	1,585	434
France	1,728	914
Germany, West	1,440	624
United Kingdom	1,075	478
Canada	1,868	332
Netherlands	342	184
Italy	1,099	155
Australia	984	172
Belgium	398	124
Sweden	1,090	135
Switzerland	415	84
Portugal	239	24
Denmark	169	63
Austria	307	11
Norway	239	36
Total	14,846	6,665

a. Values for this column were obtained as follows:

$$\sum_{i=1}^{18} P_i \, x_i \quad \text{where}$$

i is the commodity category, p is the probability that one dollar of aid-generated exports of the ith commodity group goes to the jth donor country, and x is the quantity of aid available to the recipient countries to purchase commodities of the ith group.

b. OECD, 1972.

probability values depend on the comparative advantage that each country holds in the production of various commodity categories. This advantage depends on relative factor endowments which are unlikely to change in the short run.

PROSPECTS FOR THE FUTURE

This chapter has presented some of the key issues facing the transfer of resources between developed and developing countries. Two methods were described as possible ways to transfer resources—via bilateral exchanges, which usually imply tied aid and/or via multilateral exchanges which usually imply untied aid. The chapter dealt particularly with the U.S. position on these issues and with the manner in which the aid-giving systems evolved from one of untied to tied aid and then back again to untied aid. Despite the recommendations of the OECD, the United Nations, and various private and government-sponsored studies, the major donor countries have been reluctant to untie their foreign assistance programs. The United States has been a major exception to this when it implemented legislation aimed at channelling a larger proportion of U.S. foreign assistance through multilateral agencies. The statistical results presented in this chapter indicate, however, that every donor country except the United States would tend to gain from an untied aid system. Yet important donor countries have been unwilling to untie. Certain countries such as France and to a lesser degree the United Kingdom have used their foreign assistance programs to maintain a political influence over their former colonies. There is no way to quantify such political advantages accruing to the donor countries but they are perceived to be important by the policy makers in the donor countries. Domestic opposition to untying measures have been less prevalent with foreign donors than with the United States. The political advantages of tied aid tend to accrue to the central governments of donor countries, but in foreign countries labor and industry have tended to support untied aid as a way to enhance export earnings and domestic employment opportunities.

It appears that the opposition of U.S. labor and of certain domestic industries to untying is well founded. The model developed showed that, under a totally untied system, adopted by all donor countries, the United States would tend to lose about $1 billion in export earnings yearly. Since the devaluation of the dollar, however, in February 1973, and its subsequent weakening in foreign exchange markets, U.S. commodities have become more competitive in world markets and the $1 billion figure is probably inflated given existing relative cost structures. Thus, some of the opposition to untying may be eroding. However, for multilateralism and untied aid to become fully implemented, international institutions will have to become immune to the political pressures exerted upon them by member states. Furthermore, these institutions will have to be reorganized. They have already undergone extensive change to increase their efficiency in transferring resources. Nevertheless, inadequacies persist. These raise a variety of policy problems for the donor countries. The international agencies continue to possess different membership, varied organizational structures, different means of financing, separate secretariats, and often operate in different spheres. Further consolidation will have to take place before donor countries will adhere to the idea of untied aid.

NOTES

1. AID, which is the most important of the three organizations, was created in 1961. Its predecessor agencies were the Economic Cooperation Administration (ECA) from 1948 to 1952, the Mutual Security Agency (MSA) from 1951 to 1953, the Foreign Operations Administration (FOA) from 1953 to 1955, the International Cooperation Administration (ICA) from 1955 to 1961, and concurrently the Development Loan Fund (DLF) from 1957 to 1961.

2. The bank was created in 1934 to assist in financing U.S. exports to both developed and developing countries.

3. In the hope of giving more concentrated attention to development problems, UNCTAD was created with headquarters in Geneva. It held its first conference in Geneva in 1964, its second in New Delhi in early 1968, and its third in 1972 in Santiago, Chile.

4. The U.S. government defines lower-income countries as countries whose per capita GNP is below $1,000 per annum.

5. See AID Manual Order Amendments C to Aid Regulation 1 (1971 edition, Title 22, Washington, D.C., 1971).

6. From December 1972 to December 1974, the U.S. dollar has depreciated by ·thirteen percent in terms of the Special Drawing Right (SDR). From December 1974 until the end of February 1975, a further depreciation of three percent was registered. Since the value of the SDR is determined by a weighted average of a basket of sixteen currencies, the depreciation of the dollar in terms of the stronger currencies of the basket is larger. Thus, for example, in the two years from December 1972 to December 1974, the U.S. dollar lost twenty-five percent of its value in terms of the deutschemark and fourteen percent in terms of the French franc.

7. The seven countries were: Australia, Belgium, France, the Netherlands, Portugal, Switzerland, and the United Kingdom. In 1974, following the Putsch, Portugal withdrew from the DAC.

8. A fourth group comprises private voluntary and relief organizations such as the Ford and Rockefeller Foundations, CARE, and so forth. In 1968, private U.S. organizations contributed $491 million to developing countries. While a certain proportion of these funds was expended through multilateral organizations, these private groups, however, are not world institutions.

9. A sister organization of the World Bank, the IMF, which promotes and monitors international monetary cooperation, is not discussed here. It does not provide short-run assistance in the normal developmental sense but does permit countries to draw or purchase foreign exchange from the Fund, with their domestic currencies for balance of payment purposes. The main technique used by the IMF is the stand-by arrangement under which the Fund gives advance assurance that a stated amount of resources will be available in case of need to support a program of action presented by the country.

10. In 1972, the following countries were classified by the United Nations as least developed: Botswana, Burundi, Chad, Dahomey, Ethiopia, Guinea, Lesotho, Malawi, Mali, Niger, Rwanda, Somalia, Sudan, Uganda, Tanzania, Upper Volta, Afghanistan, Bhutan, Laos, Maldives, Nepal, Sikkim, West Samoa, Yemen, and Haiti.

11. Despite its name, the Maritime Trades Department of the AFL-CIO has little to do with the maritime industry. It is composed of some forty-four unions and includes such diverse organizations as the United Telegraph Workers and the American Guild of Variety Artists.

12. The next section of the chapter presents estimates of expected values of aid-generated exports for a number of countries under untied conditions.

13. Until very recently, U.S. agriculture held the first rank in subsidy receipts.

14. The Cargo Preference Law was passed by Congress in August 1954 as an amendment to the 1936 Merchant Marine Act. See U.S. Congress (1970).

15. The Labor-Management Maritime Committee is a Washington-based organization that represents members of the National Maritime Union and subsidized operators of the maritime industry.

16. In actuality, this breakdown requirement is not enforced. In 1970, the respective percentage breakdowns were 49.2, 44.7, and 50.5, with a weighted average across the three categories of 50.5. See the 1970 Report of the Executive Board of the AFL-CIO Maritime Trades Department, page 36.

17. This assumes that every country is either aid-giving or aid-receiving.

18. This implicitly assumes that the jth country is capable of supplying that volume of exports. It may be that the jth country's economy is too small to provide

$$\frac{1}{n} \sum_{j=1}^{n} Y_j$$

dollars' worth of exports which would make the expected value equation inappropriate for that country. Note that the aforementioned expression is equal for all donor countries.

REFERENCES

IBRD (1972) World Bank Operations. Baltimore: Johns Hopkins University Press.
IBRD: Articles of Agreement, Article III, Section 5(a).

IDB (1971) Social Progress Trust Fund, 11 Annual Report. Washington, D.C.

JACKSON, R. (1969) A Study of the Capacity of the United Nations Development System. Geneva.

——— (1959) "An international development authority." Foreign Affairs 37.

MIKESELL, R. F. (1969) The Economics of Foreign Aid. Chicago: Aldine.

OECD (1971) "Development assistance: efforts and policies of the members of the development assistance committee." Paris.

PEARSON, L. B. (1969) Partners in Development: Report of the Commission on International Development. New York: Praeger.

PETERSON, R. (1970) Report to the President from the Task Force on International Development. Washington, D.C.

ROCKEFELLER, N. A. (1969) The Rockefeller Report on the Americas. Chicago: Quandrangle.

Transportation Institute (1971) The Economic Impact of Untying Aid. Washington, D.C.

TVA (1974) World Fertilizer Market Review and Outlook. Muscle Shoals, Alabama.

United Nations Development Program (1974) Report of the Administrator for 1973. New York.

U.S. Congress (1970) House Committee Print: The Merchant Marine Act of 1936 (as amended), 49 stat. 1985, Section 901b, U.S. Market Vessels, Cargo Preference, 49 stat. 2015. Washington, D.C.

World Bank/IDA Annual Reports (1971).

Chapter 7

ACCESS TO SUPPLIES: A NEW CONCEPT
IN U.S. COMMERCIAL POLICY

CHARLES W. HULTMAN

University of Kentucky

Increased dependence on foreign sources for a variety of raw materials, sharply rising prices of many basic commodities, and the petroleum embargo imposed by the OPEC countries have contributed to a situation in recent years that warrants a reevaluation of U.S. commercial policy with regard to a wide range of essential raw materials. In view of a possible danger of serious internal dislocations as a result of increased use of external supplies of such materials, it has become necessary to consider steps to prevent disruptions within the U.S. economy.

In response to this potential danger, the Trade Reform Bill, passed by the Congress and signed in early 1975 by the President, contains an "access to supplies" provision (Section 108 of Public Law 93-618) that calls for the development of arrangements with foreign countries to guarantee American access to supplies of articles of commerce that are not readily produced domestically. Although much of the discussion, debate, and controversy over the Trade Reform Bill centered on the Jackson Amendment relating to the application of most favored nation treatment to the USSR, implications of a late amendment dealing with access to supplies are probably of far greater concern to the world economy. The purpose of this study is to explore the access to supplies provision through an examination of its nature, background, problems of implementation, and resulting implications for affected countries.

NATURE AND BACKGROUND

As the United States became increasingly industrialized over the years, the composition of its external trade changed in accordance with a shifting factoral availability and comparative advantage. The gradual change in the U.S. economy from a raw material producer in the late 1700s and early 1800s to a major industrial producer in the mid-1900s has affected the composition of both exports and imports. Crude materials, which in the early 1800s were the major U.S. export, have been replaced by finished manufactures. Finished manufactures, a major import category in the early 1800s, is now substantially less significant, in part offset by imports of crude material and semi-manufactures. The growing dependence on foreign raw materials reflects continuing industrialization and growing incomes in the United States, a new need for some materials never available in this country, and the depletion of the U.S. supply of some materials. This increased reliance on imported materials is a natural outgrowth of a shifting comparative advantage and efforts to use scarce resources efficiently.

Despite the growing dependence on foreign sources for a variety of materials, previous U.S. commercial policy placed emphasis on access to foreign markets rather than on access to supplies. Generally, in past years, Congress has been primarily concerned with protectionist commercial policies of foreign governments; it has promoted efforts that would retain the U.S. share of world export markets and thus encourage U.S. exports.

Although U.S. legislation in the past focused largely on the availability of export markets, some concern both here and in Western Europe has been evidenced regarding the continuing availability of raw materials and the unjustified use of export controls. Thus included under Title IV of the Atlantic Charter is the goal of "access on equal terms to the trade and to the raw materials of the world." In addition, the proposed Charter for an International Trade Organization contained provisions dealing with international commodity agreements and reasonable price and supply stability of commodities. U.S. stockpiling of a wide range of strategic materials after World War II is another indication of this concern.

Although U.S. dependence on foreign supplies of certain items had been realized for some time, the potential dangers may not have been fully appreciated until late 1973 and throughout 1974, with the petroleum embrago and subsequent sharp rise in petroleum prices. In recognition of this possible threat, the Mondale-Ribicoff amendment to the trade bill directed the President to develop arrangements through GATT (General Agreement on Tariffs and Trade) or other international institutions that would include rules governing access to supplies of food, raw materials, and manufactured products. Basically, the intention is that no country or group of countries be allowed to impose arbitrary export controls, withhold supplies, or raise prices on commodities regularly exported to and needed by the United States. The Mondale-Ribicoff amendment (Mondale, 1973: 1) reflected a set of proposals regarding access to external supplies, as well as the implementation and enforcement of provisions through presidential action and through international organizations. The key provisions finally included in the Trade Reform Act of 1974 are relatively succinct and for purposes of exactness are reproduced as follows:

SEC. 108.   ACCESS TO SUPPLIES.

(a) A principal United States negotiating objective under section 102 shall be to enter into trade agreements with foreign countries and instrumentalities to assure the United States of fair and equitable access at reasonable prices to supplies of articles of commerce which are important to the economic requirements of the United States and for which the United States does not have, or cannot easily develop, the necessary domestic productive capacity to supply its own requirements.

(b) Any agreement entered into under section 102 may include provisions which—

(1) assure to the United States the continued availability of important articles at reasonable prices, and

(2) provide reciprocal concessions or comparable trade obligations, or both, by the United States.

SEC. 121.   STEPS TO BE TAKEN TOWARD GATT REVISION: AUTHORIZATION OF APPROPRIATIONS FOR GATT

(a) The President shall, as soon as practicable, take such action as may be necessary to bring trade agreements heretofore entered into, and the application thereof, into conformity with principles promoting the development of an open, nondiscriminatory, and fair world economic system. The action and principles referred to in the preceding sentence include, but are not limited to, the following—

. . . .

(7) the improvement and strengthening of the provisions of GATT and other international agreements governing access to supplies of food, raw materials, and manufactured or semi-manufactured products, including rules and procedures governing the imposition of export controls, the denial of fair and equitable access to such supplies, and effective consultative procedures on problems of supply shortages.

SEC. 301.   RESPONSES TO CERTAIN TRADE PRACTICES OF FOREIGN GOVERNMENTS.

(a) Whenever the President determines that a foreign country or instrumentality—

. . . .

(4) imposes unjustifiable or unreasonable restrictions on access to supplies of food, raw materials, or manufactured or semimanufactured products which burden or restrict United States commerce, the President shall take all appropriate and feasible steps within his power to obtain the elimination of such restrictions or subsidies, and he—

(A) may suspend, withdraw, or prevent the application of, or may refrain from proclaiming, benefits of trade agreement concessions to carry out a trade agreement with such country or instrumentality; and

(B) may impose duties or other import restrictions on the products of such foreign country or instrumentality, and may impose fees or restrictions on the services of such foreign country or instrumentality, for such time as he deems appropriate.

In essence, the legislation is a congressional mandate that the U.S. government enter into agreement with foreign countries to assure supplies of essential articles at reasonable prices and to include rules against denial of equitable access to supplies of materials.[1] The authority to retaliate is also provided to the President to cover violations of the rules.

IMPLEMENTATION OF THE ACCESS PROVISION

The establishment or development of arrangements to implement the access to supply provision could be accomplished through one or more international institutions, although GATT would probably be the logical choice. Such an agreement, of course, would apply to all other "contracting parties" to GATT as well as to the U.S. In all likelihood, such an arrangement will be considered and may be adopted at the negotiating session of GATT recently convened in Geneva. There is some indication (Golt, 1974: 53) that the strongest sentiment for negotiating an access arrangement has come from the United States.

Presently GATT includes over eighty countries as "contracting parties"; it also includes many but not all important basic commodity producers. Among countries not included are Saudi Arabia, Libya, Iraq, the USSR, Thailand, Mexico, and several East European countries. However, a declaration at the 1974 preparatory meeting of GATT made it clear that participation in the forthcoming negotiating sessions would be available to all countries whether or not they were actually members.

An effective agreement would require the international acceptance of a comprehensive set of guidelines that specified the nature of continued availability of items at reasonable prices, justifiable and unjustifiable restrictions on supplies of commodities, and the nature of retaliatory measures and circumstances under which they could be used by injured importing countries.

GATT, in addition to providing a basis for multilateral negotiations since the mid-forties, already consists of a set of rules or code of behavior to guide member countries in various facets of their commercial policies. Among the principles incorporated into GATT are unconditional most favored nation treatment and, under most circumstances, the prohibition of quantitative restrictions.

Article XI of GATT also prohibits the imposition of export quotas or other controls on exports, unless one of a number of stated exceptions applies. In fact, it would appear (Smith, 1973) that GATT is more prohibitive of export controls than of import controls. The exceptions under which export controls may be used pertain to instances in which commodity agreements prevail, to preserve national security, to assist domestic price-control programs, or to prevent a critical shortage of foodstuffs or other products essential to the exporting contracting party. The inclusion of an access agreement would in a sense partially duplicate the intent of existing rules prohibiting export controls. Yet in addition to the likelihood of being more comprehensive, an access agreement focuses attention on both the rights of importing countries and the obligations of exporting countries.

The General Agreement also has provisions to help enforce its code of behavior. For example, each member country is under moral and economic pressure to avoid violating the code. Heavy reliance is placed on the willingness of each country to consult with others before it alters its commercial policy to the disadvantage of other countries. If certain countries feel they are damaged, the situation is investigated and the country in violation may be asked to modify its position. If this is not acceptable, remaining countries damaged by the violations of a given country have the right to withdraw tariff concessions they have granted in the past. Generally, the last step has rarely proved necessary, which, according to some observers, points to the efficacy of this form of consultation. In addition, GATT serves as a forum through which grievances are aired in the presence of a worldwide audience. The inclusion of an access to supplies provision as part of the General Agreement would also require agreement on the conditions under which economic sanctions would be used, although it would be hoped a settlement would be resolved before arriving at this stage. To be meaningful, sanctions would have to be applied on a relatively broad basis and would require concerted action on the part of many of the importing nations. Concerted action has rarely been taken against countries through international organizations; one illustration of this type of action was the United Nations economic sanctions applied to Southern Rhodesia.

Section 301 of the Trade Reform Act requests the President to respond to unjustifiable or unreasonable restrictions placed by foreign countries on access to supplies of various types of commodities. Presumably such retaliation might be imposed either unilaterally or in cooperation with other GATT participants. It would involve all steps the President would deem appropriate and feasible to eliminate such restrictions.

In its present form, GATT is not considered (Committee on Finance, U.S. Senate, 1974) to be an adequate guide to the solution of problems arising in the regular commerce of nations. Conditions relating to international finance, the internationalization of production, and the availability of both primary commodities and finished goods and services are significantly different from those prevailing at the time the initial GATT rules were constructed. Although the GATT rules and organizational framework may not be adequate, they represent a foundation upon which a structure capable of coping with current problems can be developed. The Special Advisory Panel to the Trade Committee of the Atlantic Council (1974) suggest that a Code of Trade Liberalization be established to support GATT procedures. Two specific provisions of the Code would reinforce existing GATT provisions: (a) countries applying for export restrictions for short supply reasons would consult with other countries and consider ways in which the supply can be shared fairly with other countries; and (b) important producing and consuming countries would create stockpiles where appropriate to prevent future shortages and to promote price stability.

While these principles might usefully apply to instances of commodities in short supply and needed domestically, they do not cover instances in which countries withhold supplies in an effort to raise prices, to expand foreign exchange earnings, or to secure some other economic or political advantage. Coping with the latter is likely to prove most difficult.

In general, if GATT is to be effective in implementing an access provision, specific guidelines must be established regarding the use of export embargos and related controls, and the procedures to be followed in the use of retaliatory measures. Furthermore, the entire arrangement must find widespread acceptance among participating countries.

IMPLICATIONS OF ACCESS AGREEMENT

If there is widespread agreement that international cooperation is essential to prevent export controls and to assure continuing access to supplies, then the initial agreement specifying prices, quantities, and other conditions could conceivably be established without extensive delay. In past years, for example, several commodity agreements were initiated to influence or control the production, sale, or price of a primary commodity. These agreements included the major importing and exporting countries and involved coffee, sugar, tin, and wheat. The complexities, gains, and shortcomings of these past commodity agreements will provide useful experience and information in implementation of the access to supplies provision. Difficulties in the past have centered on factors relating to equitable prices, allocation of quotas, assurance of continuing supplies, and maintenance of membership on the part of major exporting and importing countries.

Whether or not a more comprehensive access to supply agreement can be established depends upon what the exporting and the importing countries expect to achieve, what each can offer in the way of concessions, and the good faith and willingness of all parties to support such a program.

POSSIBLE DISADVANTAGES TO THE UNITED STATES

Although an international arrangement may be a necessary alternative to prevent economic warfare and possible economic strangulation of dependent importing countries, a number of difficulties may have to be overcome. Governments may be unwilling to cooperate fully in implementing an arrangement if certain disadvantages may be inherent in it, in some instances to the developed countries, in others to the developing world.

For example, an international agreement to create certainty of access to supplies will create an obligation as well as a gain to the United States. A U.S. decision to reduce or stop sales of soybeans and other feed grains, scrap metals, or computer machinery, as was the case in 1973 and 1974, could be considered in violation of such an agreement and would be met with retaliatory measures from foreign importing nations. It would be difficult to argue, for example, that a group of underdeveloped countries desperately in need of foreign exchange earnings should not attempt to increase export prices when at the same time the U.S. government feels it is appropriate to use export controls to protect the domestic economy from the excessive drain of scarce materials.

Specifically, it may be difficult to accomplish the intent of the access to supplies provision of the Trade Reform Act along with that of Section 3 of the U.S. Export Administration Act which states that it is the policy of the United States to use export controls "to the extent necessary to protect the domestic economy from the excessive drain of scarce materials and to reduce the serious inflationary import of abnormal foreign demand." Export controls imposed by the United States even in the genuine belief that they are essential to the domestic economy may not be completely acceptable to foreign importing countries that have become dependent on this source of supplies. One writer (Diebold, 1974) suggests that the most difficult question to determine is the extent to which the U.S. will be willing to give up freedom to control its exports as a condition for getting comparable commitments from other countries.

For political and national security reasons, the United States has also imposed export controls in past years under the Export Control Act, the Munitions Control Act, and the Trading with the Enemy Act. In addition, under the Battle Act, the United States attempts to enforce export controls by applying pressure on foreign countries to utilize controls similar to those of the United States against Communist countries.[2] Thus, Senator Mondale (1973), in proposing the access amendments, noted:

> Nations have obvious concerns about guarding the domestic supplies of raw materials when threatened by shortages or other national emergencies. Although the United States used such justifications last spring to impose export controls on soybeans, oilseeds, and other products, in taking such steps without prior consultation with our traditional trading partners—Japan and Europe—we set a bad example for the rest of the world.

U.S. failure to consult with its trading partners appears to have violated a GATT principle noted previously.

Certainly a major problem in negotiating an access to supplies agreement is that of making it consistent with export controls authorized under the Export Administration Act. However, given the change in the position of some raw material producing countries and the recognition of the interdependency of the world economy, the U.S. administration now appears to recognize officially its obligations concerning access to supplies—that "We as a major supplier must examine the impact of our own practices " (Flanigan, 1974: 170), and "We must be prepared to practice it and not just apply it where it is to our own benefit." (Kissinger, 1974: 495)

ATTITUDES OF DEVELOPING NATIONS

It must be further realized that many raw material producing nations may be reluctant to participate in an arrangement that they might perceive as an obstacle to their efforts to maximize foreign exchange earnings. This is particularly true when there is a pervasive belief in the existence of a severe economic imbalance in the relationship between the raw material producing developing nations and the more industrialized developed countries. Evidence from the UN Conference on Trade and Development indicates that the developing countries will demand preferential treatment from the advanced countries particularly with regard to industrial exports. They expect easier access to external markets, greater opportunities to increase their earnings from external commodity sales, and assistance to help diversify their economies. The developing countries have asserted their right to achieve a more favorable price for their exports and to protect an inalienable right to permanent sovereignty over their natural resources. The extent to which individual countries have permanent sovereignty over natural resources has been considered but not resolved. The matter was studied and debated in the United Nations within the context of the legality or illegality of nationalization of foreign investment in extractive industries. Eventually United Nations Declaration 1803 (XVII) was adopted (December 14, 1962); it acknowledged "the inalienable right of each State to dispose freely of its natural wealth and resources pursuant to its national interests." There is some evidence (O'Keefe, 1974) that this resolution does not deal effectively with the concept of sovereignty over natural sources. However, in the context of an access to supplies provision, it does focus attention on a basic condition that must be recognized in efforts to reach an acceptable arrangement.

The desire and efforts of the developing countries to achieve changes in the world economic structure should not be underestimated. For example, in a *Declaration and Programme of Action* adopted by the sixth special session of the General Assembly of the United Nations on May 1, 1974, it was again emphasized that the developing countries must protect their inalienable right to permanent sovereignty over their natural resources. Perhaps more important was a declaration (1974) that the developing countries should:

> ·support the establishment and/or improvement of an appropriate mechanism to defend the prices of their exportable commodities and to

improve access to and stabilize markets for them. In this context the increasingly effective mobilization by the whole group of oil-exporting countries of their natural resources for the benefit of their economic development is to be welcomed.

Apparently, although the major industrial powers may have regarded the imposition of the embargo over oil as an unreasonable restriction of access to supplies, this view was not universally held. A critical point is that, under existing conditions and practices, it may not be readily determined what is or is not justifiable action. One writer (Shibata, 1974), for example, argues that in the use of the embargo, "The Arab oil exporting countries were in fact following the steps of a great number of other states which have used their export regulations to further their foreign policies."

Basically, export controls have been used by countries for four major reasons: (1) to raise prices and increase foreign exchange earnings, (2) to implement an international commodity agreement, (3) to achieve a political objective, and (4) to help alleviate a domestic shortage. The developing countries have generally attempted to use import controls for the first two reasons; the United States, for the last two reasons. As far as increasing prices or redistribution of income is concerned, such controls are regarded (Law, 1975: 114) as inferior to other forms of aid. Yet access to supplies from the raw material producers' point of view may come to involve what they perceive as a more equitable distribution and sharing of the world's technology, natural resources, income, and wealth.

Until an agreement and some guidelines are established, it is not possible to know the exact circumstances under which the developing countries either singly or in groups could exert control or influence over supplies and prices of their export commodities without conflicting with the access rights of importers. It has been suggested, for example (Erb, 1974-1975), that there be a congressional specification of the conditions under which a foreign country's imposition of export controls would be unacceptable to the United States and therefore subject to retaliation by the United States. Under Section 301 of the Trade Reform Act, the President is authorized to withdraw the benefits of trade concessions to such countries and to impose duties and other restrictions on the products of such countries.

There are, of course, wide variations in the economic positions and strengths of individual developing countries. Some are in a strong position with an abundance of petroleum, bauxite, or other commodities required by the industrialized countries. But a great many either have limited natural resources or else export food and other primary commodities that do not represent a critical import item for other countries. A large number are also heavily dependent on imported petroleum, fertilizers, and other items and have been seriously damaged by the high prices of such products.

FOREIGN USE OF EXPORT CONTROLS

Raw material and other commodity shortages may arise in different ways, the most dramatic being a boycott established by a group of producing countries in order to achieve a political objective. Or such a cartel might attempt to withhold supplies in order to increase commodity export prices and the value of foreign exchange earnings. Countries with depletable resources may attempt to extend their sources of exchange earnings over as long a period as possible. Finally, the natural depletion and consequent rising prices of some types of basic materials will occur depending upon the rate at which such materials are consumed. Shortages may be made even more severe under any of these circumstances by the efforts of purchasing countries to hoard and expand their inventories (Eckstein, 1974).

Although shortages may develop as a result of several factors, the most disruptive situation would occur if a supply scarcity were artificially and deliberately created rather than as the result of a more gradual, long-term free market development. The most critical factor determining the ability of a group of countries to achieve effective results in withholding export supplies is the geographic concentration of such supplies. Where a large share of reserves of a material is held by a few countries, all other things remaining equal, the greater the chance of a more successful cartel. Or, if one country has a cost and transportation advantage over other producers in its sales to importing nations, it may be able to achieve a partial monopoly status.

Still other factors are relevant in determining the ability of a group of countries to withhold supplies to achieve political or economic results. The Morgan Guaranty Survey (1974) lists several factors which weaken the potential to control supplies:

(a) ability of importing nations to develop substitutes or synthetics;
(b) different ideologies, or political and economic philosophies of pro-
    ducing countries which preclude coordination of activities over an
    extended period of time;
(c) insufficient exchange reserves to withstand a temporary reduction in
    export earnings while the boycott is in effect;
(d) a large share of the exporting nations' work force dependent upon
    sales abroad to cover their payroll;
(e) demand instability in the importing nations.

There are other factors that may have some influence on the
ability of raw materials exporting nations to withhold supplies.
Stockpiles of raw materials in the United States and other major
importing nations is a critical factor. Dependence upon the United
States for certain types of commodity needs may also inhibit the
action of raw material suppliers.

In general, however, it would appear that formation of an effective
cartel of raw material producers for an extended period of time may
require conditions that do not frequently prevail. This does not
mean, however, that the possibility can be ignored. Rather, the list of
products that could be withheld may be relatively narrow; hence, a
strategy needs to be developed with reference to such products. It
might be noted (Amuzegar, 1974) that, for the petroleum producing
countries, the power held is not simply one of controlling the price
and availability of petroleum, but also the holding of "petro-
currencies" which, among other things, can be switched from country to country to affect exchange rates and currency values.

ALTERNATIVE AND SUPPLEMENTAL APPROACHES

As noted earlier, the real concern for the United States is the
sudden withdrawal of supplies or sharp increase in prices of import
items. This consideration is important in evaluating the various
policy alternatives. Whether or not an international access to supply
agreement can be achieved and subsequently implemented, an indication of other alternatives and/or supplemental approaches for the
United States should be noted.

One way of coping with potential shortages is to establish bilateral
access to supplies agreements. Agreements between pairs of countries
to assure continued deliveries of commodities may be easier to

achieve and implement than similar agreements on a multinational basis. Such agreements are likely to be reached regardless of the degree of success achieved on a multinational basis. France, for example, has made an effort to establish a mutually acceptable arrangement with oil-producing states. Japan and Turkey have agreed on an arrangement whereby Japan would provide assistance for the establishment of a ferrochrome alloy plant in Turkey; Turkey, in turn, would guarantee to provide a specified volume of chrome ore to Japan for the next several years.

Stockpiling of commodities is another method of coping with temporary shortages. U.S. stockpiles already contain over ninety strategic materials, but the aggregate value has been reduced in the last several years as a result of U.S. government sales. The nature of each material must be examined carefully to determine the possibility of a foreign boycott and the potential impact on the economy. These factors, along with information on perishability, storage costs, and potential domestic production, would determine the size of the inventory.

Conservation would not eliminate, but would help alleviate, a problem with regard to some items. The energy shortage of 1973-1974 provides ample evidence of an ability to conserve on energy. It is estimated that, for some sectors of the economy, petroleum supplies could be reduced as much as fifteen percent without affecting output. In addition, the 1974 Energy Policy Project of the Ford Foundation has developed three sets of projections concerning energy usage. Under one set of projections (zero energy growth), energy consumption would increase about 1.7 percent annually through the mid-1980s and then the growth rate would decline to zero. Zero energy growth would require a sharp departure from past consumption trends; dramatic changes would be anticipated in life styles and energy use, but an "austerity" program would not be required.

Recycling may also help alleviate potential shortages of some items. The ready availability of many materials and energy at a low cost in the past has not been conducive to economical recovery of basic materials from discarded products. Although cost considerations eventually will lead to a greater recycling of many items, the process might be accelerated through appropriate subsidies.

Another approach is the achievement of self-sufficiency in items of strategic importance to the U.S. economy and which are also produced in a small number of countries that could conceivably control the supply at any time. Such an approach is already considered a goal with regard to petroleum. At the present time, there are possibly four basic raw materials that are imported and also supplied by a small number of exporters—copper, tin, natural rubber, and bauxite.

Obviously, the major disadvantage of the independence approach is the cost involved. The basic problem with economic self-sufficiency is that it reduces world specialization and the opportunity to use efficiently the supply of productive resources. Although it is true that an increased flow of world trade and investment makes the United States more dependent upon the rest of the world, it must be remembered that other countries at the same time become more dependent upon the United States. Boycotts and threats of boycotts are not a ready weapon of economic warfare for the raw material exporter who needs food, capital equipment, technology, and raw materials from the United States and that has sizable amounts invested in the U.S. economy.

Unfortunately, the use or threat of export controls induces importing countries to establish restrictive commercial policies. The United States has instituted measures to become more self-sufficient in petroleum because of the possibility of a second Arab embargo; the EEC countries are reluctant to reduce the degree of self-sufficiency in agricultural products because of possible U.S. embargo on food products when shortages arise.

Increased interdependence is a natural outgrowth of free trade and capital movements, and the exchange of ideas and information. Perhaps it is time, as suggested by Kurt Waldheim, that the world community make interdependence a positive force in world affairs. In view of potential population growth outdistancing resource availability, great caution must be used in advocating a policy inconsistent with the free flow of goods and services, international specialization, and an optimum use of world resources.

SUMMARY AND CONCLUSIONS

U.S. interest in an access to supplies agreement followed the OPEC embargo and subsequent increase in petroleum prices. The Trade Reform Act of 1974 stipulates that the President shall enter into agreement with other countries, either through GATT or some other institution, to insure an uninterrupted supply of commodities at reasonable prices. Further, the President has power to retaliate, either unilaterally or in cooperation with GATT action, against countries using export controls.

Although a continuing flow of goods and services is essential in view of the high degree of interdependency of the world economy, there are several factors that may make it difficult to establish and implement such an agreement. Even if there were widespread support for such an arrangement, the final determination of equitable prices and reasonable access may be difficult to achieve. However, conditions of a more basic nature may prove to be the stumbling blocks. The President has legislative power and already uses export controls to restrict the supply of commodities to foreign buyers for both economic and political reasons; the United States would have to forego the general application of export controls if it is to reflect a spirit of cooperation in formulating an access to supplies agreement.

Equally important is the widespread dissatisfaction on the part of many developing, raw material producing countries with their share of the benefits of world trade and investment. This dissatisfaction, combined with the asserted inalienable right to permanent sovereignty over their natural resources, suggests that the developing countries are not likely to participate in an access to supplies agreement in the absence of substantial concessions on the part of the developed world. Such concessions are likely to take the form of a guaranteed floor on prices of raw materials, the assurance of ready access to markets for developing countries, and more favorable access to the food, technology, and capital goods of the industrialized world.

The recent worldwide shortage of foodstuffs, raw materials, and energy sources again reinforces the need for production specialization and the free international flow of goods and services. The real danger in the future is the absence of leadership on the part of the industrialized world and a consequent effort to attempt such solutions on a nationalistic unilateral basis.

NOTES

1. For a brief summary of attitudes—most of which were generally favorable to the access to supply provisions during congressional hearings—see Committee on Finance, U.S. Senate, (1974).

2. For a summary of legislation supporting U.S. import controls, see Grub and Peterson (1971).

REFERENCES

AMUZEGAR, J. (1974) "OPEC in the context of the global power equation." Denver Journal of International Law and Policy 14 (Fall): 221-228.
Committee on Finance, U.S. Senate, (1974) Summary and Analysis of H.R. 10710–The Trade Reform Act of 1973. Ninety-Third Congress, Second Session, February 26: 107-108.
DIEBOLD, W., Jr. (1974) "Global scarcities in an interdependent world," in Committee on Foreign Affairs, Hearings Before the Subcommittee on Foreign Economic Policy of the Committee on Foreign Affairs. Ninety-Third Congress, Second Session, May 1, 8, 9, 15, 22: 29.
ECKSTEIN, O. (1974) "The materials problem and the development of the U.S. economy." Testimony submitted to the Permanent Subcommittee on Investigations of the Committee on Government Operations, U.S. Senate, September.
Energy Policy Project of the Ford Foundation (1974) Exploring Energy Choices: A Preliminary Report. Washington, D.C.
ERB, G. F. (1974-1975) "Controlling export controls." Foreign Policy 17 (Winter): 79-84.
FLANIGAN, P. M. (1974) "Need for reforming international economic system," p. 170, in the Trade Reform Act of 1973, Hearing before the Committee on Finance, U.S. Senate. Ninety-Third Congress, Second Session, March 4.
GOLT, S. (1974) "The GATT negotiations, 1973-1975: a guide to the issues." British-North American Committee, April: 53.
GRUB, P. D. and D. A. PETERSON (1971) "United States export controls: an overview of present regulations." Journal of International Law and Economics (January): 185-200.
KISSINGER, H. (1974) Testimony before the Committee on Finance, the Trade Reform Act of 1973, Hearings before the Committee on Finance, U.S. Senate. Ninety-Third Congress, Second Session, March 6.
LAW, A. D. (1975) International Commodity Agreements. Lexington, Mass.: D. C. Heath.
MONDALE, W. (1973) "Trade reform act of 1973." Congressional Record. Ninety-Third Congress, First Session, Vol. 119 (December 3): 1-2.
O'KEEFE, P. J. (1974) "The United Nations and permanent sovereignty over natural resources." Journal of World Trade Law 8 (May-June): 227-282.
Morgan Guaranty Survey (1974) "Foreign raw materials: how critical are they?" (March): 9-13.
"Problems of raw materials and development," Declaration and Programme of Action (Adopted at the Sixth Special Session of the General Assembly of the United Nations on May 1, 1974): 19.
SHIBATA, I. (1974) "Destination embargo of Arab oil: its legality under international law." American Journal of International Law 68 (October): 591-627.
SMITH, M. D. H. (1973) "Voluntary export quotas and U.S. trade policy: a new nontariff barrier." Law and Policy in International Business 1: 10-55.
Special Advisory Panel to the Trade Committee of the Atlantic Council (1974) "Reform of the international trade system: a proposal." Trade Reform Act of 1973, Hearings Before the Committee on Finance, U.S. Senate. Ninety-Third Congress, Second Session, March 22: 915-929.

Chapter 8

EXPORT PROMOTION IN AN AUTHORITARIAN REGIME: THE POLITICS OF THE "BRAZILIAN MIRACLE"

S T E V E N   H.   A R N O L D

American University

INTRODUCTION: THE PROBLEMS OF EXPORT PRODUCTION

Efforts by developing nations to promote the exports of manufactures are no longer dismissed as nationalistic attempts to reduce the "colonial" stigma associated with the export of primary products. On the contrary, exporting manufactures is defended on economic grounds as a logical and important consequence of the process of industrialization (United Nations, 1964; Lary, 1966; Keesing, 1967; Schydlowsky, 1967). Not only does international trade increase potential market size, creating the possibility for lower unit costs through new economies of scale, but it also opens domestic industries to greater competition, which may lead to improvements in both efficiency and quality. Exports of manufactures also provide a new source of foreign exchange, an important consideration for nations facing growth-inhibiting balance of payments constraints.

Despite these theoretical advantages, the practical problems associated with moving from the relative tranquility of a protected domestic market to the rigors of international competition present some formidable challenges. New techniques and skills are required, new cadres of experts in international marketing and advertising become essential, and new, more exacting standards are required for products to meet the specifications of the international market. Most important, the prospective exporter must be able to offer goods at prices or terms more favorable than those of the customary suppliers, in order to attract buyers who would ordinarily be reluctant to risk accepting an unknown product from a nation with a "lack of tradition" in exporting. This is a tall order for any new firm, given its relative inexperience and the problems of inadequate infrastructure, capital scarcities, and distortions in labor costs typical of many developing nations. To make prospects even more discouraging, these problems are compounded by serious obstacles to exporting at both the international and domestic levels.

One of the most well-known obstacles is the problem of access to the markets of industrialized countries, an issue of central concern in the meetings of the United Nations Conference on Trade and Development (UNCTAD). This concern has been substantiated by respected analysts such as Balassa (1965), who has documented the techniques which preserve a high degree of protection in industrialized markets, particularly in the product areas of greatest interest to developing nations. But despite UNCTAD's concerns and the consequent agreement of October 1970 to grant tariff preferences to imports of manufactures from developing countries, prospects for dramatic changes in the policies of industrialized nations appear unlikely.[1]

The difficulty in changing the international climate for trade in manufactures suggests that a nation seriously interested in breaking into the export market needs to shift strategic emphasis to the national level, using its own economic tools (such as exchange, taxation, and credit policies) to help determine the "rules of the game" under which its industries will compete abroad. But ironically, if this nation has been following a development strategy that has emphasized import substitution, it may discover that its current policies are acting as powerful disincentives to exporting. Although import substitution strategies have often been spectacularly successful in creating a domestic industrial sector, these strategies have also encouraged an economic and political climate antithetical to a successful export program.[2]

On the economic side, overvalued exchange rates and industrial protection typical of import substitution programs are strong incentives for the creation of industries by providing an opportunity to obtain imported capital goods relatively cheaply, and by protecting the newly created industries from foreign competition. But the policy of protection also reduces the incentive to operate efficiently, making it difficult for many of these industries to compete in international trade. In addition, overvalued exchange rates, while reducing the price of imported capital goods, raise the price of exports, which discourages even potentially competitive industries from entering the world market.

These economic distortions reinforce the inward-looking bias of import substitution, which, after all, does have as its primary goal the creation of industries for the domestic market. Given this domestic emphasis, it is not surprising that many industrialists devote themselves entirely to the task of supplying the home market, with little if any thought given to the possibilities of exporting, regardless of the potential benefits to themselves or the nation. Moreover, the subsidies and special benefits of import substitution programs, established to promote (and protect) domestic industrial expansion, also tend to create vested interests, both inside and outside the business sector, who have an important stake in the continuation of these benefits, and who would oppose any policy changes that appear to threaten their interests.

Promoting exports of manufactures, then, is not an easy task for a developing nation. To break into the arena of world trade with its exacting standards and protected markets requires a precisely coordinated, single-minded national effort to mobilize the economy for a massive export drive (Lewis, 1955: 352). Yet, a government contemplating the need for such an effort is often faced with a development policy that discriminates against exporting, with entrepreneurs who are uninterested in selling their products abroad, and with a variety of vested interests that may strongly oppose the types of policies needed to create an effective export program.

BRAZIL: A COMPARISON OF DEMOCRATIC AND AUTHORITARIAN REGIMES (1956-1964, 1964-1974)

Given the difficulties involved in export promotion, the success of Brazil in this field is striking. Once considered an exporter of nothing more than coffee, Brazil now exports a wide range of manufactures, from chemical products to sewing machines and automobiles. The Brazilian case is particularly interesting, since government efforts to promote exports of manufactures have been continuing for almost twenty years, but only after the military replaced the system of popularly elected democratic government in 1964 did these efforts become translated into effective results. This adds an important comparative dimension to this case study, permitting an analysis of the characteristics of the different types of political regimes as a possible explanation of this difference in success.

Like many other developing nations, Brazil followed a development program of import substitution during the postwar period, which generated a rapid rate of industry-led growth. Between 1947 and 1961, the real gross domestic product increased at an annual rate of over 6 percent, while industrial production increased at an annual rate of about 9.5 percent, enlarging the industrial contribution to GDP from 21 percent in 1947 to 34 percent in 1961.[3] As the economy began to mature during the mid-1950s,[4] President Juscelino Kubitschek formally committed the government, for the first time, to a policy of exporting manufactures, making this commitment in a dramatic speech over nationwide radio a few months after his inauguration in 1956. This marked the beginning of repeated government efforts to promote exports of manufactures, but without success. In spite of the public policy statements, the export promotion program was poorly organized, had few meaningful incentives, and was met with indifference by the private sector. For more than eight years (1956-1964), export policy-making was an exercise in failure, characterized by cycles of bold pronouncements, intense but short-lived efforts at policy change, and negligible results, leading detractors to refer to these "reforms" as "reforminhas" or inconsequential reforms.[5]

In 1964, Brazil entered a new era, both politically and economically. The democratic regime, which was facing a rapid decline in the rate of growth, a soaring inflation, and increasing political instabilities, was removed on April 1 by the military. The armed forces rationalized the coup in revolutionary terms, claiming to have replaced "partisan politics" with an "objective and rational" approach to decision-making dominated by "apolitical technocrats" (técnicos) who were to be insulated from the strong and contradictory political pressures characteristic of the previous democratic period. With the military intervention came a profound change in economic policy and a spectacular shift in export promotion programs. Although policy pronouncements in the field of exports sounded similar to those of the democratic period, the results were markedly different. Between 1964 and 1969, the military formulated and implemented a carefully organized export program for manufactures which not only contained one of the most comprehensive systems of export incentives in the world, but also was enthusiastically supported by the previously unconcerned business sector. The increase in exports of manufactures was equally dramatic, growing at an annual rate in excess of thirty percent during the military regime, as compared to twelve percent during the democratic period.[6]

Why did the military succeed in export promotion when the previous democratic regimes had failed? Did the basic policy changes which took place under the military substantiate its claim that it had "revolutionized" policy-making with a new, "rational, apolitical" model? To what extent does the Brazilian experience hold lessons for other developing nations? In order to deal with these questions, this study compares the democratic and military regimes in terms of the three issue areas most central to the problem of promoting the export of manufactures: program organization, the creation of export incentives, and the mobilization of the private sector.

ORGANIZATION OF EXPORT PROGRAMS

Given the pressures of world competition, a successful export program required a national effort that concentrated in a single-minded, efficient manner upon policies that could win customers away from traditional suppliers. To maximize the impact of these policies, it was imperative that they be coordinated. Unfortunately, this need was not consistent with the tendency for Brazilian policy-making to be poorly organized. Although decision-making has tended to focus on the executive branch, the bureaucracy itself has been highly decentralized, with only vaguely determined divisions of responsibility. In the words of one observer:

> Regardless of where one looks in the policy-making matrix, one is first struck by the proliferation of agencies with overlapping jurisdictions and interests, the complicated and lengthy processes of negotiation, the

apparent lack of continuity and coordination, and the sheer indirection
and indeterminancy of outcomes [Schmitter, 1971: 245].[7]

DEMOCRATIC REGIMES

Under the democratic regimes, this characterization certainly fits
export policy decision-making. Responsibility for export policy, such
as it was, divided haphazardly among a number of government
agencies with vague and overlapping jurisdictions, each setting its
own policy. To a certain extent, the large number of agencies
involved can be explained by the need for an export program to
involve most of the important economic tools (e.g., taxation, credit,
foreign exchange) which are often the responsibility of different
government institutions. But the extent to which the dispersion of
responsibility and vagueness of authority existed in Brazil suggests
that it vastly exceeded the limits of more "normal" bureaucracies,
prompting one highly critical government report which labeled the
export program as complex where it should have been simple, and
inconsistent where it should have been coordinated.[8]

"First among equals" of those concerned with export policy was
undoubtedly the Minister of Finance, who, as head of his ministry
and as chairman of the Superintendency of Money and Credit
(SUMOC), was centrally responsible for the most important features
of Brazilian economic policy. However, he had to insure that he
coordinated his actions with such agencies as the powerful "Foreign
Trade Department" (CACEX) of the quasi-public Bank of Brazil
(which managed to become involved in matters ranging from
financing exports to setting, in effect, special exchange rates), the
Congress, and over a dozen other agencies whose relationships, jurisdictions, and authority in relation to the Minister of Finance were, to
say the least, imprecise.

To deal with this situation, each of the democratic regimes established at least one coordinating body for exporting, in an effort to
bring together most of the various agencies involved. These coordinating bodies, however, were only advisory, representing no
improvement in the allocation of tasks or in the clarification of the
authority relations of the various agencies. As a result, these coordinating bodies quickly fell into disuse, with the agencies carrying on
much as before and the Minister of Finance (with occasional
challenges from the director of the CACEX) attempting to coordinate programs as well as was possible.[9]

The quasi-coordinator role of the Minister of Finance was complicated immensely, however, by the tendency during the democratic period for the President of Brazil to use the hiring and firing of the Minister of Finance as a way to protect his own base of political support. Whenever a general economic plan began to receive intense criticism, the President attempted to dissipate this criticism by removing the existing Minister of Finance as the person most visibly involved with the plan, and substituting someone more acceptable to the critics. This procedure of using the Minister of Finance as scapegoat for all the ills of the economic programs did apparently help to deflect hostility away from the President, but it resulted in eight ministers of finance in the 1956-1963 period. [10] This not only had a severe impact on the overall continuity of the economic program, but also made it difficult for any minister of finance to be in the position long enough to exercise a dominant personal role in policy-making. In the field of exporting, this meant that the coordinator role, which by default rested with the Minister of Finance was rarely exercised, leaving the program essentially leaderless. As a result, coordination of export programs was no better in 1963 than it had been in 1956.

MILITARY REGIMES

Under the military, the vagueness and indeterminancy of export policies was replaced by a far more unified and consistent program. Areas of responsibility and authority were now clarified, in sharp contrast to the previous system of overlapping jurisdictions. At first glance, this change appeared to have resulted from the military's promise to introduce a more rational, formally hierarchical form of decision-making. The powers of the Congress and the states were weakened, further centralizing authority in the executive. Most significantly, efforts to rationalize the executive branch to enable it to deal more effectively with exporting began almost immediately after the military took office, culminating in 1966 with the creation of a new "Foreign Trade Council" (CONCEX) which was authorized to "formulate the policy of foreign trade, as well as determine, orient, and coordinate the execution of the measures necessary to the expansion of such trade" (Law 5,025, 1966).

The impact of the rationalization program, symbolized by the creation of the CONCEX, was more apparent than real, however. This contrast between form and reality becomes particularly clear upon examination of the actual creation of the CONCEX and its present status. The task of rationalizing foreign trade (and particularly exporting) had been assigned in 1964 to the Minister of Industry and Commerce, who was by law technically responsible for the coordination of foreign trade, even though he controlled none of the most important economic policy tools involved. Realizing the impossibility of taking over these economic policies from the other agencies, the Minister of Industry and Commerce followed the more modest strategy of attempting to increase his influence on these economic tools even though they remained elsewhere (Interview, September 26, 1969).

The result of this strategy was the creation of the CONCEX, which included the heads of all ministries and agencies concerned with foreign trade, chaired by the Minister of Industry and Commerce. Under this structure, the Minister of Industry and Commerce had legally become "first among equals," coordinating the major policy-making ministries (particularly the Ministry of Finance and the Ministry of Planning), and dividing executive responsibilities between the CACEX (Foreign Trade Department of the Bank of Brazil) which regulated the domestic aspects of foreign trade in accordance with the directives of the CONCEX (issuing licenses, supervising standards, financing exports, and, in conjunction with the Ministry of Finance, preparing statistics), and the Ministry of Foreign Relations, which regulated international aspects (such as the negotiation and administration of tariff and commercial agreements). (See Figure 1.)

But although this placed the Minister of Industry and Commerce nominally in charge of a rationalized policy-making system for exporting, it was hardly a model of hierarchical authority. Effective coordination still depended upon the cooperation of the major ministries that controlled the key economic tools, since the CONCEX, although technically the policy-making agency, was authorized only to suggest measures in such crucial areas as credit, taxation, and foreign exchange (Article 4, Law 5,025, 1966). As a result, the CONCEX soon became in effect similar to the unsuccessful advisory coordinating bodies of the democratic period. Key ministers no longer attended personally, but sent their representatives, who were delegated little authority to make decisions. This, combined with the increasing tendency for key ministries to take actions affecting foreign trade without prior consultation of the

Figure 1

Scope of Authority of Brazilian Institutions in Foreign Trade
(after creation of CONCEX, 1966)

Formal Lines of Authority:

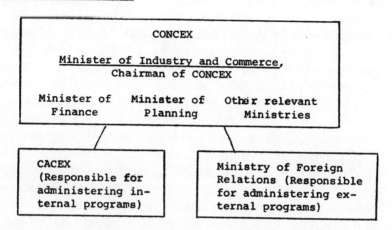

Approximate Actual Lines of Authority:

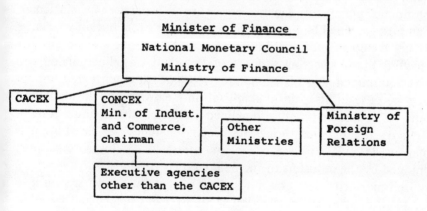

CONCEX, meant that it became increasingly less the center of important decision-making activity (Interview, August 12, 1969; de Azvedo, n.d.: 39).

As in the democratic period, the failure of the coordinating body meant that organizational responsibilities again fell by default to the most powerful minister. Normally this would again have been the Minister of Finance, who as Chairman of the National Monetary Council (formerly the SUMOC) coordinated both credit and foreign exchange policies, and as head of the Ministry controlled tax policy. For the first two years of military rule, however, the Minister of Finance, Octavio Bulhões, deferred this coordinator's role to his dynamic former student, Roberto Campos, who had been recruited by President Castello Branco to be the master architect of the economic plan and occupy the newly created "Ministry of Planning." With the change of military governments in 1967, the Ministry of Planning was headed by a less forceful individual, allowing the unofficial coordinator's role to revert back to the Ministry of Finance and its newly appointed minister, Antonio Delfim Netto, who remained through two administrations until his resignation in 1974.

Unlike the Ministers of Finance in the democratic period, Roberto Campos and Delfim Netto proved highly effective as coordinators of economic policy in general and export programs in particular. Campos was aided in pursuing his coordinator's role not only because of his technical skill and dominant personality, but also because he enjoyed the unswerving support of President Castello Branco, who was determined that his economic program, although highly unpopular because of its painful stabilization measures, should be carried out. As a result, Campos remained in office throughout Castello Branco's tenure, even though he became at times the "least popular man in Brazil." This was a sharp contrast to the insecure support enjoyed by the ministers of the democratic period.

Delfim Netto, an economics professor at the University of São Paulo who, prior to his selection as Minister of Finance had served as the new President's economics tutor (Schneider, 1971: 209), was not initially as well-known as Campos had been, but he soon established himself as the central force in economic policy, combining the power of his office and an unexpectedly polished skill at bureaucratic politics. Despite occasional rumors of his imminent departure, Delfim Netto remained from 1967 to 1974, which gave him the time to extend his control through persuasion, personal contacts, and bureaucratic maneuvers, so that he completely dominated virtually every aspect of the economy.

Illustrative of his dominance was the discrepancy between the formal and actual lines of authority in the field of export policy. Although in theory the Minister of Industry and Commerce coordinated export programs as head of the CONCEX, in fact it was Delfim Netto who eventually took charge, utilizing the control of key policy tools and informal personal contacts and friendships with the heads of key agencies, particularly the CACEX. The divergence between formal and informal lines of authority was finally resolved, after a fashion, by having the Minister of Industry and Commerce informally clear all policy initiatives through the Minister of Finance before submitting them to the CONCEX for consideration (See Figure 1).

In summary, it appears that the ability of the military regimes to improve export coordination in the unruly Brazilian bureaucracy was not achieved by the introduction of the formal reorganization plan. On the contrary, the coordinating body for foreign trade (CONCEX) was essentially a façade, with actual coordination depending, as it had in the democratic regimes, upon the attention and skill of a powerful minister who operated behind the scenes. The reason that this informal coordinator was more successful during the military period was partly due to the recruitment and retention strategy, in which the Minister was not fired as the scapegoat when policies became unpopular. Secure tenure was only part of the answer, however, guaranteeing the Minister enough time in office to dominate the policy-making process. Equally important was the fact that Campos and particularly Delfim Netto demonstrated unusual (and unexpected) skill at bureaucratic politics, which was essential in order to be an effective coordinator. Although both Campos and Delfim Netto had been recruited on the basis of economic expertise (as well as personal contact with the respective presidents), the fact that they also possessed political acumen so essential to their success was apparently a fortunate accident, and not a factor that had been considered in their recruitment.

EXPORT INCENTIVES AND ECONOMIC RATIONALIZATION

In addition to the need for efficient coordination of the policy-making process, an equally important problem was the formulation and implementation of policies to promote exports of manufactures. In the Brazilian case, it soon became clear that simply creating a series of standard export incentives (e.g., tax rebates, subsidized credit, etc.) would not deal effectively with this problem. If such incentives were to be effective, they would have to be preceded by basic changes in the economy, such as the reduction of the spiraling inflation, the liberalization of imports, and the rationalization of prices. Without such changes, potential exporters not only were plagued with high costs, but were unable to carry out such basic functions as quoting firm prices for their products. But since major structural changes in the economy could be politically painful, the success of the export program depended upon the extent to which the policy makers could devise a strategy that could bring about the economic reforms without damaging one's base of political support.

DEMOCRATIC REGIMES

The democratic regimes had a particularly difficult time dealing with any major structural changes in the Brazilian economy because of an important political "reality"—those who formed the base of political support were also those who had the most to lose from any wholesale program of economic rationalization. The process of industrialization through import substitution had created as early as the 1930s a loose coalition (termed the "ins" by historian Thomas Skidmore) which had learned to receive high payoffs from the government economic programs and which managed, with minor interruptions, to remain the dominant force in Brazilian politics. [11] The opposition (or "outs") consisted of those (particularly in trade, commerce, and some sectors of the middle class) who had not been able to benefit from the government programs. Instead of the strategy of import substitution, the "outs" generally favored a slower, more careful process of industrialization through a return to freer trade and a less regulated domestic economy. They argued that this would not only create more efficient industries, but would also reduce the possibilities for corruption, political deals, and favoritism allegedly enjoyed by the "ins" under the program of import substitution. The "ins," in return, dismissed the charges of the "outs" as reactionary and anti-development, arguing that the only way to become a truly industrialized economy was to continue full-scale the development programs based on subsidized credit for industry, increased spending on public works, and protection of industry from foreign competition (Skidmore, 1967: 55-62).

The clash between the "ins" and the "outs" intensified during Kubitschek's presidency (1956-1960). The government programs to stimulate industry were proving to be increasingly inflationary. This was compounded by a long-term decline in the price of coffee, Brazil's principal export, which began in 1954. This price decline not only hurt the balance of payments, but threatened to boost inflation still higher since the foreign exchange earned from coffee had been counted on as an essential source of financing for the development program. This produced a dilemma: How could one continue to pursue simultaneously a policy of development (defined as subsidies for industry), stabilization (defined as a containment of the rate of inflation), and balance of payments equilibrium (defined as an increase in export earnings)?

Regardless of Kubitschek's inaugural promise (echoed by subsequent presidents) for "development with stability," [12] it soon became clear that the need to maintain the political support of the "ins" meant that development (i.e., maintenance of the subsidies of the import substitution system) would take precedence. Stabilization efforts were repeatedly tried, but the measures involved (such as credit restrictions, import liberalization, and reductions in public spending) inevitably threatened the payoffs of the "ins," who created strong political pressures to have the stabilization programs eliminated. [13] Export promotion took third place in this implicit goal hierarchy. Given the genuine fears about increased inflation, any new program (such as exporting) that did not directly affect the payoffs of the "ins" could be pursued *only* to the extent that it was not seen as inflationary. This in effect eliminated the possibility of any major new incentives to exports (such as massive exchange develuations, extensive tax rebates, or large-scale subsidized credit), inevitably limiting the export program to marginal changes at best. [14]

This does not mean that dissenting voices were not heard. Within the bureaucracy, a minority of middle-level técnicos and even some of the ministers of finance appointed during the democratic period expressed a strong interest in stabilization and exporting, with particular emphasis upon a major reform in the exchange rate system. [15] But regardless of the heated discussions within the executive and the preferences of some of the ministers of finance for major reforms, the final policy outcomes clearly demonstrated the inflexibility of the hierarchy of goals. As a result, the policy became one of buying time and putting off decisions, rather than one of fundamental reforms. Policy statements regularly made it clear that although exporting was seen as an important objective, any major effort (which would inevitably have some inflationary impact) had to be put off until stabilization efforts were successful.[16] Stabilization, for its part, was also postponed, however, since it could not be reconciled with the demands of the "ins" for development subsidies. Given the inflexibility of this import substitution model, the democratic regimes found themselves forced to face an increasingly precarious economic situation with no effective stabilization or export policy. As a result, inflation increased almost unchecked, while possibilities for reducing the balance of payments problems rested essentially on the futile hope of better coffee prices and a further reduction of imports through increasingly high-cost import substitution.

MILITARY REGIMES

The military coup marked the end of the old pattern of domination by the "ins" of the setting of policy priorities. The process of increased military control was uneven, alternating periods of increased authoritarianism with periods of relaxation, but the overall effect was that of a "ratchet" in which all channels of formal civilian control were gradually rendered ineffective. Political rights of many citizens, including the three previous presidents, were cancelled for ten years. In addition, the President of Brazil was now elected indirectly, and was in fact chosen by the military. The supreme court was packed, traditional parties were dissolved and reorganized into two official parties, and Congress was closed, and then reopened in a severely weakened position.

The new power of the military, although dominant, was not monolithic, however. Like the coalition of "ins," it included factions representing different interests and ideologies, complicated by additional cross-pressures such as interservice rivalries, rank, and personal struggles for power. At the risk of some distortion, one can view the differing military factions in terms of two polar opposites. At one extreme was the group composed primarily of the minority of generals with an intellectual and internationalist orientation which had become closely associated with the Brazilian "Superior War College" (Escola Superior de Guerra—ESG). Over the years, the military-civilian staff of the ESG had developed a comprehensive ideology regarding the needs of Brazilian development, which stressed an internationalist outlook and an emphasis on technical efficiency. More specifically, this approach favored a generally free enterprise economy, with a reduction of controls and regulations, encouragement of efficient foreign investment, and management by a government stressing "technical" and "realistic" (rather than "political" and "irrational") solutions to problems. At the other extreme was a less coherent faction generally referred to as the *linha dura*, or hard line. Although they were more difficult to characterize, they generally were less internationalist in scope, less favorable toward uncontrolled free enterprise, and particularly opposed to the ESG philosophy which, in the interests of technical efficiency, advocated the opening of the Brazilian economy to large amounts of foreign investment and international competition (Stepan, 1971: 231, 255).[17]

For the first two years of military rule, the ESG faction dominated policy-making, at least partly because they had the only detailed, comprehensive plan for the development of Brazil. In essence, this new plan shifted the policy priorities from those of the "ins" to those of the "outs," with stabilization now taking precedence over development via import substitution. With the firm support from President Castello Branco, Minister of Planning Roberto Campos carried out a severe stabilization program, sharply reducing public credit and government spending in order to control inflation, carrying out exchange devaluations and liberalization of import restrictions (thus exposing industry to increased outside competition) in an effort to rationalize domestic price levels, and opening Brazil to large doses of foreign investment to help development and the balance of payments.[18]

This program did help to make prices more internally consistent and snapped the inflationary spiral, but its drastic nature also increased alarmingly the number of bankruptcies, restricted the incentives for economic growth, and created a great deal of public dissatisfaction. In addition, its reliance on foreign competition (through import liberalization) and foreign investment proved distasteful to many in the military who were more nationalistic than the ESG faction. Responding to this dissatisfaction, the hard line helped to insure that the next military president would not be from the ESG. After a process of internal negotiation within the military,

Arturo Costa e Silva became the President of Brazil in 1967, promising a "humanization of the revolution" which was generally interpreted to mean a reduction of the tight controls used to restrict inflation, and an increased voice for the general public in the government.

Although it is doubtful that "humanization" improved political communication, it is clear that the single-minded commitment to stabilization was relaxed. The new economic "czar," Minister of Finance Delfim Netto, followed a more pragmatic policy, still taking care to ensure that inflation did not again get out of control, but simultaneously establishing considerable incentives for industrial growth, especially encouraging growth through the exporting of manufactures. In particular, these new export incentives included a new subsidized credit program, a new "mini-devaluation" program to adjust the exchange rate more frequently to domestic price levels, and, most important, a whole range of highly lucrative tax subsidies which greatly increased the potential profits in exporting. [19] This was in sharp contrast to Roberto Campos, who, in the interests of price rationalization, had created some tax rebates which had helped exports, but had rejected as inflationary the types of subsidies established by Delfim Netto. Delfim Netto, however, could success-fully pursue his less restrictive program since the Campos policy had already reversed the inflationary trend. Although under Delfim Netto all new programs were still carefully examined for their inflationary impact, he saw his margin for maneuver as far less limited. In effect, this meant that Delfim Netto no longer saw himself faced with the dilemma of choosing between the three policy goals of development, stabilization, and exporting, but instead pursued all three simul-taneously. [20] As a result, it was relatively easy to devise export incentives, many of which had already been proposed in the Campos period (and even during the democratic period), but had not been adopted due to the pressure they would have added to a mounting inflation.

This comparison of the military and democratic regimes suggests that the strength of the military regime was not in its creative ability to establish bold new export subsidies. Although a few of the incentives established by Delfim Netto were somewhat unusual, most were of the type commonly used in other nations, and even the most unusual were essentially refinements of programs already in use in other nations or programs that had been previously proposed in the democratic period. [21] More important was the ability of the military to implement, over increasing public objection, a stabilization of the economy which in effect made it possible to establish subsequently a far-reaching program of export incentives. At least temporarily, the military (or at least the ESG faction) was able to ignore the opposition of the traditionally dominant group of "ins" in carrying out its stabilization program. Although this program eventually forced a crisis within the military, leading to the removal of the ESG faction from control, its short tenure of two years was enough time to lay the groundwork for a reduction of the rate of inflation and a rationalization of the price structure. This enabled the military to reemphasize development once again, but without rekindling the previous inflation.

In retrospect, it once again appears that accidental circumstances had an important impact on the success of the economic policy. To formulate the preconditions for exporting (and growth in general), it was important to begin with a program of stabilization, which made Campos' single-mindedness in pursuit of this goal a valuable asset. However, this needed to be combined eventually with a more development-oriented program to avoid stagnation, a role well-suited to Delfim Netto and his more pragmatic and eclectic approach.

MOBILIZING THE BUSINESS SECTOR

Regardless of a government's skill in formulating and implementing policy, ultimate success of any economic program in a private enterprise economy depended upon the cooperation of the private sector. Any efforts to mobilize the business community in Brazil, however, needed to come to terms with the reality that formal government-business communications were not particularly well developed. Although there was an elaborately institutionalized interest group system, [22] relations between government and business were permeated by a mutual lack of trust, with businessmen feeling that they had little impact on policies that were decided from the top by insensitive government técnicos and government administrators suspicious that suggestions from individuals or groups in the business community reflected personal rather than national interests. [23]

These mutual suspicions were in part well-founded. The business community, for example, was itself divided by mutual distrust, due to the conflicting interests of different economic sectors and regions, and the competitive pressures among those in similar fields. As a result, interest groups, though numerous, were weak and unable to agree on common policies. Moreover, this lack of trust meant that those who attempted to move into positions of group leadership were often viewed (sometimes with reason) as interested not in the general welfare of the group, but in using the group to further the particularistic interests of their own firm or clique. The resulting lack of group cohesiveness on common policies was reinforced by the narrow perspective of most businessmen, who found it difficult to deal with the broad issues of economic policy since they were not able to see how these related to the problems of their own specific firms (Leff, 1968).

But although businessmen were not particularly concerned about abstract economic policy, they were notably interested in the day-to-day treatment they received from government administrators responsible for interpreting regulations, expediting requests, granting subsidies, and passing on "inside information" vital to the survival or at least the competitive position of the firm. Consequently, a business executive's major attempts to contact the government were at this highly informal, particularistic level, with the main efforts directed not toward making general policy, but toward making individual contacts for personal advantage. Interest groups, then, became an important instrument not for formulating policy, but as one way (along with use of family and friends) for expanding one's contacts through attendance at the interest group luncheons and other informal meetings held with government administrators concerned with the regulation of business. For government to improve business confidence, then, attention had to be paid not only to the formal level of interaction, but, most important, to this particularistic, informal level as well.[24]

DEMOCRATIC REGIMES

During the democratic regimes, contacts between government and business were weak at the formal level and personnel were distrustful of each other at the informal level, at least in the field of export policy. Operating within the implicit parameters established by the need to avoid additional inflationary pressures, export policies were essentially set by government técnicos who formulated programs without extensive outside consultation and then announced them to a surprised (and often confused) public. [25] Efforts were made to attempt to improve formal government-business contacts in policy-making by placing representatives of business on the various coordinating committees that were periodically established to improve the organization of export policy. [26] But business members made up only a small minority of these committees, which remained dominated by government técnicos. More important, these committees were only advisory, quickly falling into disuse when it became clear that they were largely peripheral to the decision-making process. [27] Other formal efforts by business groups to influence policy-making also met with little success, as group position papers, pronouncements, and communications (such as telegrams) were generally ignored by government policy makers. [28]

Informal relationships are harder to document, but it appears that this was also a frustrating experience for the would-be exporter. Although there were reports of some groups or cliques using particularistic contacts to their advantage, [29] in general the day-to-day contacts between government representatives and business executives were not very rewarding. Not only did the complex rules governing export policy require exporters to visit a wide variety of offices (with conflicting jurisdictions and policies), but often in these offices the exporter was greeted with suspicion. Exporters often found themselves scrutinized as potential smugglers, subject to intense inspection, a holdover from previous days when some exporters of primary products had engaged in a variety of dishonest practices (such as under-invoicing) in order to send capital abroad illegally. So carefully did exporters have to follow the technicalities of the complex and confusing legislation and so unpredictable were the interpretations of these technicalities by the government officials, that many potential exporters gave it up as not worth the effort. [30]

MILITARY REGIMES

The military regime marked a significant change in efforts to mobilize the business sector, utilizing changes in the economic rewards as well as in business-government communications. In terms of economics, the most obvious change was the lucrative export incentives; but, due to a widespread ignorance of these programs and general reluctance to leave the tranquility of the domestic market for the rigors and uncertainties of world trade, additional measures were needed to encourage businessmen to cross the threshold into the world market. As a result, the military structured some of the economic programs so that it was not only economically advantageous to export, but it became a necessity in order to maintain the competitive edge of the firm.

The first example of this "carrot and stick" policy occurred in 1965. This was the height of the Campos stabilization policy, in which domestic demand had been severely restricted as a method of reducing inflation. Faced with reduced domestic demand for their products, many industries were in essence forced to undergo the initial costs and risks of exporting to avoid a serious drop in production and profits. With Campos' encouragement (and the new export incentives), many firms did break into the world market in 1965 and, once start-up costs were absorbed and it became apparent that the incentives helped assure a profit abroad, a large majority continued exporting even with the resurgence of domestic demand. [31]

A second example of this method of encouraging exports occurred in 1967, with the creation of a new tax incentive which allowed exporters to receive rebates not only for taxes paid on exported products, but also for taxes paid on a specified portion of goods sold in the *domestic* market as well. In effect, this gave the firm that exported a competitive edge in the domestic market, since competing firms that did not export did not benefit from this tax rebate on domestic sales. A similar proposal had been suggested in 1963, but it had been rejected on the grounds that it gave an unfair competitive advantage domestically to exporting firms. In 1967, however, this competitive advantage was no longer seen as unfair, but as a way to force *all* firms in a sector to export once one of the firms had begun exporting (Interviews, September 19, 1969; October 13, 1969).

Establishing such rewards and sanctions, however, did not end the efforts of the government to mobilize the business sector. A careful program of consultations with businessmen was begun in an effort to win their confidence for this new program. This new effort began at the formal level with the government's inclusion of three businessmen with the right of vote on the new (1966) Foreign Trade Commission (CONCEX) which was supposed to formulate and coordinate export policy. This prompted a prominent business executive to comment on how this could change the traditional pattern of policy-making:

> Direct business representation on the new CONCEX will mean that business will, for the first time, participate in the debates concerned with the working out of the basic policy directions, rather than just being consulted after all basic problems are resolved within the government. [32]

This effort to improve formal contacts was short-lived, however, with the pattern reverting back to one that resembled the democratic period. Not only did the CONCEX lose its central role in policy-making, but it also became increasingly clear that the government members who dominated the CONCEX felt that the three representatives of the business sector, who had voting rights as full members, had, in the words of one técnico, a privilege that "was not proportional to their contribution" (Interview, September 26, 1969). Consequently, the CONCEX was reorganized in 1968, placing the businessmen on an advisory commission rather than giving them a direct vote and full membership. This advisory council was in fact powerless, and had ceased to meet within a year (Interview, July 17, 1969). Government suspicions of the policy-making competence of the business community were also demonstrated by its lack of interest in formal proposals made by business organizations. In 1968, for example, a major conference of businessmen was held on the problem of foreign trade, focusing upon the problem of exports. At the close, it had drafted over one hundred recommendations, which were presented to the government and to the CONCEX. Rather than use these as the immediate basis for policy-making, however, the CONCEX considered the resolutions briefly, then proposed that they be studied later, in order to consider and approve "those that would really improve the dynamism of foreign trade" (*Journal do Brasil,* August 23, 1969).

This general rejection by government of increased formal contact in policy-making for business continued to be based on the suspicion also prevalent in the democratic regimes that businessmen were not always interested in the broad national interest. This perception was certainly in part accurate, as the particularistic conflicts within the business sector that characterized the democratic period remained during the military regimes. Efforts by the private sector to coordinate existing business groups interested in exporting in order to present broader proposals to the government were rarely successful, with businessmen from one group or clique inevitably criticizing those of another as attempting to control the cooperative organization for their own interests. [33] Instead of cooperation, in fact, the reverse occurred, with individuals in existing organizations splitting off to found new ones that they could control. This led to the creation of a number of small, competing groups with virtually identical functions. [34]

Given this tendency toward particularistic fragmentation, it is not surprising that the government efforts at formal, coordinated consultation with business groups were abandoned. However, this did not mean that businessmen were ignored. Particularly after Delfim Netto became the Minister of Finance in 1967, a new broad-scale program of consultations with a wide variety of businessmen was initiated, utilizing the informal, particularistic approach. [35] General policy was still formulated from within the bureaucracy, but the government took pains to insure that business groups felt consulted, particularly with regard to small details and the implementation of programs.

This technique was particularly evident in the important area of tax policy. The normal approach used by Delfim Netto was to draft legislation for export tax rebates within the government, and then informally circulate the drafts to a variety of different business groups for their comments and suggestions on minor points. This gave the businessmen the feeling that they were involved in policy-making that affected them, while at the same time preserving the basic government draft virtually intact. [36] This process did not always operate smoothly, [37] but it was a vast improvement over the relationship in the democratic period. Even in such a sensitive area as exchange policy (in which deliberations are usually secret to avoid windfall profits from advanced knowledge of exchange devaluations), Delfim Netto made it a point to contact major businessmen hours before public announcement of a major new policy (the 1968 "mini-devaluation" program) in order to explain the new program fully and once again give business leaders the feeling of having been personally consulted. [38]

Contrasting the democratic and military regimes, it seems clear that the military was far more effective in mobilizing the business sector. Not only was it able to construct a more efficient program of economic rewards and sanctions to encourage businessmen to cross the exporting threshold, but it also was more successful in increasing business confidence through informal, if not formal, government-business contacts. Although it is difficult to determine the impact of the government policy to consult with business, it does seem clear that the economic programs, by themselves, were not enough to guarantee business cooperation. In fact, the potential advantages of the new incentives for exports had to be sold, at least initially, to businessmen who were generally satisfied with supplying only the protected domestic market. Although this selling process was partly accomplished by the use of the economic rewards and sanctions, it was facilitated by the process of informal consultations.

CONCLUSIONS

How does one explain the success of the military in promoting exports of manufactures? Had the military, as it claimed, revolutionized policy-making by insulating its key decision makers from partisan politics, enabling them to formulate and implement policy on purely technical grounds? The evidence is mixed. In some respects, decision makers were more removed from the pressures of politics under the military regimes, which partly explains the ability of the military to create and implement a consistent export promotion strategy. More interesting, however, are the important qualifications of this general conclusion, which emphasize the continuities between the democratic and military regimes.

PROGRAM ORGANIZATION

By any standard, the export programs were far better organized under the military regimes. than they had been in the democratic period. But this improvement was not a result of the institution of a rational decision-making system, and only partly the result of the use of technical rather than political criteria for the recruitment and retention of key decision makers. The military attempted to rationalize decision-making, but these efforts were not effective. The reduction of the authority of the Congress and the states merely accentuated a tendency already prevalent in the democratic period for concentrating export policy decision-making in the executive branch, which itself was marked by divisive struggles by different agencies to protect or enlarge their spheres of influence. Formal efforts to eliminate these bureaucratic power struggles in the field of export policy (through the creation of the CONCEX) proved no more successful than had the previous efforts of the democratic regimes to establish "coordinating" agencies for foreign trade. As a result, any hope for effective coordination of export programs depended, as it had in the democratic regimes, upon the ability of one individual (usually the Minister of Finance) to use both personal skills and the strength of the office to coordinate the program on an informal, personal basis.

To a certain extent, the improved organization of exports in the military period can be traced to the technically oriented recruitment and retention criteria used to evaluate these key coordination ministers. Although personal contacts played a role in recruitment, technical competence clearly was the crucial factor, insuring that the individual in question understood the fine points of economic policy. Most important, the Minister of Finance (or Planning) did not serve as the "scapegoat" to be sacrificed if economic policy proved unpopular, as had occurred in the democratic regimes. This significantly reduced the turnover of these key ministers during the military regimes, which gave them the time to establish personal dominance over economic policy.

But technical competence, a powerful office, and strong support did not fully explain the ability of Roberto Campos and Delfim Netto to be effective in coordination of export policy. Equally important was their political skill, particularly in the bureaucratic arena. This suggests that technical criteria alone were inadequate in order to recruit effective ministers. Fortunately for the military, both Campos and Delfim Netto possessed the political acumen necessary, but this was apparently accidental rather than the result of the recruitment criteria used. In addition, it is also important to point out that although both Campos and Delfim were técnicos, they had very different views as to the priorities needed for economic policy. Once again, it appears to have been a fortunate accident and not the result of this recruitment criteria that Campos and Delfim Netto, whose contrasting approaches matched the needs at their particular times, were recruited as the economic "czars."

IMPLEMENTATION

It is in the field of implementation of policies that the military most clearly changed the existing political realities by insulating key decision makers, at least temporarily, from the political coalition of "ins" which had dominated the democratic period and had success-fully blocked the painful economic reorganization and stabilization necessary for a successful export program. However, the elimination of the previously dominant "ins" did not create a complete political vacuum. To a certain extent, policy makers had to please the new dominant group, the factionalized military. Equally important, successful implementation also had to face some of the bureaucratic battles that spilled over from the area of policy formulation to the area of implementation.

MOBILIZATION

The political skill of key decision makers was also crucial in mobilizing the private sector to export. In both the democratic and the military regimes, attempts were made to improve the confidence of the business sector by giving them a feeling of participation in policy-making. Efforts at the formal level were a total failure in both periods, characterized by a lack of communication and trust. During the military regimes, however, communications were vastly improved at a more particularistic, informal level. Although policies continued to be formulated by the government, elaborate efforts were made to use the informal clientele network to give businessmen the feeling of being consulted, often by permitting them to make minor changes in draft legislation. This process of increasing business confidence through informal consultations was clearly important in helping to mobilize the business sector, particularly when used in conjunction with the available economic rewards and sanctions that had been developed. Once again, this demonstrates the importance of political skills in the success of the export program.

The general conclusion that emerges from this study is the crucial and multifaceted role of the top técnico decision makers in the military regimes. In some ways, the military was able to insulate these decision makers from public pressures by assuring them a secure position and the power to implement decisions regardless of public support. But this did not mean that these técnicos were apolitical. On the contrary, success depended not only on technical expertise, but also on the ability to use persuasion, manipulation, and other techniques of bureaucratic infighting and clientele politics. In short, although the military did bring some important political changes, in many ways the success of the export program still depended on the abilities of new actors to play "old" politics.

Does the Brazilian experience hold any lessons for other nations seeking to break into the export market? More specifically, must one inevitably draw the uncomfortable conclusion that the requirements for success in exporting are so difficult that an authoritarian regime is essential? A rapid review of other recent success stories (e.g., Indonesia, South Korea, and Taiwan) may lend support to this argument, but a detailed analysis of the Brazilian case suggests that even with an authoritarian regime, success is not certain and may depend on a few fortunate accidents. Moreover, depending on the problems to be faced, it is possible that a less coercive system might also be effective. Although generalizations drawn from a single case must be considered highly speculative, the Brazilian experience does seem to suggest a variety of alternative possibilities.

If the main problem that a nation faces is simply the creation of export incentives and the mobilization of the business sector, the increased coercive capacity of an authoritarian regime is probably not important. Regardless of the type of regime, a wily leader could probably create the type of incentives needed to make exporting profitable, and could engage in the types of political persuasion and manipulation needed to encourage the business sector to cooperate.

If, however, the main problem is one of restructuring the economy as a prerequisite for the creation of effective export incentives, the Brazilian case suggests that a major shift of political power may be required to overcome resistance to the economic changes. Theoretically, this change could be carried out in a democratic system if a group supporting policies conducive to export promotion (such as, perhaps, the "outs" in Brazil) could wrest complete control away from those who felt threatened by the types of economic changes that were needed. But if the group opposed to major economic changes is well entrenched in power, and if it faces little challenge (due to a general lack of interest in export promotion), it appears unlikely that major changes will occur without a more authoritarian solution.

If coordination of programs is the central problem, it is not clear which type of regime will be most effective. In general, it appears that success depends upon the extent to which the person responsible for coordinating export programs has both the necessary skills and the long-term political support needed to coordinate the various competing bureaucratic agencies involved in the formulation of export policy. In the Brazilian case, the military was required to provide adequate support for the técnico in charge of coordinating the export program. But, given different circumstances (a less chaotic bureaucracy, or a system which did not make a scapegoat of the person in charge of economic policy), it is possible that even in a more open system characterized by partisan politics a skillful coordinator could survive.

In sum, this study of the Brazilian case may help to deflate some of the exaggerated claims of the proponents of the military-authoritarian approach to policy-making, but it does not provide precise guidelines for the nation contemplating the uncertainties of export promotion. But although exact guidelines are not available, the Brazilian case does give an insight into the types of problems, both political and economic, that a nation is likely to face, and outlines some of the political tactics that may be required to achieve success. Most important, it emphasizes the fact that export promotion of manufactures is not an easy goal to achieve, requiring a single-minded national commitment regardless of the type of political system used or the kinds of political tactics employed.

NOTES

1. A cautious and generally discouraging view of the extent to which preferences can be expected to improve market access to industrialized nations is given by Cooper (1971). The problems of tariff reductions among developing nations as evidenced in the increasing difficulties faced by the Latin American Free Trade Area (LAFTA) and the Central American Common Market (CACM) are clearly described in Wionczek (1970).

2. A clear and comprehensive explanation of the impacts of import substitution policies in Latin America is given by Baer (1972).

3. GDP and industrial growth are calculated from data collected by the Fundàçao Getulio Vargas, presented in *Contas Nacionais do Brasil,* and selected issues of *Conjuntura Economica.* Contribution of industry to GDP (1947–constant prices) from Baer (1965: 71). The most useful studies for the period of import substitution include Baer (1965), ECLA (1964a, 1964b), Gordon and Grommers (1962), and a more pessimistic view of the costs and benefits of the Brazilian import substitution program by Morley and Smith (1971).

4. Two separate analyses by Donald Huddle, "Postwar Brazilian Industrialization; Growth Patterns, Inflation, and Sources of Stagnation," in Baklanoff (1969: 86-108), and Bergsman (1970), although differing in details, support the idea that the Brazilian industrial sector was already well-advanced by the mid-1950s.

5. Approximately every two years during this period, new efforts were made by the government to encourage exports, with the President or the Finance Minister initiating the campaign. But despite the rhetoric, little was accomplished (see appendix).

6. This continued growth in excess of thirty percent is even more striking, when it is realized that the twelve percent rate in the previous period is somewhat exaggerated since it started from a very small base (see appendix).

7. A similar theme is also presented by Daland (1967) and ECLA (1964a).

8. This conclusion was reached by the Brazilian Conselho Nacional de Economia (1958). The standard procedure for exporting clearly acted as a powerful disincentive. First, exporters had to go to a government trade office (CACEX) for an export license, which required that they verify that they had accurately quoted the price, weight, and specifications of the product. They then made the rounds of various state, federal, and municipal offices to pay at least five different taxes. After additional stops for various seals, stamps, and approvals, the product had to clear customs, which required the inspection process (previously done by the CACEX) to be carried out again by a separate agency associated with the Ministry of Finance.

9. Coordination committees created by the democratic regimes included the "Working Group to Increase Exports" (FOEXP), created by President Kubitschek in 1957 and resurrected in 1958; the "Commission to Increase Exports" created by President Quadros in 1961; the "Executive Group to Increase Exports" (GEFEX), created by President Goulart in 1961; the "Interministerial Working Group to Study and Propose Measures for the Increase of Brazilian Trade with New Markets," created by Goulart in 1963; and the "Coordinating Council of Foreign Trade," created by Goulart in 1963. All of these were "mixed commissions," including representatives from private enterprise as well as a majority of government officials. Each had as its objective the coordination of foreign trade, with particular emphasis on exports.

10. There were three ministers of finance under President Kubitschek, one under Quadros, and four under Goulart (or five, if one individual is included who briefly exercised the duties of the ministry although he was not officially appointed minister).

11. In addition to Skidmore (1967), see also Graham (1968), for an analysis of the politics of this period.

12. For Kubitschek's platform, see Presidencia da Republica (1959-1960: 13). For Quadros, see Observador Economico e Financeiro (October 1960: 11).

13. On this point, see Skidmore (1967: 158-162, 174-182, 193-200, 234-272) and Kahil (1973). It is interesting to note that apparently even Quadros, who was elected by the "outs," could not establish an effective stabilization program despite his strong inclinations in this direction. The reasons for this remain to be fully documented, but it appears that part of the problem was that the "ins" still controlled the Congress as well as the bureaucracy.

14. Exporting was considered inflationary for two reasons. First, assuming inelastic supply, it was thought that widespread exporting of a product would increase its domestic price. Second, it was felt that the increased earnings that exporters would receive under any export promotion program would add to the excess demand already causing inflationary pressures.

15. The advisory National Economic Council began emphasizing the need for export expansion as early as 1951. (See its annual report, entitled Exposição Geral da Situação Economica do Brasil, particularly for the years 1951-1963.) These reports were widely known in various government circles (Correio da Manha, May 13, 1956). In addition, it was

privately acknowledged by the Minister of Finance that, within the government, there was a major and continuing debate over the need for major reforms (Associação Comercial, 1956: 44-45) leading one observer to comment that there appeared to be "two teams of técnicos in the government, one supporting major reforms, and one opposed" (Diario de São Paulo, October 11, 1958).

16. For example, two ministers of finance in the Kubitschek era who sharply disagreed with each other over the theoretical need for stabilization sounded remarkably alike when faced with the "real world" situation which demanded a "reforminha" strategy—in both cases, they said that it was impossible to carry out a major exchange reform before containing the inflation (Interview with Jose Maria Alkmin, Correio da Manha, May 13, 1956, and the policy statement of Lucas Lopes, Correio da Manha, October 5, 1958).

17. Much of the information on the military is from Stepan's insightful work.

18. Roberto Campos, who was closely identified with the Superior War College (ESG), had been an advocate of strong stabilization policies even during the democratic regimes, and had served as the director of the "Committee to Increase Exports" (FOEXP) under stabilization-minded Minister of Finance Lucas Lopes during the major stabilization effort of the Kubitschek regime (Correio da Manha, October 5, 1958). The Minister of Finance under the military regime, Octavio Bulhoes, had also been a critic of the democratic regimes' economic policies, arguing that a more fundamental exchange reform was needed (Estado de São Paulo, May 22, 1956).

19. Assuming that all tax exemptions were shifted to the consumer, Tyler (1969) estimated that these exemptions could reduce the price of an exported product by over forty percent.

20. Given current world inflation and shortages along with new internal consumption pressures, it is possible that it will be increasingly difficult for Brazil to pursue all three objectives simultaneously. There are already signs that the actual inflation in Brazil may be higher than the government's reported figures. Also, it should be pointed out that one reason that the three goals could be pursued in the past was that wage levels were kept very low.

21. For example, the "mini-devaluation" or "crawling peg" exchange system was a variant of systems that had been previously tried in Chile and Colombia, and which had been suggested to Brazil by the IMF.

22. An elaborate government-sponsored interest-group system has flourished since its initiation in the 1930s when then-President Vargas experimented with the idea of turning Brazil into a "corporate" state. For a description of this system, see Bureau of Labor Statistics (n.d.).

23. According to a number of authors (Hirschman, 1963; Weiner, 1962; Riggs, 1964), this lack of linkages and the presence of mutual suspicion outside one's own clique may be a characteristic of developing nations generally.

24. Concern with more general principles of economic policy was generally confined, in the private sector, to a few business leaders and the técnicos working in the private interest groups.

25. Virtually all the policy changes in the field of export policy during the democratic period came as a surprise to most businessmen. To a certain extent, this can be explained by the fact that most changes concerned exchange policy, which had to be kept secret in order to prevent windfall profits arising from the advanced notice of exchange devaluations. But the general confusion created by these policy changes, even after they were announced, suggests a lack of effective communication between the government and the private sector in this field.

26. The standard pattern was to include three representatives from business on the coordinating committees: one representing industry, one representing commerce, and one representing agriculture.

27. For example, during the Kubitschek period, the "Working Group to Increase Exports" (FOEXP), which included representatives of business, was supposed to have as one of its responsibilities the discussion of exchange policy. In fact, new exchange policies, which formed the core of the export program, were not discussed in the FOEXP, but were discussed secretly elsewhere within the government. When the new exchange policies were announced, they were as much a surprise to the business representatives on the FOEXP as they were to the general public (Jornal do Brasil, October 7, 1958).

28. The best example of this was the textile industry, which, for a variety of reasons, began to accumulate large inventories that could not be sold domestically. Although this was a severe crisis, causing the unemployment of as many as 100,000 workers, and although the textile association attempted every formal lobbying technique (telegrams, position statements, formal delegations to the President or the Minister of Finance), their requests for special treatment to ease the crisis were initially ignored by the government. Special treatment was finally granted, but was quickly withdrawn shortly thereafter, much to the consternation of the textile industry, which had not been informed or consulted. (This episode is covered in Observador Economico e Financeiro, beginning with the December 1956 issue, and continuing through the December 1958 issue.) A second example that demonstrated the difficulties of influencing the government was the observation by one of the major interest groups that it had taken "years of work" to get the government to accept a relatively minor addition to existing export policy (Associação Comercial, 1958: 41-43).

29. For example, the Estado de São Paulo (May 20, 1956) pointed out that one of the programs proposed by Kubitschek would particularly benefit a highly restricted number of steel producers who were located primarily in Kubitschek's home state.

30. For example, one request for an export license was refused because the "port of exit" had been listed as "São Paulo Airport," rather than by its formal name, "Congonhas Airport." An additional problem was that some customs inspectors did not know the technical name for a product. When they saw a common article listed by its technical name, they might refuse approval on the grounds that the two were not the same thing. The only redress for the exporter was the time-consuming legal process (Almeida, 1962: 13). This unsympathetic attitude toward exporters was generally prevalent throughout the bureaucracy, only occasionally relieved by the appointment to office of such individuals as Roberto Campos as executive director of the FOEXP in 1958, and Juvenal Gomes as Director of the CACEX in late 1963. Only under Gomes did exporters have a direct input into the decision-making process, as he acted as a spokesman for their ideas in the government discussions of export policy (Correio da Manha, May 22, 1963, and December 15, 1963; and Interview, September 19, 1969).

31. For information on the Campos policy of export promotion to use the "idle capacity" created by the stabilization program, see CIAP Subcommittee on Brazil (1967: 22-24) and FIEMG (1966: 28).

32. José Mindlin, quoted in "CONCEX Vem para Centralizar," in Direcão (July, 1966: 19-20).

33. The mutual suspicion was clearly demonstrated in the failure of three major São Paulo interest groups concerned with exporting (Federation of Industry, Federation of Commerce, and National Association of Exporters) to work together to present a unified program to the government. The one effort at a joint coalition for exporting quickly broke down amid charges that one group was trying to use the coalition for its own purposes (Interview, July 17, 1969). This type of mutual suspicion may also help to explain the relative lack of success of the "Foreign Trade Conferences" that have been organized by individuals in the private sector over the years in order to bring together businessmen from all over Brazil to formulate a coherent trade policy. Some exporters, for example, were suspicious of the motives of the conference organizer, suggesting that his purpose in setting

up the conference was to make himself well-known so that he could increase the size of his export business.

34. A particularly good example of fragmentation can be seen by tracing the origin of currently competing export groups. Initially, the Federation of Industries in São Paulo created a "National Association of Exporters" to deal with the questions of exporting manufactures. The president of this association, however, amid mutual charges of bad faith, separated this organization from the Federation of Industries, with the Federation of Industries responding by increasing the size of its existing foreign trade section, thus creating two organizations. The National Association of exporters then attempted to expand to other cities, but these new organizations soon became independent of the parent organization in São Paulo, and followed their own policies reflecting the particularistic interests of their own directors.

35. In contrast to Delfim Netto, Roberto Campos did not establish close relations with industry, and, in fact, was opposed by many industrialists due to the stabilization program. During this period, industry contacts were made less directly, through the Minister of Industry and Commerce, Daniel Faraco.

36. The minor impact of business can be seen by a comparison of the initial government drafts and the final law. In all cases, the differences were marginal, without changing the essential nature of the government proposal.

37. Even with the special effort, the tax policy did not run perfectly smoothly. Due to government delays in implementing legislation, some incentive programs expired before others could be implemented, leading to confusion and frustration among businessmen who were already depending on the incentives to make their exporting profitable. However, this was corrected quickly by the personal intervention of Delfim Netto, after hearing complaints from businessmen about this problem. This was in sharp contrast to the democratic period, when government inconsistencies went unchanged regardless of pressure from private enterprise.

38. Revista das Classes Produtoras, September, 1968: 79-80. However, Delfim Netto, in giving this advance warning, had made certain that exchange offices were already closed to insure that no windfall profits could be made from the advanced information. Because of such "consultations," some businessmen claimed more influence than in fact they had on export policy. In reality, however, export programs were generally drafted as technical studies within the government.

39. The two years with a significant increase in exports during this period were 1960 and 1961. For the former, virtually all the increase can be explained by a temporary increase in textiles, and the beginning of a modest export trade in ethyl alcohol. For 1961, it can be explained by the initiation of a small export trade in motor vehicles. After 1964, however, major increases begin to occur in virtually every product category. Foreign Trade statistics are presented in CACEX and Ministerio do Fazenda (SEEF), Comercio Exterior, published annually by the Brazilian government.

40. See note 4.

REFERENCES

ALMEIDA, B. S. P. de (1962) A Exportação Brasileira: São Paulo.

Associacão Comercial do Rio de Janeiro e Confederação das Associacoes Comerciais do Brasil (various years) Relatorio.

DE ASVEDO, O. (n.d.) Carta Memsal. Rio de Janiero.

BAER, W. (1965) Industrialization and Economic Development in Brazil. Homewood, Ill.: Richard D. Irwin.

BAER, W. (1972) "Import substitution industrialization in Latin America: experiences and interpretations." Latin American Research Review 7 (Spring): 95-122.

BAKLANOFF, E. N. [ed.] (1969) The Shaping of Modern Brazil. Baton Rouge: Louisiana State University Press.

BALASSA, B. (1965) "Tariff protection in industrial countries: an evaluation." Journal of Political Economy 73 (December): 573-594.

BERGSMAN, J. (1970) Brazil: Industrialization and Trade Policies. New York: Oxford University Press.

Bureau of Labor Statistics (n.d.) Labor Law and Practice in Brazil. Report No. 309.

CACEX and Ministerio da Fazenda (SEEF) (various years) (Estatistica do) Comercio Exterior.

CIAP Subcommittee on Brazil (1967) Domestic Efforts and the Needs for External Financing for the Development of Brazil (Call No. OEA. Ser. H/XIV/CIAP/162 [English]).

CLARK, P. G. (1967) "Brazilian import liberation." Williamstown, Mass.: Center for Developmental Economics, Williams College. (mimeo)

––– and R. WEISSKOFF (1967) "Import demands and import policies in Brazil." USAID, Office of Program Coordination. (mimeo)

Conjuntura Economica (various issues) Rio de Janiero: Fundação Getulio Vargas.

Conselho Nacional de Economia (various years) Exposição Geral Sobre a Situação Economica do Brasil.

COOPER, R. N. (1971) "The Third World tarrif tangle." Foreign Policy 1 (Fall): 35-50.

Correio da Manha (various issues) Rio de Janiero.

DALAND, R. (1967) Brazilian Planning: Development, Politics, and Administration. Chapel Hill: University of North Carolina Press.

Dairio de São Paulo (various issues) São Paulo.

Direção (1966) "Conxex Vem para Centralizar." (July): 19-20.

ECLA (1964a) "Growth and decline of import substituion in Brazil." Economic Bulletin for Latin America 9 (March): 1-59.

––– (1964b) "Fifteen years of economic policy in Brazil." Economic Bulletin for Latin America 9 (December).

Estado de São Paulo (various issues) São Paulo.

FIEMG (1966) Anais da "Semana de Comercio Exterior."

Fundação Getulio Vargas. Contas Nacionais do Brasil, 1937, 1947-1967, Vols. I and II.

GORDON, L. and E. GROMMERS (1962) United States Manufacturing Investment in Brazil: The Impact of Brazilian Government Policies, 1946-1960. Cambridge: Harvard University Press.

GRAHAM, L. S. (1968) Civil Service Reform in Brazil: Principles versus Practice. Austin: University of Texas Press.

HIRSCHMAN, A. O. (1963) Journeys Towards Progress: Studies of Economic Policy-making in Latin America. New York: Twentieth Century Fund.

Jornal do Brasil (1969) August 23.

KAHIL, R. (1973) Inflation and Economic Development in Brazil. New York: Oxford University Press.

KEESING, D. (1967) "Outward-looking policies and economic development." Economic Journal 77 (June): 303-320.

LARY, H. B. (1966) "Trade of the LDC's: manufactures point the way." Columbia Journal of World Business (Summer): 66-82.

LEFF, N. (1968) Economic Policy-making and Development in Brazil, 1947-1964. New York: John Wiley.

LEWIS, W. A. (1955) Theory of Economic Growth. London: George Allen & Unwin.

MORLEY, S. A. and G. W. SMITH (1971) "Import substitution and foreign investment in Brazil." Oxford Economic Papers 23 (March): 120-135.

Observador Economico e Financeiro (various issues) Rio de Janiero.

PEARSON, C. S. (1971) "Evaluating integration among developing countries: LAFTA as a case study." Ph.D. dissertation. Cornell University.

Presidenca da Republica (1959-1960) Sintese Cronologica. Rio de Janiero.

Revista das Classes Produtoras (1968) (September) Rio de Janiero.

RIGGS, F. (1964) Administration in Developing Countries: The Theory of Prismatic Society. Boston: Houghton Mifflin.

SCHMITTER, P. C. (1971) Interest Conflict and Political Change in Brazil. Stanford: Stanford University Press.

SCHNEIDER, R. M. (1971) The Political System of Brazil. New York: Columbia University Press.

SCHYDLOWSKY, D. M. (1967) "From import substitution to export promotion for semi-grown-up industries: a policy proposal." Journal of Development Studies 3 (July): 405-413.

SKIDMORE, T. E. (1967) Politics in Brazil, 1930-1964: An Experiment in Democracy. New York: Oxford University Press.

STEPAN, A. (1971) The Military in Politics: Changing Patterns in Brazil. Princeton: Princeton University Press.

TYLER, W. G. (1969) "Export diversification and the promotion of manufactured exports in Brazil." Rio de Janiero. (mimeo)

United Nations (1964) "Toward a new trade policy for development." Report by the Secretary-General of the United Nations Conference on Trade and Development. New York.

WEINER, M. (1962) The Politics of Scarcity: Public Pressure and Political Response in India. Chicago: University of Chicago Press.

WIONCZEK, M. S. (1970) "The rise and decline of Latin American economic integration." Journal of Common Market Studies 9 (September): 49-66.

NOTE: Additional information was gained through personal interviews with selected members of the Brazilian academic, government, and business elites who were knowledgeable about exporting. To protect their anonimity, these interviews are listed by date only in the text and notes.

APPENDIX

The conclusions of this paper rest on two basic assumptions: (1) The policies of the military regimes were significantly different from those of the democratic regimes regarding export programs. (2) These policy changes were directly related to a significant change in export performance. The purpose of this section is to examine carefully these two assumptions.

TABLE A.1

Total Remuneration to Exporters of Manufactures, 1953-1969
(exchange rate plus tax incentives)

	A. Real, Effective Exchange Rate[a]	B. Tax Incentives[b] (%)	C. Tax Incentives (expressed as index, 1953=100)	D. Total Remuneration (A. x C.) / (100)	E. Total Remuneration (expressed as index, 1953=1.000)
1953	23.36	—	100	23.36	1.000
1954	23.06	—	100	23.06	.987
1955	31.92	—	100	31.92	1.366
1956	28.44	—	100	28.44	1.217
1957	28.25	—	100	28.25	1.209
1958	34.03	—	100	34.03	1.457
1959	34.43	—	100	34.43	1.474
1960	39.70	—	100	39.70	1.699
1961	38.26	—	100	38.26	1.638
1962	37.92	—	100	37.92	1.623
1963	31.04	—	100	31.04	1.329
1964	38.63	1%[c]	101	39.02	1.670
1965	35.79	9%[d]	109	39.01	1.670
1966	32.55	19%[e]	119	38.73	1.658
1967	31.09	28%[f]	128	39.80	1.704
1968	30.10	33%[g]	133	40.03	1.714
1969	30.10[i]	34%[h]	134	40.33	1.726

a. Tyler, 1969: 117.

b. Tyler, 1969: 139.

c. Effect of ICM tax exemption in São Paulo.

d. Effect of above, plus IPI tax exemption, plus Financial Operations tax exemption.

e. Effect of above, in effect for full year.

f. Effect of above, plus expansion of ICM tax incentive to all states, plus income tax exemption.

g. Effect of above, plus special 50% IPI tax rebate on domestic sales.

h. Effect of above, plus increase of special IPI rebate on domestic sales to 100%.

i. Estimate, based on 1968 rate.

TABLE A.2

Ratios of Indexes of Effective Exchange Rates to Indexes of
Domestic Prices by Use Classes 1953-1967

Year	Class 1 Non-Dur. Consumer Goods	Class 2 Durable Consumer Goods	Class 3 Fuels	Class 4 Metallic Intermed. Goods	Class 5 Non-Met. Intermed. Goods[a]
1953	1.000	1.000	1.000	1.000	1.000
1954	1.073	1.028	1.028	.928	.932
1955	1.295	1.037	1.399	1.101	1.152
1956	1.426	1.201	1.248	.927	1.168
1957	1.503	1.274	.997	1.106	1.228
1958	2.182	1.764	1.977	1.690	1.538
1959	1.972	1.578	2.097	1.484	1.370
1960	1.934	1.322	1.899	1.496	1.391
1961	2.099	1.553	1.957	1.644	1.340
1962	1.777	1.371	2.022	1.233	1.083
1963	1.913	1.223	1.990	1.206	.964
1964	2.000	1.403	2.045	1.232	1.136
1965	1.698	1.115	1.906	.992	.897
1966	1.133	.974	1.885	.764	.754
1967	.816	.746	1.573	.735	.716

Year	Class 6 Construc. Material	Class 7 Capital Eq. for Agric.	Class 8 Capital Eq. for Industry	Class 9 Capital Eq. for Transport	Total Imports
1953	1.000	1.000	1.000	1.000	1.000
1954	1.033	1.072	1.060	1.066	1.017
1955	1.536	1.418	1.348	1.388	1.233
1956	1.469	1.296	1.350	1.391	1.231
1957	1.542	.995	1.507	1.563	1.253
1958	1.334	1.824	1.335	1.322	1.600
1959	1.401	1.734	1.303	1.233	1.581
1960	1.388	1.801	1.327	1.267	1.555
1961	1.377	1.858	1.416	1.441	1.659
1962	1.221	1.739	1.268	1.265	1.519
1963	1.128	1.563	1.133	1.124	1.391
1964	1.545	1.924	1.383	1.411	1.546
1965	1.252	1.437	1.093	1.094	1.329
1966	.913	1.187	.901	.870	1.025
1967	.761	1.316	.860	.799	.959

a. Indexes used in computing ratios exclude wheat.

Source: Clark and Weiskoff, 1967: 51; and Clark, 1967: Tables 4A & 4B.

TABLE A.3

Exports of Manufactures from Brazil 1953-1969

Year	Total Manufactured Exports[a] (U.S. $1,000,000)		Annual Increase (%)		Percentage of Total Exports	
1953	8.8		–		.6	
1954	9.4		6.8		.6	
1955	15.2		61.7		1.1	
1956	13.1		−13.8		0.9	
1957	12.7		−3.1		0.9	
1958	12.2		−3.9		1.0	
1959	13.2		8.2		1.0	
1960	21.2		60.6		1.7	
1961	35.6		67.9		2.5	
1962	33.1	(46.0)	−7.0		2.7	(3.8)
1963	37.4	(48.9)	13.0	(6.1)	2.7	(3.5)
1964	69.9	(91.4)	86.9	(87.1)	4.9	(6.4)
1965	109.5	(153.6)	56.6	(68.0)	6.9	(9.6)
1966	96.8	(151.4)	−11.6	(−1.4)	5.6	(8.7)
1967	142.7	(202.5)	47.4	(33.8)	8.6	(12.2)
1968	130.0	(201.0)	−8.9	(−0.7)	6.9	(10.7)
1969	182.2[b]	(283.3)	40.2[b]	(40.9)	7.9[b]	(12.3)

a. Exports defined as all products in Classes V, VI, VII, and VIII of the Brazilian Merchandise Nomenclature. This is a highly restricted definition of the term "Manufactured Product" which has been used until recently by the Brazilian Government. For purposes of comparison, the figures in parentheses represent manufactures using a definition more closely approximating the more inclusive U.S. definition (including parts of Classes II, IV, and IX of the Brazilian Nomenclature).

b. Provisional data.

Source: Calculated from Ministerio de Fazenda, Servico de Estatisticas economica e financeira. Estatistica do Comericio Exterior, 1953-1968. (Figures from CACEX, as recorded by E. F. daSilva, USAID/Brazil.)

EXPORT POLICIES

Comparison of export incentive policies for manufactures in 1956-1963 with those in 1964-1969 (the last years for which complete data are available) reveals striking contrasts. Generally speaking, the policies of the first period were ad hoc, piecemeal, and at times inconsistent, centering almost exclusively on the exchange rate as the implementing tool. Occasional tax and credit incentives developed were ineffective and unused. In the second period, a far more comprehensive program was established, with exchange policy supplemented by extensive tax and credit incentives, along with efforts to reduce administrative "red tape." Policies of this latter period were not completely coordinated or consistent, with some parts appearing to have proceeded by trial and error. But in comparison with the first period, it was a far more comprehensive, coordinated, and consistent attack on the problems involved in exporting manufactures.

The contrast in the two periods can be illustrated more quantitatively by calculating changes in remuneration to exporters of manufactures in the two periods. Although this is difficult to measure given the variety of different factors that must be included, the general conclusion that one draws from this exercise is that exporters in the 1964-1969 period benefited not only from higher remuneration, but also from more stable remuneration, which was necessary for long-term planning of an export program.

This can be illustrated through an analysis of changes in the exchange rate and tax incentives as a rough measure of effective remuneration. Tyler (1969: 129-138) has calculated the effective exchange rate for each year by dividing the cruzeiro value of exports of manufactures by the dollar receipts for these exports. To adjust for inflation, this calculation was then adjusted by a deflator calculated from the Brazilian wholesale industrial price index.

$$\frac{\text{earnings in cruzeiros}}{\text{earnings in dollars}} \cdot \frac{1}{\text{wholesale industrial price index}} = \text{"real" effective exchange rate}$$

Since there is no base, this calculation does not give the remuneration to exporters in absolute terms. However, it is useful for estimating in a crude way the changes in remuneration from year to year.

A more complete picture of total remuneration to exporters, however, also requires the inclusion of subsidies, the most important of which are tax rebates. To gain some measure of the effects of tax changes, Tyler (1969: 129-138) has calculated the total possible tax incentives for each year (rebates on sales and income taxes available to exporters). This was then converted to an index number, with the years 1956-1963 equal to 100 (since no tax incentives were available then). Tyler's calculations were then combined into a general index of remuneration, using the following formula:

$$\frac{\text{"real" effective exchange rate} \cdot \text{index of taxes}}{100} = \text{estimate of total remuneration to exporters}$$

It should be stressed that this is a very crude calculation, since it assumes that exemptions applied to direct taxes and indirect taxes will have equivalent effects, and also assumes that changes in the exchange rate are similar to changes in tax incentives (when in fact the former affects earnings while the latter affects costs).

The results are summarized in Table A.1. Examining "total remuneration" for the 1956-1963 period clearly shows that remuneration was less than in the 1964-1968 period. Interestingly enough, however, this improved remuneration in the 1964-1968 period is not due to the exchange rate, which is lower than during most of the previous period, but due to the new tax incentives, which managed to offset the gradual decline in the exchange rate that occurred in the 1964-1968 period. The authorities in the military regime, then, were able to use a combination of tools (tax and exchange policy) to guarantee a high and stable remuneration.

This analysis is incomplete, since it does not consider other incentives, such as credit and bureaucratic reform. These are difficult to include in any index of remunerations. However, the evidence suggests that credit programs, though small, are increasing under the military regime. Concerning "red tape," improvement can be roughly measured not only by the reduction of agencies directly involved but also by an exporter's estimate that the time needed to arrange an export shipment has been cut from days (or weeks) in the 1950s to about forty-eight hours in 1969.

In addition to the issue of export incentives, an equally important problem facing the exporter is the series of price distortions in the economy caused largely by the structure of trade protection used to establish the import substitution program. Although protection was necessary to establish new industries, it can inhibit the possibilities for exporting in several ways. First, a protection policy makes it profitable to invest in import-substitution industries, which may shift resources away from existing industries that are already exporting or planning to export. Second, protection often reduces the stimulus to competition in affected industries, increasing inefficiencies and costs which price the firm out of the world market. Finally, even efficiently run industries may find it difficult to export if they must rely on high-cost protected industries for their inputs.

The relative change in protection over time has been measured by Paul Clark (1967; Clark and Weisskoff, 1967), whose analysis includes the impact of all major forms of import protection, including tariffs, deposits and surcharges, premiums, quantitative restrictions, and the import exchange rate. As Table A.2 indicates, his calculations show a steady, if irregular, increase in protection levels until 1961, followed by a dip and a second peak in 1964. Only after 1964 did the protection levels begin a steady decline, finally in 1967 reaching protection levels below those of 1953. This analysis reinforces the conclusions reached in the analysis of export incentives, demonstrating that the military regime was consistent in implementing programs which were potentially useful to exporters.

EXPORT PERFORMANCE

These policy changes had a significant impact on export performance. In the 1956-1963 period, exports of manufactures grew only slowly and irregularly, at about twelve percent per year. Moreover, this twelve percent figure actually exaggerates the increase, since this growth was from a very small base, never reaching even three percent of total exports, and can be accounted for by the entry of a very few industries on the export market. [39] After 1964, however, exports began a dramatic and sustained growth in excess of thirty percent per year, with dips in the growth pattern explained by temporary increases in domestic demand in 1966 and 1968 (see Table A.3). Although prior to 1964, only a very few industries had managed to enter the export market, after 1964 many different industries, in a wide variety of fields, began to export on a regular basis.

Before assuming that this can be attributed to export policies, however, it is important to examine other possible causes. Two possible factors are the creation of the Latin American Free Trade Area and the general expansion of world trade, but these do not seem to be able to explain more than a small fraction of the spectacular Brazilian increase (Pearson, 1971).

A second possibility could be the maturation of Brazilian industry.

Under this assumption, it could be argued that only after 1964 were the "infant industries" created by import substitution sufficiently mature to compete abroad. A definitive answer to this question requires unavailable industry-level price data. However, two considerations make the "maturation of industry" argument implausible as more than a partial explanation of export performance. First, a great deal of Brazilian industrialization had already occurred by the mid-1950s, with the later stages of import substitution confined to the capital goods sector. [40] Although this does not guarantee that the industries developed prior to the mid-1950s were efficient, it does at least hold out the possibility that they had had enough time to mature by the late 1950s. This is reinforced by the nature of the export expansion that began after 1964. The change in export policies brought an almost immediate response from industries in a wide variety of industrial sectors. If the maturation of industry argument were correct, one would expect that industrial sectors would begin to export at different times, as each would mature at a different rate. This is a clear contradiction of the Brazilian experience, in which most sectors began exporting simultaneously, beginning in 1964 and 1965.

In conclusion, the evidence clearly suggests that changes in policies during the military regimes were an important factor in explaining changes in export performance. Although the measures of the impacts of export policies are not as precise as would be desirable, the dramatic impact of the policies is so overwhelming as to be registered even in these rather crude indicators. Given the problem of establishing base figures, there is no way of estimating the relative impact of policies to increase incentives versus policies to reduce distortions. However, this is of secondary interest, as under the military regime these policies were all moving in the direction of increasing export potential.